Politics and Bureaucratic Administration

Politics and Bureaucratic Administration

Durgesh Pande

CYBER TECH PUBLICATIONS
4264/3, Ansari Road, Daryaganj, New Delhi-110002 (India)
Ph.: 011-23244078, 011-43559448 Fax: 011-23280028
E-Mail: cyberpublicationsdelhi@yahoo.com
Website: www.cybertechpublications.com

POLITICS AND BUREAUCRATIC ADMINISTRATION

Durgesh Pande

First Edition 2011

Published by :

G.S. Rawat for Cyber Tech Publications
4264/3, Ansari Road, Daryaganj, New Delhi-110002 (India)
Ph.: 011-23244078, 011-43559448 Fax: 011-23280028
E-Mail: cyberpublicationsdelhi@yahoo.com
Website: www.cybertechpublications.com

CONTENTS

Preface

1. Introduction 1
2. The Search for Meanings 39
3. Politics in a Postmodern Age 63
4. Clash of Civilizations 103
5. Case for Collaboration 117
6. Urban Democracy in Action 122
7. Educational Governance and the New Public Management 132
8. Managing from the Inside Out 143
9. Decentralization and Educational Reform 153
10. Research Design, Methods and Data Analysis 159
11. Management of Semi-public Organizations in Complex Environments 174
12. The Management of Schools as Public Organizations 192
13. The Development of Nongovernmental Organizations 226
14. Rogue Corporations, Corporate Rogues and Ethics Compliance 235
15. University, Industry and Government Alliances 250

Bibliography 271

Index 272

Preface

Public administration can be broadly described as the development, implementation and study of branches of government policy. The pursuit of the public good by enhancing civil society and social justice is the ultimate goal of the field. Though public administration has historically referred to as government management, it increasingly encompasses non-governmental organizations (NGOs) that also operate with a similar, primary dedication to the betterment of humanity.

Differentiating public administration from business administration, a closely related field, has become a popular method for defining the discipline. First, the goals of public administration are more closely related to those often cited as goals of the American founders and democratic people in general. That is, public employees work to improve equality, justice, security, efficiency, effectiveness, and, at times, for profit. These values help to both differentiate the field from business administration, primarily concerned with profit, and define the discipline.

The multidisciplinary nature of public administration is related to a third defining feature: administrative duties. Public administrators work in public agencies, at all levels of government, and perform a wide range of tasks. Public administrators collect and analyze data (statistics), monitor fiscal operations (budgets, accounts, and cash flow), organize large events and meetings, draft legislation, develop policy, and frequently execute legally mandated, government activities. Regarding this final facet, public administrators find themselves serving as parole officers, secretaries, note takers, paperwork processors, records keepers, notaries of the public, cashiers, and managers. Indeed, the discipline couples well with many vocational fields such as information technology, finance, law, and engineering. When it comes to the delivery and evaluation of public services, a public administrator is undoubtedly involved.

The forty-five articles included in the text are all reprinted from the International Encyclopaedia of Public Policy and Administration. These accessible, interesting articles have been assembled to cover an overview of public administration, policymaking, intergovernmental relations, bureaucracy, organization behaviour, public management, strategic management, performance management, human resources management, financial management, auditing and accountability, and ethics. The articles provide definitions of the vocabulary of public policy and administrations as it is used throughout the world-- from the smallest towns to the largest national bureaucracies.

—Author

1

Introduction

The world wide globalization process supported by stronger orientations towards open markets, open highways of information, growing levels of organizational learning and interdisciplinarity in the social sciences have also made their impact on the study of our bureaucracies. Yet by all definitions public administration in the beginning of the 2000s still lacks the sense of identity that other fields of the social sciences has long since obtained. In other words, the field is looking back and down into its individuality, searching for orientations and signs that can direct it on its way forward. Today, public administration is already very different from what it used to be forty, thirty, and even twenty or ten years ago. In the coming years it is going to be even more different.

THE DILEMMA OF INDEPENDENCE AND INTERDISCIPLINARITY IN PUBLIC ADMINISTRATION

For many years public administration has struggled for its independent position in the social sciences. While in its early years it was part of the more conservative fields of Law, Politics, and Economy, it has been developed today to a unique field, independent in many ways but still enjoying mutual contributions of other disciplines in the social sciences. Moreover, in the last century it has developed a theoretical but also an impressive practical agenda that created remarkable achievements in different ways. The public sector, both as a science and as a profession is responsible for much of these achievements.

At the dawn of the new millennium, however, various new social problems still await the consideration and attention of the state and its administrative system. The question of independency of public administration as a science seems today less important than in the past. Instead, there are many calls to take advantage of multi disciplinary orientations in the social sciences and to find better ways to integrate them in the current ethos of public administration. It is also suggested that such interdisciplinary ideas, tools, and methods can help to overcome social problems and create effective remedies for the new type of state maladies. Interdisciplinarity is also translated into is cooperation, collaboration, and a share of information and knowledge. The multi-level, multi-method, and multi-system analysis with a look towards the future are the main frontiers of modern public administration.

The interdisciplinary view endeavors to provide an insight into the complexity of the field by combining different levels of analysis into an integral whole, which better accords with reality. This knowledge may well serve our understanding of how the state, and its executive branches, is managed and of the obstacles to better public performance. An important task is to illuminate cross-disciplinary principles for greater effectiveness and efficiency of public management in future generations, when environmental pressures will grow, together with an increase in citizens' demands and needs. An interdisciplinary approach to public administration may thus be of merit for a contentious field in a state of rapid change. It may stimulate new and viable thinking that can lead to additional positive innovation in the old type of bureaucracies.

The central assumption of this essay is that slowly and gradually, but constantly and extensively, a change is being nurtured in public systems and in the attitudes of public managers, politicians, and citizens to the conservative role of public institutions. These transformations carry many challenges, as well as risks, that citizens, governments, an administrators of the future will have to confront and address. They all represent new alternatives for the evolution of public administration as an art, perhaps also as a science and as a profession (Lynn, 1996). Our task, as stemming from such a perspective, is to understand better the changes ahead, which have the potential of building bridges into the future of modern democracies. A core assumption, as will be developed here, is that this goal can be achieved only through cooperation among the public, private, and third sector organizations that collaborate through mutual efforts and combined knowledge available in all the relevant social sciences.

PUBLIC ADMINISTRATION IN TRANSITION

The Evolutionary Process

The foundations of modern public administration can be discerned thousands of years ago, across cultures, and in various nations around the globe. The Bible mentions a variety of hierarchical and managerial structures that served as prototypes for governance of growing populations. Ancient methods of public labor distribution were expanded by the Greeks and the Romans to control vast conquered lands and many peoples. The Persian and Ottoman empires in the Middle East, like India and imperial China in the Far East, and the Mesoamerica cultures paved the way for public administration in the modern age, wherein European Christians, and later Christians of the New World, were in the ascendant.

All these, as well as other cultures, used a remarkably similar set of concepts, ideas, and methods for governing and administrating public goods, resources, and interests. They all employed professionals and experts from a variety of social fields. They all used authority and power as the cheapest control system for individuals, governmental institutions, and processes. All of them faced administrative problems close in type and in nature to problems of our own times: how to achieve better efficiency, effectiveness, and economy in government, how to satisfy the needs of the people, and how to sustain stable political hegemony despite the divergent demands and needs of sectorial groups. Not surprisingly, all the above cultures and nations also used similar managerial tools and methods to solve problems of this sort. They all used, fairly effectively, division of work, professionalism, centralization and decentralization mechanisms, accumulation of knowledge, coordination of jobs, complex staffing processes of employees, long-range planning, controlling for performance, and so on. Intuitively, one feels that nothing has really changed in the managerial and administrative process of public organizations for centuries, possibly millennia. But this feeling is of course exaggerated. Some major changes have taken place in recent centuries to create a totally different environment and new rules, to which rulers and citizens must adhere and by which they must adjust their operation. In fact, a new kind of governing game has taken shape, in which public administration plays a central role.

Despite basic similarities, the public administration of our times is entirely different from public services in the past. These differences can be summarized in 7 key points:

(1) It is *larger* than ever before, and it still expanding;

(2) It is more *complex* than in the past, and becoming increasingly so by the day;

(3) It has many more *responsibilities* to citizens, and it still has to cope with increasing demands of the people.

(4) It is acquiring more *eligibilities*, but must restrain its operation and adhere to standards of equity, justice, social fairness, transparency and accountability.

(5) Modern public administration is considered a social *science,* a classification that carries high esteem but also firm obligations and rigid constraints.

(6) For many individuals who decide to become public servants it is also a *profession and occupation* to which they dedicate their lives and careers.

(7) Public administration is one of the highly *powerful institutions* in modern democracies.

Thus, it is evident that public administration of our time wields considerable power and influence in policy framing, policy making, and policy implementation. Hence it is subject to growing pressures of political players, social actors, managerial professionals, and the overall economic market.

An Eclectic Science

Public administration is an eclectic science. It was born towards the end of the 19th century when the business of the state started to attract social-academic attention. The revolution turning public administration into an independent science and profession is traditionally related to the influential work and vision of Woodrow

Wilson (1887) and Frank J. Goodnow (1900). These scholars were among the first who advocated the autonomy of the field as a unique area of science that drew substance from several sources. In the first years, law, political theory of the state, and several "hard sciences" such as engineering and industrial relations were the most fundamental and influential mother disciplines. Over time, these fields strongly influenced the formation and transition of public administration but the extent and direction of the influence were not linear or consistent.

Kettl and Milward (1996:7) argued that traditional public administration, as advocated by the progenitors of the discipline, consisted in the power of law. Representatives of the people make the law and delegate responsibility to professional bureaucrats to execute it properly. Highly qualified bureaucrats, supported by the best tools and resources, are then expected to discharge the law to the highest professional standards, which in return produces good and accountable managerial results that best serve the people. According to Rosenbloom (1998), the legal approach views public administration "as applying and enforcing the law in concrete circumstances" and is "infused with legal and adjudicatory concerns." This approach is derived from three major interrelated sources:

(1) administrative law, which is the body of law and regulations that control generic administrative processes;
(2) the judicialization of public administration, which is the tendency for administrative processes to resemble courtroom procedures; and
(3) constitutional law, which redefines a variety of citizens' rights and liberties. Several legal definitions argue that public administration is law in action and mainly a regulative system, which is "government telling citizens and businesses what they may and may not do" (Shafritz & Russell, 1997:14).

However, with the years it has become obvious that law in itself does not maintain satisfactory conditions for quality public sector performances to emerge. Constitutional systems furnish platforms for healthy performance of public administration, but do not account for its effectiveness or efficiency. Put differently, good laws are necessary but not sufficient conditions for creating a well-performing public service. They only highlight the significance of other scholarly contributions.

One such important contribution came from the classic "hard sciences" of engineering and industrial relations. In its very early stages public administration was heavily influenced by dramatic social forces and long-range developments in the western world. The ongoing industrial revolution in the early 1900s, which was accompanied by political reforms, higher democratization, and more concern for the people's welfare, needed highly qualified navigators. These were engineers, industrial entrepreneurs, and technical professionals who guided both markets and governments along the elusive paths to economic and social prosperity.

Various fields of engineering, the subsequent evoking area of industrial studies, and other linked disciplines such as statistical methods became popular and crucial for the development of management science in general, and were also gradually found useful for public arenas. The link between general management and public administration has its roots in the understanding of complex organizations and bureaucracies, which have many shared features. Here, much contribution was made in non-American societies such Germany, France, and Britain. In fact, early American public administration was influenced by the works of various European. Thus, the current state of public administration can not be covered without adequate understanding of the seminal works by Max Weber (1947), Henry Fayol (1925), Lindel Urwick (1928), and others. Their ideas and theoretical development of the field are considered today as core-stones for the emergence of modern public administration and management.

With time, dramatic changes occurred in the nature and orientation of general organizational theory, and in its application to public administration of modern societies. A major transition resulted from the exploration by the Hawthorn studies in the 1920s and 1930s, conducted by a well known industrial psychologist from Chicago University, Alton Mayo.

A behavioral apparatus was used to drive a second revolution, beyond the revolution of its original emergence, which swept the young science into its first stages of maturity. Today, trends and developments in the public sector cannot be fully understood without adequate attention to behavioral, social, and cultural issues. These aspects conjoin with questions of policy making and policy evaluation, as well as with managerial, economic, and organizational contents, better to illuminate public systems. The human and social side of public organizations became central and critical to all seekers of greater knowledge and comprehension of the state's operation. People and groups were placed at the heart of the discussion on organizational development and managerial methods. The human side of organizations was made an organic part of the art of administration. Still today it is an indispensable facet of the craft of bureaucracy. All who are interested in the healthy future and sound progress of public organizations and services both as a science and as a profession have to incorporate humanistic views well in their basic managerial ideology.

However, major transitions still lay ahead. International conflicts during the 1930s and the 1940s wrought immense changes in national ideology and democratic perspectives in many western societies. Consequently, public administration and public policy had to be transformed as well. During the Second World War theoretical ideas were massively supported by advanced technology and higher standards of industrialization. These were pioneered by professional managers and accompanied by new managerial theories. Ironically, the two world wars served as facilitators of managerial change as well as accelerators and agents of future developments and reforms in the public sector. The political leaders and social movements of the victorious democracies were convinced that the time had come for extensive reforms in the management of western states.

The assumed correlation of social and economic conditions with political stability and order propelled some of the more massive economic programs in which the state took an active part. The rehabilitation of war-ravaged Europe involved governmental efforts and international aid, most of it from the United States. Major attention was dedicated to the creation of better services for the people, long-range planning, and high-performance public institutions capable of delivering quality public goods to growing numbers of citizens. To build better societies was the goal. A larger and more productive public sector was the tool. In many respects the utopian vision of a better society generated by the post-war politicians and administrators in the 1940s and 1950s inexorably crumbled and fell during the 1960s and 1970s.

A sizable number of governments in the western world could not deliver to the people many of the social promises they had made. The challenge of creating a new society, free of crime and poverty, highly educated and morally superior, healthier and safer than ever before, remained an unreachable goal. So during the 1970s and 1980s, citizens' trust and confidence in government, and in public administration as a professional agent of government, suffered a significant decline. The public no longer believed that governments and public services could bring relief to those who needed help, and that no public planning was good enough to compete with natural social and market forces.

The promises of modern administration, running an effective public policy, seemed like a broken dream. Political changes took place in most western states, largely stemming from deep frustration by the public and disapproval of government policies. By the end of the 20th century the crises in public organizations and mistrust of administrators were viewed both as a policy and managerial failure (Rainey, 1990). In addition, this practical uncertainty and disappointment with governments and their public administration authorities naturally diffused into the academic community.

Theoretical ideas for policy reforms in various social fields that once seemed the key to remedying illnesses in democracies have proven unsuccessful. Within the last decade the search for new ideas and solutions for such problems has reached its peak, as premises originally rooted in business management have become increasingly adjusted and applied to the public sector. Among these ventures are re-engineering bureaucracies (Hammer and Champy, 1994), applying benchmarking strategy to public services (Camp, 1998), re-inventing government (Osborne and Gaebler, 1992), and the most influential movement of New Public Management (NPM: Lynn, 1998; Stewart and Ranson, 1994). These are receiving growing attention accompanied by large measures of skepticism and criticism.

TRANSFORMATIONS IN THE ACADEMIC REALM

Throughout those years public administration as an academic field was also in transition. Today, many examples exist in universities of independent public administration units; some operate as schools and some as free-standing faculties. But in at least an equal number of universities, public administration programs on all levels are only part of larger units such as Political Science departments, Business and Management schools, or even Public Affairs schools. This disciplinary schizophrenia certainly yields a science that is more complex and heterogeneous, but also more challenging and full of promise.

The scientific background and identity of public administration in the late 1990s and early 2000s is still not stable and has not overcome its childhood ailments. On the contrary. Identity conflicts have only intensified with the years. Some 30 years ago, Waldo (1968) noted that ongoing transformations in public administration reflected an identity crisis of a science in formation. During the last three decades Waldo's diagnostics on public administration as a science struggling with a pernicious identity problem has not changed much. The evolution of alternative sub-disciplines inside and around the field (e.g., policy studies, public personnel management, information management, etc.) carried promises but also risks for its position and role as a central field of social study.

As recently noted by Peters (1996), modern public administration greatly reflects lack of self-confidence both as a science and as a profession. This lack is expressed in many ways, the most significant being incapacity to guide governments through a safe circuit of public policy change. Much of the accumulated wisdom in the science of public administration has been obtained through social experiments, the commission of policy errors, and sometimes even learning from them about better ways to serve the people. But mistakes cost money, much money, money from all of us, the taxpayers.

Like good customers in a neighborhood supermarket, citizens should and have become aware of the services they deserve, of the high prices they are asked to pay, and of governmental actions that should be taken to produce useful changes. Demands for better operation are generally aimed at governments, but they should be, and are, also targeted at the science and at academia. Science has the potential of exploring new knowledge, generating better explanations for relevant administrative problems, applying sophisticated and useful professional methods, and most importantly directing all available resources to produce successful and practical recommendations for professionals.

Its prime goal is to design a comprehensive theoretical view of public systems that is clear, highly efficient, effective, thrifty, and socially oriented at the same time. This cannot be achieved without extensive understanding of the diversity, complexity, and interdisciplinarity of the science of public administration.

THE CONTRIBUTION OF AN INTERDISCIPLINARY VIEW TO PUBLIC ADMINISTRATION IDENTITY

In many ways the persistent public mistrust of governmental services and institutions, together with the marked instability of public administration as a science, inspired us in the present venture.

The fragile status of the theory of public administration is a port of departure for a different kind of discussion, which is broader and multi-perceptional. Our core argument is that one can find many ways to depict the administrative system, its functionality, and its relationship with the public. But the identity crisis of public administration cannot be solved until many approaches are combined and coalesce to explain the very basic constructs that modern societies encounter at the start of the new century.

A foremost assumption of this chapter is that only mutual efforts and quality combination of critical knowledge from a variety of social disciplines and methods can yield a real opportunity for overcoming public administration's post-childhood problems. Such a crisis of identity, which has existed for more than a century now, carries risks, but also promises, which must be well isolated, assessed, analyzed, and only then fulfilled. The translation of science into operative acts by government must rely on such wisdom, which can be sufficiently accumulated from various social branches.

Interdisciplinary Heredity

The desired comprehensive understanding of public administration, as portrayed earlier, should rely on the accumulated wisdom and knowledge of its sister disciplines (and not necessarily the conventional mother disciplines) in the social sciences. Unfortunately, so far most writing on public systems has adopted a uni-dimensional viewpoint. Public administration was frequently understood through the eyes of policy analysts or political scientists. Alternatively it was considered a specific field of management science or as an organizational studies domain.

While the roots of the administrative process are definitely, and with much justification, identified with political science, policy studies, and managerial constructs of public institutions, it would be greatly in error to point solely to these arenas in portraying the domain and nature of public administration. An integrative approach has much merit and potential in this case, and it must be well developed to conform to the complex reality of serving the public.

More specifically I argue that the administrative science is a discipline in transition that involves politics, but not only politics. It deals with policy, but reaches much farther and deeper than policy questions. It incorporates sociological and cultural aspects that change rapidly in a mass communicative global world, but it goes even beyond these issues. It deals with people as workers, as citizens, as clients, and as consumers, as leaders and managers, as well as with a variety of other human constructs that fuse into a unique branch of knowledge. A multi-disciplinary approach is evidently required to explain better what every scholar already knows from his or her personal perspective: that the truth about public administration has many faces and no monopoly exists any longer on the discipline's status and orientations.

In light of the above I identify three main disciplines that serve today as core sources of knowledge in the study of public administration.

(1) *Policy analysis, Political science, and Political Economy;*

(2) *Sociology, Cultural studies, and Community studies;*

(3) *Management and Organizational studies;*

Policy, Politics, and Political Economy

The political approach to public administration was depicted by Rosenbloom (1998) as stressing the values of representativeness, political responsiveness, and accountability to the citizenry through elected officials. These values are considered necessary requirements of democracy, and they must be incorporated into all aspects of government and administration. Wallace (1978) argued that ultimately public administration is a problem in political theory. It deals with the responsiveness of administrative agencies and bureaucracies to the elected officials, and through them, to the citizens themselves. Shafritz and Russell (1997) provide several politics-oriented definitions of public administration: it is what government does (or does not do), it is a phase in the policymaking cycle, it is a prime tool for implementing the public interest, and it does collectively what cannot be done so well individually (pp. 6-13). Hence it is impossible to conduct a politics-free discussion of public administration. This political debate in public administration is also heavily influenced by the sub-field of political economy. Questions of budgeting and financing the public sector (Wildavsky, 1984) as well as bringing more economical rationality to decision making processes usually conflict with political considerations (Jackson & Mcleod, 1982). However they also put them under economical restraints and enhance "checks and balances" to a system mostly monitored and controlled by politicians, political parties, and other federal or national institutions, rather than professionals and practitioners.

Yet, politics is definitely the heart of public administration processes. Politics focuses on citizens as members of groups or on highly institutionalized organizations that sound the public's voice before political officials and civil servants. The politics approach to public administration involves strategies of negotiating and maneuvering among political parties, public opinion, and bureaucracies. It involves an incremental change in society, which relies on open debate, a legitimate power struggle, distribution and redistribution of national resources and budgets, and a heavy body of legislation and law to regulate these processes.

Perhaps the most obvious linkage between politics and public administration stems from policy making and policy implementation processes. It is naive to distinguish political systems from professional administration systems in regard to public policy. As Rosenbloom (1998:13) suggested, "public administrators' involvement in the public policy cycle makes politics far more salient in the public sector than in private enterprise. Public administrators are perforce required to build and maintain political support for the policies and programs they implement. They must try to convince members of the legislature, chief executives, political appointees, interest groups, private individuals, and the public at large that their activities and policies are desirable and responsive".

The theoretical contribution of political science to the study of public administration is therefore multi-faceted. It invokes better understanding of the power relations and influence dynamics that take place inside and among bureaucracies (Pfeffer, 1992) and determine their operative function as well as outcomes. It also employs a rather vast knowledge from economics and rational thinking. Party politics acknowledges that the investigation of pressure and interest groups, and the better understanding of conflict relationships among various players of the state, are used to build models of decision making and policy determination that are rational and realistic. In addition, political psychology is implemented more thoroughly to explore personality traits of political leaders as well as public servants. For the same reasons, budgetary studies and policy analysis methods are an integral facet of the political approach, which assumes limited rationality as well as high constraints of time and resources on the administrative process.

From a somewhat different perspective, Ellwood (1996: p.51) argued that political science has simultaneously everything and little to offer public management scholars, hence also public administration scholars. Everything, because both fields deal with political behavior, processes, and institutions. Little, because political science deals only with the constraints forced on the administrative process with no practical contribution to the managerial improvement of public systems. Ellwood further concurs that both fields rely on other academic disciplines, employing techniques of anthropology, economics, game theory, historiography, psychology, and social psychology, as well as sociology. In line with this it would be only natural to conclude that the relationship between political science and public administration is described as an on-again, off-again romance. Kettl (1993, p.409) suggested that "the importance of administration lay at the very core of the creation of the American Political Science Association..when five of the first eleven presidents of the association came from public administration" and played a major role in framing the discipline.

As Ellwood puts it, with the years, public administration became public but also administration. It shifted its focus to a more practical and client-service orientation, which necessarily incorporated knowledge from other social disciplines like personnel management, organizational behavior, accounting, budgeting, and so forth. The methodological contribution of a political approach to public administration studies is also meaningful. Here a macro analysis is necessary if one seeks an understanding of the operation of large bureaucracies and their coexistence with political players. A political approach delivers these goods by means of comparative studies, policy evaluation methods, rational choice models, and simulations, as well as content-analysis techniques and other tools useful for observation of the political sphere.

Sociology, Culture, and Community

Studying public administration is also a social issue. Thus, another approach that is highly relevant to the understanding of public administration bodies and processes rests on a sociological apparatus. It has a very close relationship with the political approach, so it is sometimes defined as a socio-political view of public systems or as a study of political culture (Shafritz & Russell, 1997:76). Yet its core prospects are beyond the political context. The voice of society has a special role in the study of public administration arenas not only for democratic and political reasons but also because of its fundamental impact on informal constructs of reality such as tradition, social norms and values, ethics, life style, work standards, and other human-cultural interactions that are not necessarily political.

The theoretical contribution of a sociological and cultural approach to public administration consists of several elements. An essential distinction must be drawn between inside and outside cultural environments. An outside cultural sphere incorporates informal activities and behaviors of small groups as well as of larger social units which interact with the administrative system. Included in this category are customers' groups, private organizations, not-for-profit volunteering organizations, and citizens at large. Considerable attention has been turned to communities and to the idea of communitarianism (Etzioni 1994; 1995) as well as to the emergence of the third sector as rapidly changing conventional structures and beliefs in modern societies (Gidron, Kramer, and Salamon, 1992). An inside cultural environment is related to internal organizational dynamics and to the behaviors of people as work groups. Thus, it is sometimes termed organizational culture, or organizational climate (Schein, 1985). Like the outside organizational environment, it has some observable constructs but it mostly expresses many covert phases. In many ways, "culture is to the organization what personality is to the individual – a hidden, yet unifying theme that provides meaning, direction and mobilization" (Kilmann et al., 1985). It includes basic assumptions as to what is right and what is wrong for a certain organizational community, norms and beliefs of employees, unseen social rules and accepted codes of behavior, as well as tradition, language, dress, and ceremonies with common meaning to all organizational members. All these distinguish "us" from "them", promote group cohesiveness, and improve common interests.

Several sociological sources can be effective in analyzing public administration dynamics. First is group theory, which is also closely related to the study of leaders and leadership. Second are ethnic studies, which concentrate on minorities and race questions such as equity, fair distribution of public goods, and integration in productive public activity. Third is communication and the technological information revolution, which have had a radical effect on society, public policy, and public administration units and structure. Information networks and communication have become an immanent feature of the cultural investigation of bureaucracies. For many years a plausible approach in management science and in the study of public administration called for the formulation of a universal theory in the field, one that is culture-free and applicable across all nations. With the passage of time and with giant technological developments this perception became ever more anachronistic.

Today, the goal of a universal administrative paradigm is hardly achievable. An alternative viewpoint is more balanced and contingent. It argues that basic similarities do exist between public organizations and public administration mechanisms, but at the same time intra-organizational and extra-organizational culture fulfills a major mediating role. Culture in its broad context constantly affects the operation of bureaucracies as well as political systems that interact with them. Examples like Theory Z of W. Ouchi (1981) and lessons from a more recent Chinese and east European experiences stimulated the scientific community and initiated culture-oriented ventures in general management inquiry (Hofstede, 1980).

They especially promoted the investigation of work values and culture-oriented management in private but also in public arenas. Many scholars became convinced of the necessity of incorporating social and cultural variables as core elements in the administrative analysis of public arenas. A sociological and cultural approach to public administration also made an important methodological contribution. It initiated culture-focused surveys of individuals and groups who work in the public sector or of citizens who receive services and goods. Culture-focused observations and analyses possess the merit of being sensitive to people's (as citizens or employees) norms, values, traditions, and dispositions, and sometimes they overlap other politics and policy-oriented studies the better to explore dynamics in public organizations.

Finally, several ethical considerations should be included under any sociological understanding of the public sector. Ethical dilemmas are frequent in public administration and relate to cultural aspects, to norms, and most importantly to the individual behaviour of public servants. For example, hand-in-hand with governmental operation, questions of ethical standards, integrity, fair and equal treatment to clients, or appropriate criteria for rewards to public servants become more relevant. Today, public services in Europe are wider than ever before (Gladstone, 1995; De-Leon, 1996).

As a result, public servants are taking care of growing budgets. They control the transference of more capital to and from the state treasury. This exposes many of them to ethical dilemmas as to how to properly manage, distribute and redistribute economical wealth. Other ethical difficulties arise as a result of the instability between business and social requirements in the public environment. For example, when the cost of certain medicine is too high for citizens to purchase, should the state take responsibility and help them? When state prisons are full of convicted prisoners, should the state release some of them to create more places for others? Responding to such moral issues is difficult. However, public policy which neglects considerations of ethics, equal treatment of the public, or basic justice and fairness among its members is initiating a self-destructive process which may damage its functioning in the long run (Wilenski, 1980).

Management and Organization Studies

The third core-stone of public administration is based on knowledge from management and organizational sciences. A managerial definition of public administration proclaims that it is the executive function in government or a management specialty applied in public systems (Shafritz and Russell, 1997:19-23). Although public sector management is distinguished from private sector management, in many ways the two systems share a surprisingly broad area of similarities (Rainey, 1990). For many years, differences stemmed from the nature of services each sector customarily provided, from diverse structures and functions, but mainly from discrepancies in the environment. However, when the environment started rapidly to change, organizations had to change as well. Modern societies have become more complex, flexible, and dynamic. Cultural, industrial, technological, economic, and political environments of organizations have undergone rapid transformations that are still in progress today. On the one hand, public and private organizations have to adjust and comply with similar changes in the environment to safeguard their interests and existence. But on the other hand, the starting point of public organizations is far inferior and urgently calls for rethinking and reinventing (Osborne and Gaebler, 1992).

Conventional wisdom accepted a classic assumption regarding the relatively stable and unshakable structure of public organizations. Drawing on the Weberian approach, hardly anyone disputed the need for large bureaucracies in modern democracies. Moreover, the advantages and disadvantages of large bureaucracies were well known among academics and practitioners. A weighty bureaucracy was considered an axiom of public administration.

Only with the emergence of new management trends in old bureaucracy were these basic assumptions questioned. For example, Kettl and Milward (1996) stated that management in the public sector matters. It matters because citizens' demands increase and because the standards of performance expected from governments are higher than ever before. Performance is related in the minds of people and in scientific studies to quality of management, quality of managers, and the administrative process between them. Accordingly, it has much to do with the human aspects of administration. Perhaps this perception has led to some recent developments in public administration, making it client-oriented and more businesslike. Scholars frequently define these shifts as the principal change in public administration and its transition into a revised field of study named public management.

PRESENT SCENARIO

What is the future of modern public administration and what new frontiers are awaiting ahead? The wisdom of managing states and communities in the 21st century relies on manifold disciplines and multiple sources of knowledge. The information era and the immense technological advancement with which our nations struggle necessarily create higher levels of accessibility, availability, and transparency to the public. The emergence of e-government is no more a fantastic dream but blatant reality. Public administration in America and in the world is moving through reforms and changes that are aimed at downsizing, privatization, de-bureaucratization, higher professional managerialsim, and above all strict dedication and aspirations to become a better "science" by improving measurement tools and adhering with positivism and empiricism.

Since the early 1980s much work has been conducted in public administration theory and practice that claimed to go beyond the conservative approach in the field. This "liberalization" of public administration is recognized today as the "New Public Management" (NPM) trend. The self-identity problem of public administration was greatly aggravated by the launching of the idea of NPM. As noted by Kettl and Milward (1996: vii), "public management is neither traditional public administration nor policy analysis since it borrows heavily from a variety of disciplines and methodological approaches". Mainly drawing on the experience of the business/industrial/private sector, scholars have suggested taking a more demanding attitude to the dynamics, activity, and productivity of public organizations. However, "competing academic disciplines dueled to establish bridgeheads or, worse, virtually ignored each other as they developed parallel tracks on related problems" (p. 5). Consequently, a cross-fertilization, which could have accelerated learning and improved performance of public systems, was delayed.

What are the roots of NPM, and in what way is it actually a *new* arena in the study of the public sector? Several theoretical foundations, as well as practical factors, can answer these questions. The first, and probably the deepest source of NPM emerges from the distinction between two proximate terms or fields of research: administration and management. As noted earlier, since the late 1880s the monopoly on the term administration has been held by political scientists. Scholars like Goodnow and Wilson were those who perceived public administration as a separate and unique discipline that should consist of independent theory, practical skills, and methods. However, the term management referred to a more general arena, used by all social scientists and mainly by those who practice and advance theory in organizational psychology and business studies. Consequently, conservative administration science tends to analyze the operation of large bureaucratic systems as well as other governmental processes aimed at policy implementation. Management, on the other hand, refers to the general practice of empowering people and groups in various social environments and in handling multiple organizational resources to maximize efficiency and effectiveness in the process of producing goods or services.

NPM has indeed become extremely popular in the theory and practice of contemporary public administration. Still, it is not clear if we can define it as a long-range revolution in public administration theory. Some will say that NPM has only revived an old spirit of managerialism and applied it in the public sector. Others will argue that this in itself has been a momentous contribution to public administration as a discipline in decline. Relying on an extensive survey of public management research in America, Garson and Overman (1983:275) argued that this increasing popularity was due to the more virile connotation of the term management than administration.

Over the years, a growing number of political scientists came to perceive public administration as an *old* and declining discipline. It was unable to provide the public with adequate practical answers to its demands, and moreover it left the theoreticians with epidemic social dilemmas awaiting exploration. Interesting evidence of this process could be found in many schools of public administration that during the 1980s and 1990s decided to become schools of public management. Looking for alternative ideas, management theory was proposed as the source for a new and refreshing perspective. It was suggested that public management rather than public administration could contribute to a new understanding of how to run the government more efficiently, hence to surmount some of its pandemic ailments.

Thus, Perry and Kraemer (1983) stated that a greater impact of new ideas and methods from the field of public management on the administrative science was essential and natural. It reflected a special focus of modern public administration that was not to be ignored. Rainey (1990:157) claimed that this process was a result of the growing unpopularity of government during the 1960s and 1970s. Ott, Hyde, and Shafritz (1991:1) also stated that public management was a major segment of the broader field of public administration since it focused on the profession and on the public manager as a practitioner of that profession. Furthermore, it emphasized well-accepted managerial tools, techniques, knowledge, and skills that could be used to turn ideas and policy into a (successful) program of action.

During the last two decades many definitions have been suggested for NPM. Yet nothing seems wrong with the relatively old perception of Garson and Overman (1983:278), who defined it as *"an interdisciplinary study of the generic aspects of administration...a blend of the planning, organizing, and controlling functions of management with the management of human, financial, physical, information and political resources"*. As further discussed by other scholars (e.g., Lynn, 1996:38-39), six differences exist between public administration and public management that make the former a new field of study and practice. These are:

(1) the inclusion of general management functions such as planning, organizing, control, and evaluation in lieu of discussion of social values and conflicts of bureaucracy and democracy;

(2) an instrumental orientation favoring criteria of economy and efficiency in lieu of equity, responsiveness, or political salience;

(3) a pragmatic focus on mid-level managers in lieu of the perspective of political or policy elites;

(4) a tendency to consider management as generic, or at least to minimize the differences between public and private sectors in lieu of accentuating them;

(5) a singular focus on the organization, with external relations treated in the same rational manner as internal operations in lieu of a focus on laws, institutions, and political bureaucratic processes;

(6) a strong philosophical link with the scientific management tradition in lieu of close ties to political science or sociology.

While the emergence of NPM is frequently related to the increasing impact of positivist behavioral science on the study of politics and government (e.g., Lynn, 1996:5-6), the practical aspect of this process should also be considered. Practical public managers (Golembiewski, 1995), as well as political scientists, will refer to the difficulties in policy making and policy implementation which faced many western societies in Europe, America, and elsewhere during the 1970s. These practical difficulties are viewed today as an important trigger for the evolution of NPM.

Reviewing two recent books on NPM (Aucoin, 1995; Boston, Martin, Pallot, and Walsh, 1996), Khademian (1998:269) argues that American and Westminster advocates of the field find common ground in explaining why such reforms are necessary. The problem of an inflexible bureaucracy that often could not respond efficiently and promptly to the public needs conflicted with some basic democratic principles and values in these countries. Peter Aucoin elegantly summarizes a "trinity" of broadly based challenges with which western democracies have struggled, and will probably continue to struggle in the future, partly through management reform. These are:

(1) growing demands for restraint in public sector spending,
(2) increasing cynicism regarding government bureaucracies' responsiveness to citizens' concerns and political authority and dissatisfaction with program effectiveness, and
(3) an international, market driven economy that does not defer to domestic policy efforts.

These challenges have apparently led many western governments, in America, Britain, New Zealand, Canada, and elsewhere, to the recognition that firm reforms and changes in the public service should be made.

There is no doubt that at least some of the accumulated wisdom of the private sector in many countries is transferable to the public sector (Pollitt, 1988; Smith, 1993). In an attempt to liberate the public sector from its old conservative image and tedious practice NPM was advanced as a relevant and promising alternative. NPM literature has tried to recognize and define new criteria that may help in determining the extent to which public agencies succeed in meeting the growing needs of the public. NPM has continuously advocated the implementation of specific Performance Indicators (PIs) used in private organizations to create a performance-based culture and matching compensatory strategies in these systems.

It has recommended that these indicators be applied in the public sector (e.g., Smith, 1993; Carter, 1989) since they can function as milestones on the way to better efficiency and effectiveness of public agencies. Moreover, citizens' awareness of the performance of public services was suggested as a core element of NPM since it can increase the political pressure placed on elected and appointed public servants, thereby enhancing both managerial and allocative efficiency in the public sector. Scholars who advocate NPM liken this process of public accountability to stakeholders/ citizens to the role adopted by financial reporting in the private/ corporate sector (Smith, 1993). As in that sector, increasing exterior-related outcomes can have a profound impact on internal control mechanisms, as managers and public servants become more sensitive to their duties and highly committed to serve their public customers.

Thus, Lynn (1998:231) suggested that the NPM of the late 1990s had three constructive legacies for the field of public administration and for democratic theory and practice. These were:

(1) a stronger emphasis on performance motivated administration and inclusion in the administrative canon of performance-oriented institutional arrangements, structural forms, and managerial doctrines fitted to particular context, in other words, advances in the state of the public management art;

(2) an international dialogue on and a stronger comparative dimension to the study of state design and administrative reform; and

(3) the integrated use of economic, sociological, social psychological, and other advanced conceptual models and heuristics in the study of public institutions and management, with the potential to strengthen the field's scholarship and the possibilities for theory grounded practice.

While the first two "legacies" are widely discussed in contemporary literature, the third is much understudied and needs further theoretical development, empirically guided research, and practical implementation.

Moreover, Kettl and Milward (1996) argue that one of NPM's most significant contributions to public administration as a discipline in transition is the focus on the performance of governmental organizations. According to their analysis, this scientific orientation needs to draw on "a wide variety of academic disciplines for the full and richly textured picture required to improve the way government works. Only through interdisciplinary cross-fertilization will the picture be rich enough to capture the enormous variety and complexity of true public management (and administration) puzzles" (p.6).

The Journey Continues

This chapter has relied on previous works to describe public administration as a discipline in transition. In many ways it has always been in continuous movement, but not always in the same direction. Contrary to the heavy, formal, and inflexible image of bureaucracies, public sector bodies in America, Europe, and elsewhere have been in rapidly intensifying transition since the early 1990s. During the last century public administration has undergone gone significant changes resulting from crises, as well as breakthroughs in an ultra-dynamic environment. Generally speaking, Waldo's (1968) assertion that these ongoing transformations reflected an identity crisis of a science in formation is also relevant today, albeit with some amendments. Whereas in the past these crises signaled a struggle for the recognition and legitimacy of public administration as a scholarly academic field, today the identity problem leads to other dilemmas, which are beyond simple existence and legitimacy.

In recent decades the struggle over the nature and uniqueness of public administration has continued, some say even intensified. From the very early days of the discipline to the present its boundaries have been in a state of ongoing debate. To talk of the "Public", of "Administration", and of the integration of the two constructs into a useful terrain for study holds out promise as well as involving difficulties. But consensus does exist on at least one issue: the public needs a better bureaucracy, more flexible, working efficiently and effectively, moving quickly toward objectives, and at the same time responding to the needs of the people without delays and with maximum social sensitivity, responsibility, and morality. The public also expects good and skillful administrators, versed in the mysteries of quality services and effective management. Only they can produce better "public goods" and deliver them to all sectors of society in minimum time and at minimum cost. These goals are undoubtedly ambitious but they have the potential of safeguarding the structure of democratic societies. This is a revised version of the ideal type of public administration systems applicable to modern times.

However, reality seems far more complex. There is growing concern among scholars today that these goals are way beyond reach. Modern states across the world face serious problems of adhering to the public's needs. Achieving one target is usually accompanied by painful compromises on others, and limited resources are frequently cited as the main reason for failure in the provision of services. Moreover, fundamental changes are taking place in people's lifestyles, as in their beliefs and ideologies. They are multiplied through high technology, communication systems, new distribution of capital, and the rise of new civic values that never existed before.

All these lead citizens to perceive government and public administration systems differently. The role of the state and its relationship with bureaucracy and with citizens is undergoing a substantial transformation not only in the minds of the people but also in scientific thinking. In a rapidly changing environment, public administration has a major function and new aims that must be clearly recognized. It remains the best tool democracy can use to create fruitful reciprocal relationships with citizens, but on a higher and better level. To uncover the major tasks and challenges facing the new generation of public administration we require a cross-disciplinary strategy and improved integration of all available knowledge in the social sciences aimed at redefining the boundaries of public administration systems in its new era.

Today, at the beginning of the 21st century, the formation of public administration as an interdisciplinary academic field seems certain. Still, it is unfinished business due to the need and demand to make it more of a "harder social science", one which is closer to management science, economics, or even psychology. Hence, the state of the field is in dispute among academics and practitioners from across the world who seek higher and more extensive scientific recognition, by applying a higher level of empirical-based paradigm. It is argued that such inputs may produce a more accurate self-definition and better applicability of the field to rapid changes in modern life.

This process presents new challenges for public administration. Perhaps the most important is to integrate more widely existing knowledge of the social sciences with efficient public action and with quality governmental operation. In the coming years public administration will be evaluated by higher standards of theory cohesiveness and by more comprehensive performance indicators rooted in a variety of scientific fields. The exploration of new interdisciplinary horizons for public administration is thus essential, and inevitable for the successful passage of the field into the third millennium. Somewhat contrary to the concerns of Waldo (1968), the identity crises in its new form may carry a positive, not endangering, interdisciplinary merit. The interdisciplinary orientations have the potential of pulling public administration out of its perplexing-stagnating status and lead it towards a more solid scientific position.

In light of the above a consensus exists today among scholars and practitioners that modern public administration decidedly benefits, and will continue to benefit, from the seminal inputs of social and cultural motives and mainly from the impact of managerial and organizational theory. In keeping with these, modern societies question the current obligations of public personnel toward citizens, and urge them to put people and social values first. These tasks can be achieved by treating citizens as customers or clients but also through building a different value of administrative spirit (Vigoda and Golembiewski, 2001). Yet managerial tendencies draw fire from those who argue that a client orientation of the public sector breeds citizen passivity and lack of individual responsibility toward the state and its agencies. It is further assumed that today these obligations and commitments are not clearly decoded, manifested, or satisfactory implied. Consequently they yield an identity problem of the field and strive for redefinition of its unwritten contract with the people. Scholars are divided over the best way to obtain missions of good-management together with good cultural order. Still, they agree that much more can be done to improve responsiveness to citizens' needs and demands without forgoing the active role of citizens in the administrative process. Moreover, the information revolution is expected to create a growing impact on public administration of the future both as a science and as a profession. In referring to the modern public sector Caldwell suggested that "Our task for linking information, social issues, politics, policy and management is a challenge yet to be accomplished. The enthusiasm for public planning, notably in the 1930s, did not survive the Second World War. The so-called "reinvention" of government based on a market-driven model appears to be essentially contemporaneous and superficial in relation to the multiple challenges to be confronted in the 21st century."

Thus, Caldwell continues to argue that "governments and their administrators (in our time) characteristically focus on immediate situations and pressing problems. There are few political rewards for anticipating the long – range future. However, the advancement of science and an apparent growth of public acceptance, however slow, of science-based forecasts may enlarge the "educating" role of public administration. We are hardly at the end of the expansion of knowledge and information, and there is growing although limited recognition that we also face formidable challenges to a sustainable future. And so it is more realistic to see the "New Public Administration" as an evolving process continuing to become "new" as it is adapted to meeting the needs of the ever-receding future".

The Problem of School Management and Performance

Relatively recent reform and policy initiatives in the United States have renewed calls for both performance accountability and more rigorous standards in one of the nation's largest public institutions: the public schools *(Commission on Excellence in Education, 1983; Secretary's Commission on Achieving Necessary Skills, 1991; U.S. Department of Education, 2002)*. In addition, consistent comparisons of school performance in the US with those in other nations suggest that the effect of administration on the technical output of publicly-permeable organizations such as schools is largely misunderstood. These calls for accountability and international comparison also assume that the unique environment of these organizations does not influence either the managerial behavior of school administrators or the performance of individual students within these organizations. The problem presented here is that public school administrators are often evaluated on the performance of the people they ostensibly serve, namely the students. As a result, a research focus on the relationship between school administrators' managerial behavior and student performance is necessary to either validate or invalidate popular calls for multilevel performance accountability. Because school administrators are often organizationally removed from the individual and technical outcomes of schooling (namely, student performance), some argue that it is inappropriate for school administrators to be held directly accountable for the performance of students. Yet this accountability continues a long-standing appreciation for the corporate structure and system of top-down management with its accompanying accountability structure that is so often revered among school administrators *(Tyack, 1974).*

In an effort to lessen or eliminate performance disparities in the United States, in particular, some have also called for more rigorous standards for both administrators and those they manage. One way of implementing more rigorous performance standards is standardization of management and administration. Standardization is often interpreted to mean consistency, rigor, and appropriateness of the organizations' services. But standardization may also refer to the level of administrative or managerial centralization, because as standards become more consistent, they also tend to become increasingly centralized.

These international comparisons result from the underlying belief in the United States that the nation-state encourages and directs the growth of public schooling as a tool for creating productivity and citizenship *(Fuller & Rubinson, 1992, p. 11).* Therefore, the most important institutional influences on schools as organizations should reside at the national level.

In other words, organization-level influences are nested within the nationally institutionalized environments of the organization. One measure of national environmental effects is administrative control or governance, which has been shown to have significant effects on the workings of publicly-permeable organizations like schools *(Stevenson & Baker, 1991).* For instance, in administratively decentralized national systems the organizational effects on schools may be more localized, whereas in administratively centralized national systems there is much penetration from the national government and other national level institutions into organizations at the regional and local levels. In order to uncover these important contextual effects at the national level, this study uses comparative, cross-national data and multilevel regression modeling to determine both within and between system effects.

Calls for performance accountability and administrative centralization give rise to important multilevel questions:

(1) To what extent, if any, is variation in technical output associated with variation in administrators' managerial or administrative behaviors in publicly-permeable organizations? and

(2) Does administrative centralization act as an intervening influence in this relationship by affecting the amount of influence that administrators have over the methods and means leading to the technical output of their organization?

Conventional Theories of School Management and Performance

Behaviors of school administrators are often discussed in relation to their influence on the further behaviors or performance of their administrative subordinates *(Hallinger & Heck, 1996; Hallinger & Heck, 1998; Heck, 1996; Heck, Larsen & Marcoulides, 1990; Leitner, 1994; Murphy, 1988; Murphy, 1990; Ogawa & Hart, 1985; Pounder, Ogawa, & Adams, 1995)*. Because of the various avenues and influences administration may embody, connections between school administrators and the objects of their managerial behavior are both direct (straightforward from one level to the next) and indirect (filtered or enhanced either across or through levels).

Both policymakers and public stakeholders alike often assume school administrators' influence on student performance. Much of the literature connecting school administrators, managerial behavior and student performance assumes a tight linkage between organizational administration and technical output.

For example, some studies suggest that how school principals manage schools directly affects their implementation of key processes within their work structure, which then indirectly influences a schools' climate and organization hierarchy and, ultimately, student performance *(Heck, Larsen, and Marcoulides, 1990, p. 99-100).*

As public schooling becomes and remains the predominant formal mechanism through which citizens are formed, socialized, and prepared for roles in the political, cultural, and economic arenas of adult life, the administration of schools becomes increasingly essential to the social life of families, nations, and the global community. Consequently, the pressure on school administrators like principals to influence and, hopefully, raise the performance levels of students is significant.

Although schools are large public organizations from both a scope of influence and public participation perspective, theoretically-based research on school management and administration, when found, is not necessarily organizationally explicit *(Ogawa and Bossert, 1995, p. 233)*. Although school administrators' roles and managerial behaviors are often prominently figured in discussions of performance accountability, few studies explore alternative organizational perspectives concerning the relationship between school administration and organizational output such as student performance.

If, however, school administration is discussed in relation to its organizational characteristics, the technical-functional perspective is emphasized, which depicts "organizations as technically rational systems..[emphasizing] two organizational features: goals and formal structure" *(Ogawa and Bossert, 1995, p. 227)*. According to this perspective the goal of school administrators is the end product of the organizational process: high levels of technical output measured as student performance. From this perspective, school administrators are in positions of authority to affect and mold the formal structure of their schools in order to facilitate and encourage high student performance.

It is worth noting that although external forces may influence school administrators' managerial behaviors, the behaviors themselves focus on internal management of school processes, resources, and relationships. Using these characteristics of school administrators' managerial behaviors, the reform and policy argument for administrative accountability for individual level performance finds justification. Standardization of organizational procedures through centralization further emphasizes the influence that each of these categorical elements of school administrators' managerial behavior should have. By reducing the variability of organizational process through centralization, variability in school administrators' managerial behavior and influence on student performance should also be reduced, freeing them to engage in non-performance-related behaviors and activities.

INSTITUTIONAL PERSPECTIVES ON SCHOOL MANAGEMENT AND PERFORMANCE

The persistence of archetypal school management behaviors and models in spite of significant variation in individual performance levels contradicts technical-functional arguments *(for examples and further citations see Hallinger & Heck, 1996).* Among the many kinds of school organizational environments that exist, there are often pressures on school administrators to behave in similar ways and perform duties leading to similar outcomes. A neo-institutional perspective of school administration accounts for this similarity by suggesting that school administrators follow rationalized scripts designed to ensure organizational legitimacy and survival. This means that the managerial behaviors of school administrators are more related to rationalized models of legitimate organizational structures and processes than to specific outcomes, including individual-level performance.

From a neo-institutional perspective school administrative behavior is an organizational quality and as such (1) enhances an organization's social legitimacy and chances for survival, (2) finds strength in a network of roles throughout the institution, (3) relies on individuals' resources, and (4) leads to the adoption of structures that mirror an organization's cultural environment *(Meyer & Rowan, 1977; Ogawa and Bossert, 1995).* By situating school administrators in the midst of complex organizations, this perspective questions the assumed linkage between school administrators' managerial behavior and individual student performance. Instead, a neo-institutional perspective suggests that school administrators follow legitimate models of managerial behavior that determine the amount of variation in their behavior occurring between and within local organizations and national systems characterized by different levels of administrative centralization.

EXPECTATIONS AND HYPOTHESES

To summarize, a technical-functional perspective predicts an association between variation in school administrators' managerial behaviors and variation in individual student performance. By contrast, organizational and institutional perspectives suggest that individual level influences may result from technical-functional forces and reasoning, but the actual products of this reasoning may defy technical-functional outcome predictions. For example, when student performance rises, it may not necessarily be because school administrators' managerial behaviors changed or precipitated the change. Organizational managers such as school administrators may influence organizational level change without any accompanying change in outcome at the individual level. The first hypothesis tests these contrasting perspectives.

Hypothesis 1: Overall variation in school administrators' managerial behaviors associates with variation in individual student performance.

School administrators may not be accountable for individual level outcomes because these outcomes are predicted by organizational elements to which school administrators may contribute, but which are not dependent upon or significantly related to their managerial behavior. Instead, school level decisions and changes follow legitimate, rationalized models in part to ensure the survival and legitimacy of the organization in spite of rather than because of individual level outcomes such as student performance. It may be more appropriate to look at organizational level characteristics that correspond with individual level outcomes independent of school administrators' managerial behaviors than to use these organization level behaviors to predict individual level outcomes. This means that school administrators' individual resources and decision-making authority are not as significant to individual student performance as the institutionalized model or environmental context in which their managerial behaviors exist and to which they conform.

Consequently, the school environment or type of educational system in which individual students and school administrators work may be more predictive of individual-level student performance and organizational-level school administration characteristics than any causal link between school administrators' managerial behaviors and individual student performance. Organizations become structured by their environments and isomorphically change with them *(DiMaggio & Powell, 1983; Meyer and Rowan, 1977).* Of particular interest to school administrators is the probability that structure and substance, which insinuates itself among school organizations, disseminates through their managerial behaviors and activities. Rather than any sort of technical exchange between school administrators and individual students via the school administrators' managerial behaviors and the consequences of their behavior, school administrators reflect organizational models applied to and shaped by environmental contexts.

Another perspective introduced above is that rational and contextually legitimate models of schools' organizational structure, processes, and outcomes drive school administrators' managerial behaviors. Legitimate managerial behaviors depend on the institutional model incorporated into each school system. Variation in school administrators' managerial behaviors should therefore differ depending on the type of organizational environment in which they operate. Variation in managerial behavior that is contextualized to specific organizational conditions and contexts should also be more influential than managerial behaviors that follow a strictly standardized model, which limits school administrators' decision-making authority.

Hypothesis 2a: Variation in school administrators' managerial behaviors reflects their degree of independent decision-making authority and depends on the level of administrative centralization;

Hypothesis 2b: Consequently, variation in school administrators' managerial behavior influences individual student performance more in administratively decentralized than in centralized systems.

Regardless of the significance of school administrators' managerial behavioral influence on individual student performance, the level of administrative centralization should determine school administrators' ability to contextualize management within their schools. The same institutional influences that contribute to the training, education, and managerial behavior of school administrators as rationalized and legitimate models of organizational management are products of the environment and preexisting levels of student performance at least as much as they are causes of it. School administrators in decentralized systems can direct their managerial behaviors more specifically to the contexts and situations of their school and students, leading to more appropriate resources and opportunities as well as higher individual student performance.

Problems of Scope and Comparativeness

As with many other social scientific arenas, a preponderance of the administration and management literature and research focuses on a single national system's situations and concerns, specifically, and other national systems less frequently. Consequently, the literature and research on school administration in general and their managerial behavior in particular is limited in scope and generalizability across national systems.

With a frequent emphasis on the effects of globalization, researchers have begun emphasizing the benefits of international comparison more often. Epstein *(1994, p. 918)* argues that comparativists explain "why [national] systems and processes vary and how education relates to wider social factors and forces." An internationally comparative perspective allows researchers to explain phenomena not only within school systems and institutions, but also phenomena that link schooling to its unique organizational environment within national systems *(Noah & Eckstein, 1969, p. 113; Theisen & Adams, 1990)*. Internationally comparative perspectives are important because they encourage school administrators and policymakers to understand and consider the role of historical, social, cultural, political, and economic influences on schools' organizational development *(Paige & Mestenhauser, 1999)*.

Public schooling is a global phenomenon and as such the managerial behavior of school administrators has the potential to influence student performance in every nation's system. Although national system-specific analyses exist *(Dimmock & Walker, 1998; Fenech, 1994; Hallinger, Taraseina, & Miller, 1994; Heck, 1993; Paige & Mestenhauser, 1999)*, cross-national analysis of school administrators' influence on individual student performance through their managerial behavior is rare. Because this analysis considers individual level performance and organization level managerial behavior in different national contexts, it adopts a cross-system approach *(Bray & Thomas, 1995)*. This sort of analysis also affords the opportunity to adequately consider school administrators' managerial behavior in its broader sociological and political context of administrative centralization.

Data, Measures, and Models

The data for the analyses come from the Third International Mathematics and Science Study (TIMSS). Administered between 1994 and 1995 under the auspices of the International Association for the Evaluation of Educational Achievement (IEA), TIMSS represents an international sample of individual students, classroom teachers, and school administrators from more than 40 different national school systems. The TIMSS sample includes nations from most of the world's geographic regions as well as nations with both developing and developed economies.

In each country a multi-stage sampling design was used to select a nationally representative sample of math classrooms. TIMSS administered math achievement tests to all students in the selected classrooms. Students also completed surveys that included questions about their families, teachers, schools, and after-school activities. School principals completed questionnaires about their work schedule, their involvement in school and professional activities, and general school characteristics. Both achievement tests and questionnaires were designed to be comparable across classrooms, schools, and countries.

Dependent Variable

To measure student performance, these analyses use the TIMSS math achievement test scores for individual students. The TIMSS achievement tests are based on IRT (Item Response Theory) scale scores, meaning that each student was not given all of the test questions, but only a few items within each content area of each subject. The TIMSS designers used the answers to these questions to create "plausiple values" for the math achievement score each student hypothetically would have received if given all of the possible test questions.

Independent Variables

The dimensions of school administrators' managerial behavior considered for analysis are the contributions of principals' human resources, organizational rationality and legitimacy, and the distribution of curricular (and consequently organizational) power versus authority. These managerial influences are operationalized by dividing school administrators' managerial behaviors into those focusing on internal management and those focusing on external legitimacy. This division allows measurement of both administrative centralization's influence on managerial behavior as well as school administrators' managerial influence on individual student performance. The two composite measures of school administrators' managerial behavior are based on responses from the TIMSS school principal questionnaire. The first measure consists of eight items from the principal survey and indicates the number of hours per month each principal typically spends on internal school activities. The second measure consists of an additional five items from the principal survey and indicates the number of hours per month principals typically spend on external school-related activities. The two measures of managerial behavior are moderately correlated across the entire sample ($r = .330$, $p < .001$, $n = 4550$).

The centralization variable used in the analysis was constructed from information found in The International Encyclopedia of Education *(1994)* concerning curricular governance in each of the appropriate national education systems. In constructing this measure the primary concern was determining the location of administrative decision-making authority within each nation's school system. Nations were rated on a scale of 1 to 5, with 1 indicating administrative decision-making authority at the national level, 3 indicating authority at the provincial level, and 5 indicating authority at the local level. The values of 2 and 4 were assigned to intermediate systems: national-provincial for the former and provincial-local for the latter.

CONCLUSION

The results described above suggest that the managerial behavior of school administrators may be more complex than these analyses have captured. Although school administrators tailor their managerial behaviors to meet the amount of authority they are given to manage organizational processes and individual output according to their schools' organizational environment, cross-national variation in school administrators' managerial behavior is not significantly associated with variation in individual student performance or administrative centralization. There are several possible reasons for this. One is that the model for school administrators' managerial behavior is so strong that even when given authority to influence organizational processes, school administrators do not take full advantage of that opportunity and do not deviate significantly from legitimate models of managerial behavior. Another explanation is that even when variation occurs, the legitimate model of school administrators' managerial behavior is so strong and the desire for legitimacy so great that school administrators' managerial behavior is not related specifically enough to the schools' organizational and the students' individual contexts. Neither of these explanations, however, take into account the variation among national systems in spite of their level of administrative centralization. Yet another explanation is that the transitory and temporary influence of school administrators cannot outweigh the consistent influences of resource and opportunity over the course of individual students' school careers.

The evidence suggests, however, that school administrators' managerial behaviors relate to schools as organizations more than individual level outcomes such as student performance. Instead the institutionalized organizational model or environmental context determines which school administrators' managerial behaviors are legitimate and rational. As a result, the organizational environment or type of national system in which school administrators work may be more predictive of individual level performance than any causal link between managerial behaviors and individual performance. As stated above, level of administrative centralization does not significantly influence the relationship between school administrators' managerial behaviors and student performance either. This suggests that although organizations become structured by their environments and isomorphically change with them, school administrators' managerial behaviors may be even further contextualized so that standardization of managerial behavior through administrative centralization does not predict the managerial behaviors of school administrators as much as the specific needs and histories of the local schools and communities in which these they are situated. Therefore, school administrators' ability to contextualize their managerial behaviors within their schools is not related to student performance or administrative centralization as much as to the organizational environment of their schools.

The largely insignificant results of these analyses suggest that the technical-functional perspective affords too much significance to the standardization and accountability of school administrators' managerial behaviors when considering student performance outcomes. By testing the technical-functional arguments that level of administrative centralization and emphasis of school administrators' managerial behavior should influence student performance and finding no significant relationships, these analyses have shown that managerial accountability arguments are weak when applied across organizations and systems. Although qualitative and micro level analyses may provide evidence of tight linkages between school administrators' managerial behavior and student performance, these analyses suggest that taking contextually situated instances and transforming them into broadly applied policy or reform agenda initiatives is ill-informed and ill-conceived.

2

The Search for Meanings

INTRODUCTION

The enormous human tragedy of 9/11/01 has understandably been condemned the world over. The killing of innocent civilians has aroused sympathy for the victims and anger toward those who murdered them.

On that day a massive national effort was launched both to take action and to search for its meanings. The first included the war on terror and it does not have an end in sight, and the second began by asking, "why do they hate us?", and that too is unlikely to end any time soon. Framing the questions in that fashion severely limited the search for meanings, and the taking of a series of actions culminated in the expansion of the national security state. Justifications for an imperialistic role for the United States are openly being offered now (e.g., Kaplan, 2003). Sometimes the two—taking action and searching for the meanings of 9/11—were mixed. While the search for meanings has received some attention in certain publications, most of the time the information and analysis presented focused on the actions taken and/or proposed at home and abroad.

When thinking of 9/11, we wonder how a dramatic national event with monumental consequences could have been turned, as it largely has been in PA, into recommendations for more coordination among organizations at different levels of American government. Let me be more specific. First, 9/11 was clearly of central importance to PA, since that tragedy drew attention to possible failure of intelligence agencies; it required massive response on the part of city, state and federal public employees who performed in a heroic manner; and it led to the expansion of national security personnel, funding, and broad legislation.

That notwithstanding, no convincing evidence has emerged so far that these events broadened or deepened our frameworks to view this tragedy in significantly new ways. No new paradigms were offered, for example, a fact which acquires greater significance when one recalls that in calmer times—which were frequently described then, it seems awkward now to remember, as "turbulent"—such practices were not uncommon (e.g., Farmer, 1995, and Fox and Miller, 1996). When considering recent publications, one notices that although their substance has certainly changed, their frameworks, institutional preferences, and the tools relied on, with rare exceptions, remain familiar: constitutional democracy; improving performance and accountability; applying rationality; and producing better results at lower costs.

Second, it is widely believed that the study of PA is interdisciplinary, but the nature of interdisciplinarity that now dominates the field emphasizes some aspects of social sciences and leaves out other disciplines. If PA scholars had remained in touch with, and incorporated major concepts developed in, such fields as cultural studies, literary theory, and comparative politics, they would have been far better equipped to respond in different ways, understand at different levels, and interpret, perhaps even influence, the policies that are now being made and executed. It is obvious that the concept of orientalism, and the discourse that it generated, is among them. It is probably worth pausing for a brief moment to identify some aspects of it.

Orientalist discourse, as it gradually took shape during the nineteenth and twentieth centuries, had made "an assumption that the Orient and everything in it was, if not patently inferior to, then in need of corrective study by the West" (Said, 1978; pp. 40-41). Such study, as well as the power in many cases to change the reality that was being studied, was a unique Western privilege. Said continues,

Yet what has, been previously overlooked is the constricted vocabulary of such a privilege, and the comparative limitations of such a vision. My argument takes it that the Orientalist reality is both antihuman and persistent. Its scope, as much as its institutions and all-pervasive influence lasts up to the present. (p. 44)

Said presented a thorough review of orientalism's developments and its critique in his seminal work (Said, 1978). His recent death was mourned the world over. Recently, there has been a full-scale revival of orientalist scholarship; see, for example, Berman and Lewis .

Ignoring the pervasive influence of this discourse, among other developments in cultural theory, now haunts PA literature and keeps it unaware of its prejudices and its constricted vocabulary. If dramatic events like 9/11 do not provoke exploration of new theoretical frameworks, analytical categories or linguistic styles—all the tools, that is, that are expected to help in breaking out of the routines of "normal science"—the prospects for disciplinary growth and creativity, not just the fashionable talk of churning out new paradigms, are dim.

Third, the interest in the vulnerable, those who are the victims of market forces or governmental action, has not received, unfortunately, the attention in PA that it deserves. The continuing influence of that inertia is reflected in part in the way that the issue of civil liberties has been treated recently. With one exception, civil liberties in PA literature, as will be shown later, are treated in an abstract and distant fashion. That topic surfaced for discussion because of the well-founded fear that certain minority groups (Arabs, Muslims, Middle Easterners, as well as those who resemble them) may be threatened after 9/11, but paradoxically, it is these very groups that remain virtually invisible in PA literature! Furthermore, there is a strange disconnect between those muffled voices talking of civil liberties and the vast majority singing the familiar chorus of organizational design, coordination, and rationality. But perhaps that is not so strange when we recall that the generalized understanding of the Orientalized *other* has already set in motion energies that will turn the gaze of scholarly attention in some directions and not in others.

Fourth, attacks in the past, it may be useful to recall, had come fast and furious at even the slightest hint of policy being separate from its implementation in PA literature; the infamous dichotomy, which had begun to resemble a dragon, had been slain over and over, a development that no one could dare to forget. Interest in policy, in turn, meant a variety of concerns that at least included its points of origin, the forces that gave it shape and meaning, and the interpretive powers that were assigned, assumed, and enlarged; and, of late, it had begun to include issues of race, gender, class, sexual orientation, and national origin. Since at least the rhetoric demanded that one stand tall and triumphant over the slain dragon of that dichotomy, the expectation might have been high that attention will be paid to such policy issues when focusing on 9/11. It is surprising, then, that there was is so little of it on this occasion, an occasion when, if PA were serious about questioning the politics-administration dichotomy, it could have accomplished a great deal.

Some of the pressing questions that might have been pursued are (a) making major decisions in an environment of crisis, (b) backgrounds of the important actors and their likely impact, (c) effects of bureaucratic routines and standard operating procedures after an initial preference has been expressed at the highest level (and other similar insights provided by Allison [1971]), (d) intersection of such special relationships as oil interests, Religious Right, and military contractors at the highest levels of the Bush administration, and (e) understanding the goals of the terrorists.

It is hard to fathom why PA scholars did not probe such issues. Perhaps there was some comfort in moving in familiar grooves, and these grooves are said to have a tendency to get deeper with time. There is momentum of the past too that pulls in ways that are hard to detect. (I suggest later that the unchallenged acceptance of the official and dominant interpretation, along with all of assumptions that go with it, has also a lot to do with it.) Fortunately, there are exceptions as well. Melvin Dubnick (2002; p. 86), for example, stated, "In their efforts to reflect on the implications and consequences of the tragic attacks of September 11, 2001, Americans are faced with the added responsibility of having to give meaning to such senseless events." I build on a similar foundation in this chapter in the hope that exploring the diversity of meanings is in itself a desirable goal and, further, that it may lead sometimes to events becoming less senseless.

No one chapter, or perhaps even a book, can both celebrate what is valuable in that momentum and those grooves *and* inspire enough creative energy when a national tragedy demands it. I certainly do not expect in this chapter to accomplish such ambitious goals. The purpose of the chapter is to address some issues and raise others that enhance the possibilities for a plural, open, and perhaps even exciting role that the diverse meanings of 9/11 might open up for PA. The central issue is the expansion of the space for interpretive powers and alternative explanations, not to find ways to implement policies efficiently or at a lower cost. I address these issues by, first, presenting a critique of the response in PA literature to 9/11.

The special issue of *Public Administration Review* (2002, vol. 62) serves as a proxy for PA literature. That issue published more articles on 9/11 than are available in any one publication in the field; furthermore, *PAR* is often referred to as the journal of record in PA. Called here the Dominant View, the PA literature reveals the acceptance, with very few exceptions, of the decisions handed down from top officials with thoughtful recommendations about how their implementation might be improved without raising any serious questions about the origins of the crisis as well as any discussion of alternative responses to the ones quickly adopted under the existing constraints.

The second way I have tried to address this issue of expanding the space for alternative interpretations and explanations, organized here under Alternative Meanings, consists of reviewing the same events with different possibilities in mind. Fortunately, alternative interpretations and explanations are readily available, although they are often overlooked. The third part, called Civil Liberties, focuses on these liberties in view of their special significance in the post-9/11 period, and because the *PAR*'s special issue devotes a whole section to it. That part also provides a critique and suggestions for what might have been included. The chapter ends with some concluding thoughts.

DOMINANT VIEW

The search for meanings of 9/11 began to be framed soon after the tragedy occurred in a language that was exaggerated and hyperbolic; it encouraged wild generalizations that substituted slogans for analysis. Initially, it will be recalled, that President George W. Bush described the crashing of the four airplanes on that day as an act of terror, and promised that those responsible will be brought to justice. Soon after that, he called it an act of war. But even characterizing the attack as a terrorists' declaration of war on America did not seem to be enough. Ratcheting the language up further, the attack, the president (and virtually all the journalists, TV hosts, and most of the analysts) declared, had been launched on freedom, a concept that was left vague and unspecified, but was closely identified with the United States.

The terrorists, the president and pundits claimed, resented Americans for having that freedom since they did not have it themselves, and that was why they had struck. Finally, it was civilization itself that was identified as their real target, although that too was left undefined; presumably it stood for both American cherished values and cultivated refinement.

There might have been the expectation that with time calm reflection will replace the initial emotionally-charged rhetoric. Instead, that original view not only hardened, it began to be defended on the basis of escalating definition of what needed to be protected (human life, freedom, civilization) and policy and political agendas (war, oil, unipolar world, elections) with which they were linked. It also required the corresponding denigration in exaggerated ways of those who were believed to pose the threat. "Evil came to our door," stated President Bush (2002; p. 4). Since then, a variety of government officials have described the terrorist threat to be global, and nothing less than total victory is now said to be the national goal. A new temperament and vocabulary emerged which facilitated the use of words that encouraged venomous denunciation: *demonic, evil, violent, dangerous, terrorist, suspicious, Islamic*. The tendency to escalate, in language and in reliance on organized violence, is now clearly the dominant and privileged implication of 9/11.

Even Vaclav Havel, a rare individual who combines refined sensibilities with political experience, was clearly under its spell when he said in a recent speech, "Evil must be confronted in its womb and, if there is no other way to do it, then it has to be dealt with by the use of force." He did not say what evil was or where its womb was located. Similarly, an American academician, Condoleezza Rice, who was appointed as the National Security Adviser to President Bush, apparently seemed to believe that the terrorists' commitment to violence was irrevocable and irrational; military developments or other provocations did not influence their behavior. Recently, she insisted that the changed conditions in Iraq had nothing to do with the increased terrorist activity there. She dismissed the notion that the terrorists would "be minding their own business—drinking tea, having meetings" if American invasion of Iraq had not taken place. "They are fighters, they are jihadists," she said, and if they were not fighting in Iraq, she stated, they would be in the Gulf, Southeast Asia, perhaps even the U.S.

The dominant meaning is not likely to loosen its grip in the foreseeable future. Quick military victories in Afghanistan and Iraq have reinforced it. Some see in it an opportunity to erase the memory of Vietnam, and others view it as an attempt to increase the influence of the military-industrial complex. Most feel helpless or alienated when confronting the repeated messages of fear and patriotism in media now owned by a shrinking number of owners.

The dominant meaning is also reflected in a kind of essentialization that would be considered contemptible in other contexts. For example, those who would immediately challenge the idea that the behavior of a group should be understood in reference only to its cultural, racial or religious characteristics, have felt perfectly comfortable in doing just that during the last two years in reference to one distinct religious minority. I don't know anyone, for instance, who has wondered what is it about the Christian religion or white race that produces children or youth who go with guns to schools and start killing other kids and their teachers.

Similarly, how often have op-ed pieces appeared, or dinner table conversations in many households turned to, exploring a connection between the Christian faith of Timothy McVeigh and his terrorist attack on a federal building in Oklahoma City? That notwithstanding, the fact that the terrorists were Muslims continues to provide enough justification for many well educated men and women to link the terrorists' behavior with their religion. The assumption that what drove them to such extreme violence was a unified and generic Islam, not an analysis of events, or hurts and grievances that their nations endured, has by now become routinized. Perceptions based on these assumptions, which are both biased and false as Said has so often demonstrated, are repeated so frequently in official statements, media channels, and many scholarly works that they take for many the shape of solid reality and unqualified truth.

While some serious and balanced discussion of the religion of Islam and the Muslims living in a variety of societies has taken place during the last few years, far more frequent has been the daily Islam-bashing, in print and electronic media, journals and books, and movies and TV shows. One of the worst "scholarly" examples of it is Bernard Lewis's *What Went Wrong*?, as was recently pointed out by Said (2002; pp. 69-74). Instead of opening up possibilities for new meanings and understandings of who "we" and "they" are, another layer of beliefs about the Muslim world is being laid, one that selectively supplies additional beliefs to confirm the old prejudices to define it primarily in terms of its lacks and deficiencies and absences. All of this is being done in the name of increasing awareness and reducing misunderstandings about Islam! It appears that keeping the oil flowing at a low price had only temporarily dampened the orientalist discourse.

All of the recent literature in PA made no mention of such concerns. Most of it either ignored the reasons, explanations, or meanings of the terrorist attacks while focusing largely on issues of implementation or it explicitly reinforced the version that did not deviate from the dominant view. Here is an example of the first:

As we think about the best approach to creating an affordable and sustainable system of homeland security in the context of competing budgetary claims, we can and should select those programs and tools that promise to provide the most cost-effective approaches to achieve our national goals.

The second was represented well by Stephen Sloan who went beyond the already inflated official view by suggesting that the terrorists have "declared war against all." I wonder if he is aware that the number of countries that have not reported any case of terrorism is actually far greater than those that have. But human imagination is remarkably creative; it is quite capable in the present environment of producing highly original definitions of terrorism.

Chester Newland was the only author in that *PAR* special issue who recorded his views on this matter in any detail. They deserve serious consideration. He pushed farther the already very broad boundaries of the Dominant View. He stated in a matter-of-fact fashion that "terrorism seeks to force civilized society to violate its own basic values and disciplines that sustain them," and, further, that "humane society is among terrorists' chief targets". He also offered some explanations for the terrorists' behavior. "Terrorism thrives on many varied causes, though terrorist acts often are grounded most essentially in personal or borrowed longing for self-justification: *I am*!"

Newland did not provide any evidence for his conclusion that the causes of terrorists were grounded "most essentially in personal or borrowed longings for self-justifications..." In the absence of any evidence, one may speculate whether such self-justification was a widely-felt human need. If so, he left unexplained the most vital part, namely, the connection between such longings and the acts of the terrorists—e.g., why did not others also commit acts of terror? On the other hand, if such longings are rare, he might have speculated about why they occur among the terrorists more frequently than others. Could it be the memories of humiliation and betrayal, misguided understanding of current events, poor child rearing practices, foreign exploitation of resources facilitated by local stooges, or something entirely different? No, there are no such speculations. When the purpose is to condemn the *others* there is no reason to let them speak for themselves, nor is there any need to scrutinize the logical leaps in thinking when trying to understanding why they might have acted in a particular fashion. Whether called scholarship or knowledge, it can come soaked in prejudice, it can be plucked out of thin air, it can be constructed, published, and, most of time, it can escape any serious review or critique.

In the following passage, Newman gives the impression that there are other or related causes of terrorism as well. A most visible and deeply saddening inspiration for expanding global terrorism is the escalation of generations-long, tit-for-tat, more than an eye-for-an-eye conflicts between Israel and Palestine, which have blinded both to the humane roots of their historically great cultures, now plunged into mutual degradation, if not destruction. Thus [sic], through pursuits of self-aggrandizement and other causes as pretexts for being, terror flourishes.

Here Newman would have one believe that self-aggrandizement and other causes of Israeli-Palestinian conflict are serving as pretexts for some undefined phenomenon called *being*, which leads to the prevalence of terror. There are even more serious questions here than those raised above—about definitions ("being," "pretexts," "self-aggrandizement"), and the connections assumed from one step to another.

Pretexts for being, if it is possible to understand that phrase, sweep aside such major events as the Nazi atrocities during World War II; the active role in the Middle East, first, of the British and then that of the United States; the alliances formed during the Cold War; location of major religious sites in Jerusalem and the surrounding areas; Israel's security; the personalities of the major actors; and the Israeli occupation of Palestine, and the establishment of a large number of settlements. Perhaps they are folded, in a highly unique way, under "tit-for-tat, more than eye-for-an-eye," or they are to be found under the rubric of "other causes," but, then, one cannot be sure of that either. Such confusion reinforces the view that undefined and unsubstantiated negative statements tend to be allowed only about some subjects, in both meanings of the word.

Newland also attributes to the terrorists some other ideas. "Globalization, in particular, is corrupted to appear as an invader clothed as liberator." No terrorists, incidentally, are quoted that support this view, or, for that matter, any of the other views confidently attributed to them. As is widely known, critiques of globalization by now have been offered from virtually all points on the political spectrum. Even mainstream figures, such as the Nobel Prize-winning economist, Joseph Stiglitz , has offered one. And among the supporters of globalization too, its role as the liberator is not so clearly evident. Here is what Thomas Friedman, a well-known columnist for *The New York Times*, states: The hidden hand of the market will never work without a hidden fist. McDonalds cannot flourish without McDonald Douglas, the designer of the U.S. Air Force F-15. And the hidden fist that keeps the world safe for Silicon Valley's technologies to flourish is called the U.S. Army, Air Force, Navy, and the Marine Corps.

One begins to wonder who is corrupting globalization's role. Why does its role as an invader, or its dependence on the threat of the use of military power, become the corrupted version of what is actually a liberating force only when the terrorists state it, assuming that is what "they" (all of them or some factions, those based around Afghanistan or Indonesia or Saudi Arabia or Algeria ?) do believe?

Since Newman can be located within the framework of Dominant View, it may be appropriate to point out the set of unstated assumptions upon which that framework rests. One of them requires that energies and attention be directed with a sense of urgency to terrorism. Standing alone, unqualified, de-contextualized, and torn from any historical precedents or memory, such terrorism hastens the need to identify military targets. The provocation of 9/11 is thought to be a sufficient reason.

But explanations for the rise of terrorism are also offered, in an ideologically conscious manner by an increasing number of scholars, and they are repeated by those who go along with the official position, trusting their government leaders, but adding sometimes minor variations, caveats, or psychobabble.

Such explanations almost always export the problem beyond American borders: it is often Islam that is blamed or the culture of certain areas or lack of democracy and/or education. Hand in glove with such a perspective is the firmly held belief that European countries, and particularly the United States, have done no harm abroad; they have exerted a benign influence, helped the poor and the starving in other countries by providing them foreign aid and accepted refugees and immigrants from such areas. These two elements, evil comes from abroad and the United States and Europe are a force for the good in the world, are the major pillars on which the Dominant View rests. Alternative explanations will be discussed later, but at this stage it may be noted that the

Dominant View either does not entertain the possibility of different perspectives, or when it does it is for the purpose of presenting new evidence, or interpreting the old, for demolishing or considerably diminishing the significance of certain events and forces. Those events and forces are colonialism, the purpose of which was exploitation; a variety of insidious practices introduced or condoned in the so-called Third World countries in the interest of what were once called the imperatives of the Cold War; Western interference in the affairs of such countries where democratically elected governments were overthrown and dictators installed, on some occasions, and dictators removed, when they were no longer useful, in the name of introducing democracy, on others; and financing certain NGOs or other groups with a view to influencing government officials or election results.

There are certain consequences of the PA literature not questioning the assumptions of the Dominant View at least on some occasions. One of them is ignoring the considerations mentioned above. Another is implicitly accepting the view that terrorists are primitive people who are inspired by their cultures and interpretation of their religion to be violent, determined to attack innocent people abroad whose life style they envy, and committed to denying themselves the benefit of learning from Western ideas and generosity. What is expected to emerge from all that is a literature that does not raise any doubts about the policies meant to militarily crush the terrorists abroad and refine the organizational tools that thwart the security threats at home. No wonder the PA literature reflected these values and produced the results that it did.

Even in the familiar territory of policy implementation, a blowback of sorts is another consequence. The limitations of the Dominant View are being revealed in Afghanistan and Iraq in a variety of ways. First, after the predictable military success in contests between highly unequal combatants, American funding for nation-building, which was opposed until recently, may be inadequate in amount and not likely to be sustained over a sufficiently long period of time. Recent reports already reveal that while military spending in Afghanistan was high, funds promised for civilian purposes are shrinking. This imbalance has a familiar ring to it. It may be useful to recall that it was a similar imbalance, between high military spending when armed struggle against the Soviet occupation of Afghanistan was being sponsored by the CIA and the almost complete lack of interest in social and political matters after the Soviet defeat, that contributed to the instability in that area and provided the impetus for terrorist activities there in the first place.

Second, the United States' military and civilian personnel are likely to be inhibited in cooperating with, even conceding power to, the people who were, until military victory was achieved, demonized, the same people that continue, after their clear defeat and extreme hardship, to reveal remarkable tenacity of faith in their religion and pride in their culture.

The opportunity to rid themselves of all that baggage and embrace the American definition of the good, secular life is not being taken advantage of as enthusiastically as expected. Third, these inhibitions on the part of American personnel are further complicated by the fact that the quick military victories have so far produced less respect, and more hatred, for the United States among Arabs and Muslims. In Iraq, a recent survey by the intelligence branch of the Department of State, the results of which are still classified, are said by *The New York Times* to reveal that hostility toward Americans is not grounded only in the traditional Sunni loyalists of Saddam Hussein or, now, in Shiites as well because of the frequent raids in their areas. "As reasons for the Iraqi hostility, the defense officials cited not just disaffection over a lack of electricity.., but cultural factors that magnify anger about the foreign military presence."

Operating within the constraints of the Dominant View has significance for both policy making and implementation. The recent PA literature, unfortunately, does not even mention the kinds of concerns suggested above. Implementing policies by improving domestic security organizational arrangements in a geographical and cultural vacuum goes beyond ethnocentricity. Another unfortunate consequence of working within its constraints is that the slain dragon of that old dichotomy appears to be coming back to life again: policy-making, it is now being implicitly granted, is someone else's business, PA is about implementation.

ALTERNATIVE MEANINGS

The Dominant View often inspires images in the media, TV and radio talk shows, and chat rooms of blood-thirsty Muslims, instructed by Islam to kill the infidels at every opportunity. Fortunately, alternative meanings of 9/11 are readily available, even though they are often ignored. Here is one example. Under the supervision of Madeleine Albright, who was not known to be friendly toward Muslims or Islamic countries when she was the Secretary of State, the Pew Research Center and the *International Herald Tribune* conducted a survey of opinion leaders in several countries. As many as "58 percent of the foreign leaders said U.S. policies were responsible for the attacks while only 18 percent of the U.S. opinion leaders interviewed held that view."

The dominant understanding and interpretation of 9/11 invariably ends up with pointing the finger at some variant or the other of Islam (Wahabi, radical, madrassah-based, fundamentalist, politicized, jihad-oriented, the list goes on) and Muslim culture, beyond the personality and resources, that is, of Osama bin Ladin. Definitive understanding of the terrorists' motivations and sources of inspiration are not known so far. What can be said with certainty is that they were educated, young, Muslim, men who were nationals of Saudi Arabia and Egypt, and they hated the United States. For many Muslims, which might include the terrorists, the meaning of 9/11, however, is similar to the foreign respondents' views in that survey. To understand their perspective, one does not have to search for vague clues, subtle hints, or hidden messages, one only has to review some events in United States' foreign policy. For many Americans, these events may be long buried in the past and they might even appear trivial, but for most Muslims their memories are both remarkably fresh and painful.

The prominent events range from the overthrow of the democratically elected government of Iran in 1953 to the present support of Israeli treatment of Palestinians, and a great deal in between. The terrorists base in Afghanistan emerged out of a deep sense of betrayal of the *mujahedeen*, some of whom later became the Taliban. It may be necessary to recall that the *mujahedeen* were Afghans, described at one time by President Ronald Reagan as the moral equivalents of the American founding fathers. They fought the American-financed war to oust the Soviets from Afghanistan; they suffered on a massive scale, with their casualties in thousands and dislocation of population in millions. When these sacrifices had paid off and the Soviets had been forced out, the United States abruptly left the scene, leaving them feeling both exploited and abandoned. It is these feelings that were channeled into terrorism later on, and it was American weapons and training that gave them some of its lethal quality.

Furthermore, there is deep resentment about the stationing of American troops in Saudi Arabia. For many Muslims, the havoc that American-backed sanctions in Iraq caused its people, now being attributed exclusively to Saddam Hussein's policies, was a matter of very considerable concern already; it is now being reinforced by the events unfolding after the American military victory there. Reassurances from top government officials that American policies are not directed against Muslims, only those who are terrorists, are often viewed with skepticism among the Muslim communities here and abroad because in virtually all the contemporary international disputes, Muslims are on one side, and the United States is either neutral or it is on the other side: Palestine, Kashmir, Sudan, and Chechnya. The public stance of the United States that combines jingoism and revenge, on the one hand, and claims of innocence and virtue, on the other, generate among Muslims feelings of either cynicism or bitterness. This alternative explanation holds that these harsh memories of humiliation and exploitation of American policies provide the seeds from which we are reaping the current harvest of terror.

The sound of voices that rely on these kinds of analyses has been muffled by the loud proclamations of the dominant meaning, and its substance distorted by questioning the loyalty and patriotism of those who voice it. There are exceptions, of course. One of them is former President Jimmy Carter, who acknowledged the provocative nature of the recent policies. "We have thrown down counterproductive gauntlets to the rest of the world, disavowing U.S. commitments to laboriously negotiated international accords," he wrote. "Peremptory rejection of nuclear agreements, biological weapons convention, environmental protection, anti-torture proposals, and punishment of war criminals have sometimes been combined with economic threats against those who disagree with us."

The efforts to seek alternative meanings of 9/11 in recent PA literature are remarkably few, but they need to be recognized. Sloan (2002; p. 125), for example, identifies the need for a different kind of inquiry, but he does not undertake it.

But beyond the conduct of war, what is required in the long-term is the commitment of the international community to identify and seek to eliminate the root causes of a form of armed conflict and political violence that is as old as recorded history and as current as today and tomorrow analysis is to posit four alternative war narratives that are likely to surface during the post-September 11 era. As will be noted, there are indications of each during the months following the tragedy, but none has yet emerged as the dominant post-script.

His narratives are similar in some ways to the one presented here, but they are also different; they do not include the alternative meanings, for instance. The dominant view overlaps with his first two narratives.

We have wondered why interest in these alternative meanings is so rare in PA. The lingering influence of dichotomy I mentioned earlier comes to mind, which has been often slain but appears to be remarkably resilient. Furthermore, our training as well as the substance of our teaching, in most cases, limits our horizons in some ways, although we are reluctant to admit that—in fact, we have heard strong denunciation of any such allegation on several occasions. Leaving our wounded pride aside for a moment, there is no denying that the amount of interest in various aspects of policy *making* in our publications and our national conference is quite limited. To that list should be added the fact that the tradition of questioning the motives, assumptions, interests, and cultural sensitivity of policy makers is not well developed in PA literature.

CIVIL LIBERTIES

Soon after 9/11, residents in the United States from mostly Muslim countries were rounded up in large numbers, detained, and interrogated for long periods. They were not allowed to contact anyone immediately after being taken into custody; when they were located by their families, they were moved to other locations, often very far from where they originally lived; they were not informed ahead of time of the evidence that was to be used against them; and for months, many were held in solitary confinement. In a recent broadcast of "60 Minutes," those interviewed stated that they were tortured and were considering filing a class action suit to collect damages.

The exact number of individuals who were so detained has not been released, but it is thought to be between 1,500 and 2,000. The Attorney General's reason for holding them is that they are "suspected terrorists" but the grounds for suspicion are apparently so unfounded that not a single one has been charged with involvement in September 11 attacks; and with the exception of four people indicted on support-for-terrorism charges in late August, no one has been charged with any terrorists act. Those arrested on immigration charges—the vast majority—have been effectively "disappeared." Their cases are not listed on the public docket, their hearings are closed to the public and the presiding judges are instructed to neither confirm nor deny that their cases exist, if asked. Two district courts and a unanimous court of appeals have held this practice unconstitutional.

Such governmental harassment, made legal by the USA PATRIOT Act, paralleled, perhaps even encouraged, the non-governmental one that occurred on a larger scale with even more lethal consequences. The actions against Muslims and Arabs, or those who looked like them, ranged from obscene calls to three murders. It was in view of the anticipation of these events, or soon after they began, that the issue of civil liberties began to be raised, and resistance to its violations began to be noticed.

The relative lack of interest in recent PA literature in civil liberties, or sympathy for its victims, may have to do with the inadequate attention to the vulnerable generally, indifference toward an ethnic minority most Americans have little or no contact with, negative representation of them in the media, and/or Orientalist prejudices. It may also be based on the mistaken view that protections that civil liberties provide in the U.S. are limited only to its citizens. In a very recent case (*Zadvydas v. Davis*), the Supreme Court held, once an alien enters the country, the legal circumstance changes, for the Due Process Clause applies to all 'persons' within the United States, including aliens, whether their presence here is lawful, unlawful, temporary, or permanent.

But attempts continue to be made to threaten American citizens' civil liberties. Two citizens, Yasser Hamdi and Jose Padilla, were arrested and declared by the president to be "enemy combatants"; that is all that was thought to be necessary for the indefinite, incommunicado incarceration of any US citizen..This proposition is so extreme that even the US Court of Appeals for the Fourth Circuit, by far the most conservative federal circuit in the country, rejected it.

Some of those who are, or are suspected of being, Taliban fighters were captured in Afghanistan and brought to Guantanamo Bay; at one time their number was around 600. After some confusion, the legal cover found for detaining them was to give them the status of "unlawful combatants." The official reason for holding them, in conditions that some have described as resembling a human zoo, was the gathering of intelligence. Virtually all of them are Muslims but they come from more than 30 countries; those from Saudi Arabia are the largest in number. Their detention period could be indefinite. They are not allowed the protections accorded prisoners of war. Justification for keeping them in such a legal vacuum is based ultimately on military strength.

In the recent PA literature, Shamsul Haque is clearly the exception. His overview of threats to civil liberties that these changes pose to all who live the United States, citizens as well as immigrants, is highly valuable. He discusses four kinds of rights. (a) The civil rights are challenged because the USA PATRIOT Act grants to the executive branch certain unprecedented powers of "surveillance, including gathering sensitive personal records, tracking e-mail and internet usage, monitoring financial transactions, practicing sneak-and-peak searches, and using roving wiretaps". (Lisa Nelson's analysis of the impact of new technology—she examines Carnivore carefully—that filters information for intelligence gathering purposes is also important here.)

The threats to political rights consist of recent changes that affect "the protection of due process under the Fifth Amendment and the safeguards against 'unreasonable searches and seizures' guaranteed by the Fourth Amendment". Also adversely affected are freedoms of speech and association because of the Act's "broad definition of domestic terrorism, which may cover political dissent, civil disobedience, and [even] environmentalism..."

In regard to minority rights, the stereotypes of Asians and Arabs that have been created in the United States have increased intolerance toward them at home, and probably encouraged repression against Muslims in China, Chechnya, and Kashmir. (Haque does not mention the fact that under the Act, the president has the power to declare terrorist any person or organization, and, having done that, the assets of that person or organization can be frozen.

By exercising that power, two of the three largest Muslim charities have been shut down; they are said to be "under investigation." No charges have been brought against them, and the period for which these funds will remain frozen by government is not known. Giving charity or *zakat* is a religious duty of all Muslims.) (d) Social rights, which refer to entitlements to public services, suffered as well. Budgetary allocations for defense and domestic security have increased while spending on social programs has declined.

This is an incomplete account of the transformation in the civil liberties that has occurred since 9/11/. The issues touched on are grave, and they require urgent and frequent attention. For these reasons, it was gratifying to note that in the special issue of *PAR* six articles appeared in a section set aside for this topic. (Haque's was not among them; it was in another section.) On closer scrutiny, however, it became clear that one of the six articles, by Kirlin and Kirlin , brought together interesting data that revealed that citizens' propensity for civic engagement had decreased since 9/11, but it said nothing about civil liberties. Another one, by Spicer , was also not concerned with civil liberties but with the range of government operations. Spicer expressed strong preference for government as a civil association that performed only minimal functions, and acted mostly as an umpire, which was to be clearly distinguished from the dreaded vision of government viewed as a purposive association. He worried that the resources mobilized for fighting terrorism may be redirected later for the achievement of social purposes. I wondered if making food stamps available to the poor had already pushed the government into the dangerous category of a purposive association.

The remaining four articles (by Anthony Lewis, Lisa Nelson, Jon Gould, and Melvin Dubnick) do touch on aspects of civil liberties, some of them very briefly (Lewis contributed a page and a half), others in more detail. The reason for the terribly abstract, anti-septic, and distant feeling I had on reading them was not hard to locate. I was stunned to note that except for a fleeting comment in two articles, to which I will turn in just a moment, there was *no* reference to Muslims or Islam or Arabs in any of the six articles and the introduction in the entire section devoted to civil liberties! Since the obvious needs to be stated, at what decibel level in order to be heard it is hard to tell, it was the fear that Muslims as individuals or as a group may become the primary targets of violence and discrimination that the issue of civil liberties surfaced in the first place. (Non-Muslims are also threatened, but that is not widely known.) Making a passing reference to them while writing on civil liberties in a post-9/11 context is comparable to publishing an article on civil rights in the 1960s while mentioning African-Americans in a cursory fashion!

In one article, Jon Gould sought to carefully balance civil liberties against the need for government surveillance. He identified six factors that most Americans are willing to tolerate in order "to uncover those individuals who pose a threat" (p. 76). One of the six dealt with "limiting the search..to more relevant suspects might smack of illegal discrimination." He stated, "Given the demographics of the September 11th hijackers, some might call for intensive screening of young Middle Eastern men who seek to board an aircraft."

He proceeded then to reveal the findings of a poll in which 68 percent of the respondents stated that it would be a mistake to "put Arabs and Arab-Americans in this country under special surveillance" (p. 77). Since Gould moved on after this, and did not mention Arabs or Muslims again, he left behind an incomplete story. No mention was made of the several widely reported cases of Muslims who were not allowed to board airplanes for which they had confirmed reservations. Or any reference to the sweeps in Arab and Muslim neighborhoods soon after 9/11 from which a large number of men were taken into federal custody. What he leaves the reader with is a balancing act generously tipping in favor of civil liberties as reflected in a public opinion poll while completely ignoring their violations in practice.

In the other article, Dubnick (2002; p. 89) stated that while the official message coming from the White House and the administration "from September 11 onward has been a clear warning that Arab Americans and Islamics of all nationalities should not be the target of revenge or reprisal," there was also an "enemy within narrative" that could be heard as well, and the latter message was probably heard very clearly by such agencies as Immigration and Naturalization Service and FBI. It is quite remarkable that even in this one sentence in which the group under attack is identified, Dubnick could not name it accurately. Who are the Islamics? Did he mean Muslims? Islamists?

In both articles, or any of the six for that matter, the authors cannot be accused of expressing any sense of outrage over, or sympathy with, the Muslims and Arabs whose civil liberties were being violated. Maintaining such a distance is in itself worth exploring, although I will not attempt such exploration here. Clearly, we have a long way to go.

Looking to the civil rights' future, conventional wisdom holds that when the danger is over, better sense prevails, balance is restored, and the rule of law is again respected by the government. But Ronald Dworkin draws our attention to the different nature of the problem that the nation currently faces.

We are ashamed now of what we did then: we count the [Supreme] Court's past tolerance of anti-sedition laws, interments, and McCarthyism as among the worst stains on its record. That shame comes easier now, of course, because we no longer fear the Kaiser, or kamikazes, or Stalin. It may be a long time before we stop fearing international or domestic terrorism, however, and we must therefore be particularly careful now. What we lose now, in our commitment to civil rights and fair play, may be much harder later to regain. When the PA literature focuses on a variety of issues, there is a sense of comfort and familiarity—with the concepts used, the outcomes expected, the citations relied on, etc. But when the gears shift and the issues now have to include the victims of governmental overreach, there is no easy way to absorb these concerns, and there is a disconnect of sorts, since the language to name and confront it is far less fully developed.

The vitality of Dworkin's analysis for PA deserves to be widely known. Prompt and eager efforts in PA literature to institutionalize the combating of international and domestic fear, which several articles in *PAR* clearly do, may prolong, if Dworkin is right, the danger to civil liberties. The possibility that PA is complicit in this fashion is a serious issue that needs urgent attention.

CONCLUSION

We have wondered what implications would emerge for PA from including *all* these three perspectives. It is an issue that needs exploring in our professional journals and conferences. However, here are some tentative speculations. In our curriculum and research, such inclusion might lead to the incorporation of some discussion of policy frameworks within which administration takes place. The legacy of Cold War, which has rarely been emphasized, might be added for providing a historical backdrop. With the growing interest in terror, some understanding of orientalism would greatly broaden our horizons; and exploring the potential or existing culpability of PA in institutionalizing fear may broaden the interest in constitutional democracy. Some familiarity with American foreign policy could add a dimension of interdisciplinarity that we often overlook.

And who can deny these days the usefulness of knowing something about the politics, ownership, distribution, and consumption of oil. While these concerns might be spread across the curricula, they might also breathe new life into international and comparative public administration. In view of the current interest in including non-governmental actors in PA's curriculum, there are a variety of fascinating areas that have opened up: development of the institutions of PA in Afghanistan and Iraq in the context of explicitly acknowledging the national, regional and American interests; the tension between relying on NGOs, on the one hand, and private businesses, on the other; the renewed interest in industrial-military-complex; and the role of monetary payoffs in obtaining agreements of other countries, on one hand, and the support of individuals and groups within foreign countries to facilitate military occupation, on the other.

Few would argue with the proposition that broadening the scope of interpretive abilities is likely to improve our understanding of public policies. I have indicated how frequently we in PA tend to gravitate toward parochial and narrow routines of the past. I have also tried to offer a different framework for understanding the same events. I entertain the immodest expectation that such a framework when applied might develop the capacity for searching for diverse and varied meanings of events, policies, and even organizational restructuring plans. If there is any merit to this kind of analysis, I have only scratched the surface. Other possibilities were mentioned recently by Louis Menand (2002, 98) although he did so partly in jest.

> September 11th showed that the United States is hated by many good people around the world because it is an imperial bully; the United States is hated by many bad people around the world because it is a beacon of freedom and opportunity; Islam is a civilization irredeemably hostile to Western values; Islam is a civilization assimilating Western values; globalization has gone too far; globalization has not gone far enough...

The task of sorting out explanations of major events and developments along these lines—call them hypotheses, if you must—in the curriculum of PA can only enrich it. To put it differently, not doing so, will give us in many cases only monolithic versions of received wisdom, silencing many unfamiliar voices, and students in classes trying to stay awake.

It is perhaps appropriate to end with an untidy note that prevents, or at least reduces, the prospects of misunderstanding. First, I have been critical of scholars writing for the special issue of *PAR* dated September, 2002, who did not have access to some information that I have relied on, and that may appear unfair. While that may be true in some cases, my belief is that the general tendencies that I have identified are still valid.

However, nothing would please me more than to see convincing evidence that PA literature had already moved in the direction I am suggesting, and that my critique and proposals are unnecessary. Second, nothing in this chapter is meant to justify the actions of the terrorists. Those steeped in the dominant view have sometimes made unwarranted inferences of this kind when encountering dissenting opinions. Third, any kind of analysis, it needs to be readily acknowledged, if pushed to extreme limits, will produce absurd results. Search for diverse meanings does not automatically validate all of them equally. Such search has led in some instances to bizarre conclusions through convoluted reasoning. Jean Baudrillard's statement about 9/11 illustrates the problem: "We can say that they *did* it, but we *wished for* it" (quoted in Menand, 2002; p.101, emphasis in original).

3

Politics in a Postmodern Age

INTRODUCTION

Two days after American forces entered Baghdad, Arab television stations in countries like Qatar, Egypt, the United Arab Emirates and Lebanon broadcasted images of Iraqi opposition to the new occupation. To the surprise of the American people, American forces were greeted with demonstrations and not celebrations. On several occasions, American soldiers fired live ammunition at demonstrators who were just "liberated" from the brutality of the Iraqi regime. Are these quacks of occupation or liberation? Why are some Iraqis opposed to American presence and influence in Iraq? How could Arabs not appreciate the great fortune (i.e. liberation) the United States had bestowed on them? This article finds in the history of the interaction between the West and the Arab world an answer to these questions.

History of western influence and meddling in Arab countries and the relationship between the West and the East over the past century has contributed to a sense of distrust of the West by Arab peoples. This article first narrates the story of almost one hundred years of struggle by indigenous people in the Middle East for liberation – from the West and not by the West. Then, the article presents a set of proposals that would improve the relationship between Arabs and the West.

Arabs and the West: One Hundred Years of Resistance!

Over the past one hundred years, the West has not enjoyed the image of liberator among the people of the Middle East. Many

Arab national movements adopt anti-western political speech to gain popularity among their peoples (Bill and Springbord, 1990). Western interests have been at odds with the national and public interests of the Arab peoples. While decolonization would normally mean national independence, tyrants who eventually ruled Arab countries have ensured that Arabs would not achieve self-determination (Alkadry, 2002).

Alkadry and Khalil summarize the relationship between the West and the peoples of the Middle East in four instances of resistance that lasted a century. The result of these instances is a decolonized Middle East without popular sovereignty and democratic governance. Throughout these moments, western interests prevailed at the expense of human and political rights of the people of the decolonized Middle East peoples.

Betrayal

The first epoch of resistance is one of betrayal of pan-Arab nationalistic aspirations to spare western economic and political interests. In 1917, during the First World War, the Ottomans allied themselves with the Germans against the French and British empires. In what Antonios (1938/1946) refers to as 'The Arab Awakening', he describes how the Arab nations, led by the Shareef Hussein of Mecca, allied themselves with the British and the French and revolted against the Ottomans and helped put an end to an empire which has lasted more than four centuries.

The basis of the treaty between Arabs and the Allies was a British promise made to Shareef Hussein - a pan-Arab Meccan leader - that Arabs would form an independent and sovereign nation on the ruins of the Ottoman empire.

In return for this promise, the Arabs would revolt against the Ottoman empire which has fallen under the control of the 'Young Turks'. The European victors, however, had other plans for the region. Said (1993) explains that, "the Arabs after liberating themselves from the Ottomans in 1917 and 1918, took British promises for independence as the literal truth"(Said, 1993, p. 247). Antonios (1938/1946) describes what happened at the San Remo conference where British and French leaders changed the geography of the region:

Whatever else may be said of the San Remo decisions [of spring 1920, in which "the whole of the Arab Rectangle lying between the Mediterranean and the Persian frontier was to be placed under mandatory rule"], they [allies meeting in San Remo] did violate the general principles proclaimed and the specific promises made by the Allies, and more particularly by Britain. The purport of the pledges given in secret is now known: ...with that the Arabs had come into the War and made their contribution and their sacrifices, and that fact alone sufficed to turn the corresponding obligation into a debt of honor. What the San Remo did was, in effect, to ignore the debt and come to decisions which, on all the essential points, ran counter to the wishes of the peoples concerned.

The San Remo agreement between the British and the French put Arabs under direct colonial rule. Palestinian Arabs had to deal with a new settlement activity which was encouraged by the British, and which would be the cornerstone of the Arab-Israeli conflict for the last 65 years (Hourani, 1991). At the same time that the British leaders made promises to Arab leaders, they made different promises to the growing European Zionist movement in what became known as 'the Balfour Declaration.' The Balfour Declaration gave Zionists the promise of a homeland in Palestine.

The betrayal of Arabs by the West caused deep resentment and was followed by a period of cultural awakening and revival among Arabs. Hourani (1991) emphasizes the significance, at the time, of developing a revitalized Arab-Islamic identity and culture which could resist the West and "Western Imperial Impingement" on them (Said, 1993, p. 252). Said (1981) argues that the result of this double struggle, on one hand to liberate the nation from the new British colonialism and on the other to revitalize Arabic culture, mixed with western betrayal has been a discourse of 'Arab nationalism'—at the heart of which is a complex of "hope betrayal and bitter disappointment" which resulted in an unfulfilled and incomplete culture, "expressing itself in a fragmented language of torment angry insistence," often uncritical condemnation of outside (mainly western) enemies (Said, 1981).

British and French colonial forces labeled themselves as forces of reconstruction and nation building under a British and French mandate (as compared to colonialism). Arabs were betrayed when suddenly control of Arabs by Muslim non-Arab Ottomans was replaced by non-Muslim Europeans. The audacity of this situation is exacerbated by the fact that Arab activists were misled into helping Europeans achieve this colonial presence.

Inventing Borders

The second epoch was even more dramatic than the first. The French and British administrations immediately transformed the Arab world into several nation-states with arbitrary borders. Arab aboriginals were not consulted and their economic, demographic or geographic interests were of little concern to the new victors of the Second World War (Hourani, 1991). These geographic creations have resulted in many conflicts and problems that have lasted up for decades and up until our current day (Sayegh, 1958). Clapham (1985) notes that "European colonial rule has a major global impact in that it created political territories which were artificial, in the sense that they did not arise from societies which they governed but were instead imposed on them" (p.4). Alkadry and Khalil note that "this arbitrary delineation of borders is at worst an attempt to fragment the ideas of civil society and citizenship consistent with the divide-and-conquer colonial philosophy, and at best a disregard and dismissal of these two concepts by the colonial powers consistent with colonial dismissal of natives' rights to things that are civilized."

After this arbitrary delineation of borders, Arab natives were left with little options but to "[recite] a script written by someone else." There were no national identities associated with the newly created states, and the common historical, cultural and political experiences of most of these countries was a yearning for Arab or Islamic unity (Abu Jaber, 1969). In summary, the colonial forces carved up the Middle East, installed non-democratic and traditionally-alien regimes in the newly created states, and expected Arabs to dance to these newly-introduced colonial tunes.

Colonial powers, by delineating arbitrary borders to arbitrary states, affected the notion of civil society and solidarity which are very important to the Islamic tradition of Middle East nations (Antonios, 1936/1948; Mansfield, 1973; Abadi, 1983). The colonial forces created states with conflicting ethnicities and divided some coherent and existing ethnic communities among two, three or four states. For instance, the Kurds who lived in a contiguous geographic region were divided among Syria, Iraq, Iran and Turkey with borders separating siblings and cousins. Since 1922, every Iraqi regime called for correcting the colonial carving of Kuwait out of Iraqi territory after many centuries of Kuwaiti control by Baghdad (Ali, 2002). The creation of the State of Israel – created mostly by settlers who actively worked to expunge Palestinian natives from their homeland– triggered a struggle in the Middle East that has lasted and will last for decades to come (Said, 1981). The resulting Palestinian exodus into neighboring Arab states has also caused civil wars in Lebanon and Jordan (Deegan, 1994).

Colonial Practices

The British and French colonialists suppressed national movements within the colonized nations, silenced voices for national independence and self-determination and installed local puppet leaders to help suppress Arab populations in the newly created states (Bill and Springbord, 1990; Clapham, 1985). The colonial forces, especially the British, introduced western forms of monarchy regimes that are alien to the region and to the historic traditions of its peoples (Lewis, 2000). Throughout the Arab world, the colonial forces suppressed nationalist movements and attempts to hold democratic elections. In 1924, British colonial administrators opposed attempts by the King of Jordan to hold elections for a parliament (Abu Jaber, 1969).

The British also opposed elections and the formation of nationalist government in Iraq in the early 1920s, and instead installed a complacent royal regime - that of King Faisal who had been recently exiled from Damascus by French colonial administrators (Bill and Springbord, 1990). In 1942, the British forces surrounded the Egyptian Royal Palace to force the Egyptian King to remove a nationalist government and appoint a pro-British government. French colonial administrators also systematically opposed popular and elected regimes in Lebanon and Syria and rather endorsed political leaders who would be more complacent to the goals and priorities of the French imperialists (Rustow, 1963).

The Betrayal of Arabs and their colonization by the British were only made worse by the mass influx of European and other Jews into Palestine and therefore the demographic displacement of the Palestinian natives. In the late 19th century Jews accounted for less than 10% of the population of Palestine. By the 1930, they accounted for almost one-third (Said, 1981). The culmination of these two factors and the news of the Balfour Declaration, by which the British gave a promise of a Jewish state in Palestine, all gave rise to the Great Arab Revolt in Palestine which has arguably started in 1929 and lasted for almost ten years until 1939. The Great Arab Revolt in Palestine was especially important because it has mobilized thousands of Palestinians "from every stratum of society, all over the country." The Revolt was a response to British colonialism and their refusal to suppress Jewish immigration to Palestine. Young Palestinian nationalists felt that Zionism was not simply a delusion, to be, or that could be, corrected. Rather, Zionism was, part of and, "parcel of Western imperialism in the Middle East, and only the eradication of the latter could halt the advance of the former."

Resistance has occurred at all these instances of confrontation. Colonial administrations in the Middle East and in other Muslim nations faced some fierce resistance from the indigenous peoples. Examples of resistance to colonialism include the Mahdist movement led by Muhammad Ibn Abd Allah against Italian and British Conquest in Somalia, the revolt of 1920 against the British colonial administration in Iraq, the 'Abd Al-Qâder revolt against French colonialism in 1830 in Algeria, the Mahdist movement of 1821 against Egypto-British colonialism in Sudan, the revolt by Ahmad 'Urâbi against British occupation of Egypt in 1881, the Sanûsi resistance against Italian colonialism in Libya, and the Palestinian resistance to British and Zionist colonialism particularly in the uprisings of 1936, 1987 and 2000 (Peters, 1979).

Confrontation between the colonizing Europe and the colonized Arabs lasted decades and did not even end with decolonization and national independence. British colonials installed leaders and regimes in Arab countries who maintained the British influence in the region for decades after the British left. National independence did not translate into self-determination, and ultimately liberation and popular sovereignty, for the people of the Middle East, as colonial forces continued to exert influence over the decolonized people years after decolonization (Said, 1993).

Neocolonialism and Resistance to the US Instead of Europe

The fourth epoch of confrontation is perhaps the one of great significance to American scholars. In the post-colonial period, Arab confrontation with Europe and European colonialism was transformed into confrontation between Arabs and the United States of America. Arabs in the post-colonial era could be found in one of three camps: repressive regimes friendly to the United States, repressive regimes not friendly to the United States, and occupying regimes that are sustained economically and militarily by the United States (Alkadry, 2002).

By economically and politically sustaining ruthless regimes, the U.S. constrains the emancipation of Arab peoples and at the same time ensures a complacency of these regimes in their external relations. The regimes friendly to the United States include Saudi-Arabia, post-Nasser Egypt, Jordan, pre-1990 Iraq, Kuwait, United Arab Emirates, Bahrain, Qatar, Tunisia, Morocco, and pre-1979 Iran. Countries not friendly to the United States include Syria, Nasser's Egypt, Sudan, Libya, and post-1990 Iraq. Being a major source of crude oil, the Middle East became the heart pump for the world economy (Nixon, 1980, 1992). In this instance, the United States and Europe sanctioned the oppression of people in the region and the continued prevalence of royal and dictator regimes as "friendly tyrants" (Pipes and Garfinkle, 1991). With direct western support, regimes in Saudi Arabia, Egypt, Shah's Iran and Jordan continued to oppress their nationals and to suppress the formation of democratic institutions (Ali, 2002).

Egypt and Jordan - essentially dictator regimes - were cited as models of governance by the United States President G. W. Bush as he searched for complacency for US and Israeli interests by the Palestinian Authority in July 2002 (Al-Jazeera, 7/17/2002). In this moment of confrontation, the socio-political and economic theaters were directed and envisioned not by Arabs or the economic and political interests, but rather by the economic and political interests of the United States and Israel (Kubursi, 1999). The anger about American support for friendly tyrants is obvious in the fact that almost all the terrorists who attacked New York and Washington on September 11, 2001 were almost all from countries ruled by friends of ours but not of their own people (Egypt, Saudi Arabia, and United Arab Emirates). These terrorists did not come from Syria, Iraq, Iran, or Libya - countries that are not considered friendly to the United States.

Besides support for "friendly tyrants," the United States objection to unfriendly tyrants has helped these tyrants sustain themselves through nationalist anti-Zionist, anti-American rhetoric. The United States intervened to deal with unfriendly Arab nationalist movements that toppled pro-colonial regimes in many of the newly-created states. This happened in Iraq, Syria, Egypt (1952-1973), and Libya. These regimes faced what Bill and Springbord (1990) term as a process of "defensive modernization." These regimes used external threats to their national security as excuses to disallow a process of democratization as well as suppress opposition within. Some of these Arab regimes switched roles as defensive modernizers and friendly tyrants. Iraq shifted from a friendly tyrant before its invasion of Kuwait in August 1990 to a defensive modernizer afterwards. The Shah of Iran (pre-1979) was a friendly tyrant while Khomeini was a defensive modernizer. Egypt under Nasser (pre-1970) is an example of a defensive modernizer while Egypt under Mubarak and Sadat (post-1973 period) became a friendly tyrant regime.

Finally, Arabs of Palestine have been living under Israeli occupation, or in exile since 1948. Over the past 50 years, Arabs watched Israeli progress from a settler community to a prosperous state. This prosperity would have been impossible without the direct and indirect support by the United States. This support has become sharper in the post-cold war era. The United States in the 1990s used its Security Council veto power to block any sanctions on Israel, any presence of international observers to protect Palestinian rights under the Geneva Convention, or even any investigation of alleged war crimes by Israel in the occupied Palestinian territories. This unconditional support for Israel despite its violation of tens of Security Council resolutions, is paralleled by strict enforcement of all such resolutions against non-friendly

Arab states – such as Libya and Iraq. The United States used protecting Israel's right to exist as its rationale for this support. Still, the double-standard in enforcing international law and unconditional support for Israeli occupation of Arab lands are the source of great resentment of United States policies in the region (Chomsky, 2001; Said, 2001).

Western hegemony (Bin Sayeed, 1995) has also triggered some major resistance by the peoples subjected to imperialism. Bin Sayeed (1995) argues that the resurgence of this old phenomenon as "Islamic Resistance to Western hegemony in the Middle East" (p. 5). However, he only looks at resistance by self-proclaimed Islamic states specifically Saudi Arabia, Iran, and Pakistan. We submit here that the more threatening form of resistance is that of non-states - organizations such as Al-Qaeda and Islamic Jihad. These organizations are products of tyrant regimes friendly to the U.S. but not to political freedoms within their own countries. With the suppression of political organizing and oppression of opposition by oppressive regimes that are supported and sustained by the West, political Islam seems more difficult to halt because of the inseparability between religion and politics.

The Product of a Century of Confrontation

In summary, the past century witnessed the prevalence of western interests at the expense of the human and political rights of Arabs. At each period of confrontation, the resistance by Arabs was stronger than resistance in earlier periods.

This is evident in the history of the decolonized Middle East as it has experienced wars more than any region in the world for the last fifty years. The region was home to three wars between Israel and its neighbors, a war between Iraq and Iran, a war between Iraq and Kuwait, and two wars between Iraq and the United States. Several countries in the region also experienced internal conflicts: Turkey (Kurds), Iraq (Kurds), Lebanon, Sudan, and Algeria Indeed, the daily tragic pictures coming out of West Bank and Gaza Strip and the inability or unwillingness of the United States and Europe to find a just solution to the Palestinian issue make peoples of the region very suspicious of these two powers.

Colonial administrators carved up the Middle East, oppressed its peoples, and installed regimes and states with no single national identity or common definition of citizenship that would unite their peoples. Western imperialism and defensiveness against it by anti-imperial regimes in the region have ensured that the peoples of the Middle East did not experience true processes of liberation. Those national forces that toppled pro-colonial and pro-imperial regimes found themselves in defensive positions that turned them into regimes as ruthless as their colonial predecessors.

Arabs and the United States in the Post-Hussein Years

Not long ago and in the words of President George W. Bush, Americans engaged in a seemingly innocent debate of how could Arabs hate the United States. "We are so good," the American President announced. The interesting thing about this debate is that it was a debate among Americans – no Arabs invited and no historical context. This article serves to answer that question. At the same time, the article should not be construed as justification for anti-American sentiments. Instead, they are explanations of what went wrong and how long these sentiments have been in the making. Understanding the roots of a problem is the first step to surgically deal with that problem.

The past four decades were particularly damaging for prospects of peace between the United States and the Arab peoples. Reversing this hostile relationship is done not by retaining image spin-masters and purchasing television ads in Saudi Arabia, Lebanon, Egypt, Jordan, and other countries. Nor is this done through invading an Arab country to allegedly liberate its people from a friendly tyrant gone mad, while leaving the liberation of other Arabs from other Arab and non-Arab friendly tyrants contingent on the loyalty of these tyrants to the U.S. A change has to entail fundamental policy changes.

First, ending the Israeli occupation of Arab lands would help ease the tensions between the United States and Arabs. For the last 38 years, Israel has occupied the West Bank and Gaza Strip despite many United Nations resolution and outcry of the international community to end this occupation (Keeley, 2002).

For more than fifty years, Palestinians have been living as refugees in other Arab states. The Palestinian question is critical for any peace between Arabs and the United States. According to an editorial in Arab News, Saudi Arabia's first English-language daily, "while the strikes in Afghanistan have pushed the Palestinian struggle down to the second-lead position in media coverage, it remains the central issue for the region. Palestine continues to yield, every day, its dead and injured. Until that stops, all agree, there can be no peace in this region" (World Press, 2001).

Second, the US presence in Iraq has to be very transparent and its approach to dealing with Iraq must be both surgical and delicate. Alkadry and Khalil predicted that the next confrontation between Arabs and the West is at the crossroads of globalization. The US occupation of Iraq seems more appropriate as that fifth moment of confrontation. What the United States needs to ensure is that it does not follow in the footsteps of European colonizers.

Finally, additional confrontation with Syria and Iran does not serve American interests. It reminds Arabs of their helplessness in the face of United States war machinery. Unlike images of natives that are spread by western popular culture (Shaheen, 2001), Arabs are intelligent and able to identify hypocrisy when they see one evil sanctioned because of friendliness to the United States and another targeted because of non-friendliness to the United States. Therefore, any attempt to fight evil in the world must start with the friendly tyrants in the Middle East and elsewhere. Support for friendly tyrants has to end because Arabs have started realizing that western supporters and not only the tyrants is their enemy.

THE MIDDLE EAST CONFLICT

The Middle East conflict has been fiercely debated by politicians and religious and professional groups. In recent years, the Middle East conflict has been the primary source for unrest and instability in the world. Addressing this conflict objectively and rationally could reduce/eliminate bloodshed and profoundly change the direction of world politics. The conflict has led to deep resentments among people of various faiths and cultural backgrounds. Its persistence is attributed to the tremendous influence that religion and economic factors exercise upon policy. It appears that there are several groups that prefer to politicalize religion and are intended to keeping the world in a state of perpetual Jihad. In this chapter, the various perspectives of Christianity, Judaism, and Islam regarding Jihad are outlined. The origins of and the historical perspectives on Jihad are clarified. The evolution of the meaning of Jihad in each religion is outlined in the context of the rise and fall of power in each religion. Various forms of Jihad are presented. This chapter suggests that perpetual Jihad is a tragic and highly dangerous development and its consequences to the world are potentially devastating. Perpetual Jihad will fuel rather than resolve conflict and will eventually threaten world stability.

The Middle East conflict: perpetual jihad

In a sign of optimism Warren W. Christopher (1994), then U.S. Secretary of State, argued that if the forces of peace prevail and governments in the Middle East adopt free market reforms, the region will enjoy an era of economic growth that exceeds anything it has seen in the twentieth century. This same sentiment was been echoed recently by Colin Powell. Powell, among others, believes that the Middle East has all the required resources to enhance the economic welfare of its citizens and be a major economic player in the world economy. There are, however, various factors that have frustrated economic development and led to a general decline, in recent years, in the standard of living of the people there.

The UN's *Arab Human Development Report 2002* asserts that from the Atlantic to the Gulf, people experience "deprivation, in all its forms." The Report reveals that there is a widespread economic stagnation and sluggish trade performance. These have been primarily attributed to "political upheavals, military conflicts, sanctions and embargoes." All have contributed to lack of political freedom, foreign occupation, instability, and neglect of human development. Powell , accentuates the need for genuine change in the Middle East. Nevertheless, he asserts that the Middle East economies "are stifled by regulation and cronyism. They lack transparency, and are closed to entrepreneurship, investment, and trade." Both Powell and the *Arab Human Development Report 2002*, however, acknowledge that the region suffers from a mismatch between aspirations and their fulfillment. This situation has often led to alienation, apathy and discontent. Consequently, human capacities have not been nurtured and economic opportunities have been missed.

There is a consensus among Middle East Experts that the region faces deep problems and genuine challenges that have paralyzed it from moving forward politically and economically. Among the most genuine challenges is political sentiment with deep religious underpinnings. Indeed, such sentiments have perpetuated conflict, instability, and suffering in the region. These sentiments have persistently impeded progress toward political understanding and economic stability in a region where international politics and religion are intertwined. In fact, the daily usage of the term Jihad reflects these sentiments.

Jihad is among the most widely used terms in the current daily discourse on Middle East religion and international politics. Intentionally or unintentionally, various forces have given this simple word contention and meaning with far reaching political and religious implications. Jihad is an Arabic word that is derived from *juhd*—effort, exertion, strive, struggle, hard work, or hardship. In common usage and language it specifically means striving to perform a task, intense effort, or meeting a challenging goal or responsibility. For example, the Quran used it to mean efforts- *Jahidhim*- (9:79) or, even stronger, *-jahed*- (35:42) along with the common meaning, strive. Jihad is not synonymous with other Arabic words *harb*, war, *qitaal* fighting or *Muaraka* quarrel. The Arabs used the word before Islam, whether they were pagans, Christians, or Jews. Nor is the Arabic word Jihad similar to the Hebrew term *milhemet mitzvah/hovah* for obligatory war (Firestone, 2001a) or the Christian term "just war." The term Jihad was never meant to mean "holy" in Islam; theologically the Islamic tradition did not sanction the term holy or just war. In addition, the linguistic roots of Jihad "have nothing whatsoever to do with military action, violence, or warfare" (Sullivan, 2003). Nevertheless, in recent years, and especially in Western literature and among extremist religious groups, Jihad has been utilized more than ever to convey the meaning of violence or holy war; a meaning that was promoted during the era of the Crusades.

In the absence of spirited dialogue, a positive understanding of the word Jihad may give way to prevailing negative connotations. Indeed, there are competing forces in the global political arena that seek to institutionalize a highly negative translation. Sullivan , warns that there are intellectuals who promote the negative meaning of Jihad. Similarly, Pfaff asserts that these intellectuals attempt to create events that are "dangerous and potentially even more violent than they have already become. They are not a war of religion, and it is deeply irresponsible to try to turn them into one." The fact that these intellectuals and policy makers have access to various types of resources, especially the media and military, make it imperative to engage in intellectually spirited discourse in order to provide a better understanding of the various meanings of the term, and to narrow the gap of misunderstanding and suspicion across cultures.

In this chapter, we intend to assess the perspectives of Judaism, Christianity, and Islam on Jihad in the context of the rise and decline of power of the entities associated with these religions. Using historical accounts and perspectives, we intend to demonstrate that Middle East conflicts and today's Jihad are directly influenced by religious fever, especially when policy appears to be an instrument of religion. Furthermore, the chapter provides certain implications and their meaning for today's events in the Middle East and the rest of the world.

THE NATURE AND POLITICS OF JIHAD

Tom Robbins (1990, p. 52), in his history-based novel, predicts that we are witnessing a rebirth of the old crusade as a new Jihad to "..stop terrorism and take the damn oil" from the Arabs and to reclaim the Promised Land. Ironically, it is immediately after this prophecy, that the term terrorism and the Middle East issues have become the most debated topics in the political discourse (e.g., the First Gulf War,1990-91; the second Palestinian Intifada, 2000-2003; 9-11 terrorist attacks, 2001; the invasion of Afghanistan 2001; the second Gulf War against Iraq, 2003). It is possible that the abatement of the Cold War and the rise of political religion in the United States, that has evolved rapidly since the era of President Reagan, 1981-89, have created a new environment fertile for inventing a new enemy and associated terminologies. It is without doubt, however, that politicization and misreading of religion have motivated various actors to pursue seemingly divisional policies at home and abroad. Indeed, the recent rise of religious extremism among the three religions: Judaism, Christianity, and Islam has impaired constructive dialogue among civilizations and fueled the flames of Middle East sentiments. Curry (2002, p.42) argues that reflection and rationality, in the current debate on violence and war, have been "distorted almost beyond recognition by rhetoric and misunderstanding." He postulates that an important and logical understanding comes only through a clear vision of the past. Accordingly, Curry argues that the Crusaders' invasion of the Middle East provides incredible insight on today's events and their religious underpinning.

Commenting on the headline, "Pro-Israeli General Will Oversee Reconstruction of Postwar Iraq," in the Jewish weekly, *Forward*, Raban asserts that this appointment was a calculated act and "entirely in keeping with the Bush administration's policy of teaching the Middle East a humiliating lesson." Similarly, the *Washington Post*, in an editorial , indicated that the White House nomination of Daniel Pipes, a person who was accused by several civil rights organizations of anti-Muslim bias, to the U.S. Institute of Peace, was "a sort of a cruel joke." Middle East experts acknowledge that today's events are analogous to the early twentieth century, when Britain and France invaded the Arab World and to the Crusades era. Mansfield (1985, p.176) documents that Sir Mark Sykes and Francois Picot, the authors of the 1916 Sykes-Picot British-French agreement to divide the Arab east between the two countries, were heavily influenced by religion. Mansfield indicates that Sykes was delighted when the British Prime Minister, Lloyd George had "several British ministers who . . .[having] all been brought up in the spirit of nineteenth-century Bible – reading Protestantism, were attracted by the romantic idea of helping the Jewish people to 'return' to their promised land after two thousand years."

Likewise, Curry (p. 38) indicates that the Crusades in 1095 inspired more passion and enthusiasm than ever imagined in Europe and that "The idea of an expedition to reclaim Jerusalem from the unbelievers seized the imagination of people from all social classes." Curry suggests that this passion has been slow to die. When the Europeans invaded the Middle East nine centuries later, they displayed a fierce religious pride. He quoted Sir Edmund Allenby (p. 39), the British General who captured Jerusalem in 1917, declaring, "Today the wars of the Crusaders are completed."

Barnard Lewis (2002, p.9), notices that in the last two centuries the World has witnessed the Military advances of Christendom in the heart of the Muslim World, the Middle East. He argues that the two major Muslim powers, the Ottomans and the Persians, "continued to fight each other until the nineteenth century, by which time they no longer constituted a threat to anyone but their own subjects." The ultimate collapse of these two powers initiated the rise of Christian Europe as the ultimate arbiter of power in the Middle East until 1956, when the U.S. made its presence in the region remarkably noticeable.

Many analysts seem to suggest that the true dimensions of the recent war mission are no different from past wars in the Middle East: religious rivalry and economic interest. Friedman , among others, believes that the U.S. has used its power against Iraq more "to defend oil and Israel than democracy." Indeed, there are some who think that it is solely driven by a strong belief in doing God's work and serving the will of God. Writing in the *New York Times*, Maureen Dowd states that this "new fight isn't logical-it's cultural. It is the latest chapter in the culture wars." Rupert Cornwell believes that the current political atmosphere and development on the ground demonstrate without a doubt that '"the looming war with Iraq is indeed a "crusade" against Muslims."' Similarly, Barbra Ehrenreich argues that an '"invasion of Iraq and the attendant "collateral damage" will harden the impression that the United States is pursuing its own kind of jihad—against the Islamic world." Margolis (2003, p.8) succinctly summon up what he termed Jihad against Iraq and the problems in the Middle East by stating, " The real reasons North Korea is not in Bush's gun sights are, of course, that it does not challenge Israel, has no oil, and plays no role in Christian Armageddon."

The religious factor has always been important in shaping the discourse on the Middle East conflict and in understanding its true dimensions. This has been the case historically and should not be expected to diminish anytime soon. The risk, however, is that religion is more likely than any other variable, in the absence of tolerance, to lead to dogmatism and uncompromised stances. This certainly perpetuates conflicts and makes compromise and understanding a far reaching objective. In the context of the recent war in the Middle East, Neummann acknowledges that the root of the problem is the "issue of the occupation of the West Bank." But, he attributes the severity to the lack of implementation of the biblical prophecy by annexing all of the land by Israel. Pasko elaborates on this crisis when he argues that everything in the world is created for a biblical reason and consequently the invasion of Iraq "is for us-i.e. the Jews and Israel…the Torah telling us that everything that happens in the world is for the benefit of the Jewish people."

Kristof reports that the White House plan to invade Iraq and remake the Middle East has "an element of messianic vision." Milbank , quoting Richard Perle, an advisor to Bush, stated that the President, "comes from the conviction he's on the right course [and] knows exactly what he's doing." Milbank indicates that some southern Christian leaders believe that the President in this war is "on an agenda from God," and that "Divine Providence" has a role in the President's action. Rosenblatt agrees stating that , "it's ironic that President Bush, a born –again Bible reader, appears to have rejected the Christian position and adopted instead the Jewish stance on self-defense and responding to evil" in initiating a war against Iraq.

The idea that the current war and the U.S military presence in the Middle East is religiously and politically motivated is commonly held too among Middle East experts and Muslims. Edward Said (2003a) painfully acknowledges that Washington has made no secret that its plans "are to re-draw the map of the whole Arab world, perhaps changing other regimes and many borders in the process." He went on to suggest that the real objective is to please Israel and to have a vision for the region that is "based on a script written by Donald Rumsfeld and Paul Wolfowitz." Recently, Said (2003b) seems to suggest that the primary consideration of the war plans is Israeli domination. He states, "Along with Syria, Iraq once represented the only serious military threat to Israel and, therefore, it had to be smashed." Similarly, a statement attributed to Bin Laden (February 16, 2003), reiterates the religious underpinning of the war. It states, "We are following with great interest and utmost concern the preparations by the crusaders to occupy the capital of Islam . . . and to rob the wealth of Muslims and to appoint over you [Iraqis] an agent government that follows Washington and Tel Aviv, in preparation for the founding of greater Israel."

While there seems to be consensus among many experts on the underlying religious and economic motives for the current war, it is impossible to determine with absolute certainty that religious considerations have been transformed into a policy direction. But some Washington experts clearly allude to this possibility. Vulliamy insists that religion plays a significant role in shaping President Bush's Middle East policy. He indicates that Carl Rove (Bush advisor) and Paul Wolfowitz, Deputy Secretary of Defense, are the masterminds behind Bush. He states, "Rove's position dovetailed with the beliefs of Paul Wolfowitz, and the axis between conservative Southern Protestantism and fervent . . . East Coast Zionism was gorged-each as zealous about their religion as the other." This led, according to Aluf Benn, to a policy that "is still focused on transforming the Middle East into an area under U.S. protection, in which Israel will enjoy privileged status." Lind asserts that the alliance between neoconservatives and fervent Christian Zionists "took over Washington and steered the U.S. into a Middle Eastern war unrelated to any plausible threat to the U.S."

This alliance has led to an aggressive Middle East policy. According to Lind the neoconservatives are, "products of the influential Jewish-American sector of the Trotskyist movement of the 1930s and 1940s, which morphed into anti-communist liberalism between the 1950s and 1970s and finally into a kind of militaristic and imperial right with no precedents in American culture or political history." Brownstein indicates that the neoconservatives exercise a strong influence on policy formulation and direction. He argues that President Bush "seems personally most drawn to the neoconservative perspective, and that makes the neocons' thinking an important guide not only to how the administration got to Iraq but where it might go from there." Both Buchanan and Marshall also confirm that the administration's policy toward the Middle East has been completely designed by the neoconservatives.

Buchanan speculates that Washington is determined to engage in "endless wars on the Islamic world to serve" the interest of Israel and implement the neoconservatives' agenda. Many leaders of the neoconservatives do not veer away from confirming that their end goal is instability and destruction in the Middle East. Michael Ledeen , former under Secretary of State and a leading neoconservative, states, "Stability is an unworthy American mission, and a misleading concept to boot. We do not want stability in Iran, Iraq, Syria, Lebanon, and even Saudi Arabia; we want things to change. The real issue is not whether, but how to destabilize." Previously, Ledeen argued that perpetual war is the only useful option to ensure the submission of the Muslim World. He eloquently elaborates on this point, "we will not be sated until we have had the blood of every miserable little tyrant in the Middle East, until every leader of every cell of the terror network is dead or locked securely away, and every last drooling anti-Semitic and anti-American mullah, imam, sheikh, and ayatollah is either singing the praises of the United States of America, or pumping gasoline, for a dime a gallon, on an American military base near the Arctic Circle."

The appeal of the "perpetual war" appears to have a strong hold in Washington. William Kristol believes that it is the desired blueprint for a new world order. In an editorial in the *Weekly Standard*, he indicates that the successful invasion of Afghanistan and Iraq is the beginning, "The Battles of Afghanistan and Iraq have been won decisively and honorably. But these are only two battles. We are only at the end of the beginning in the war on terror and terrorist states." While this perpetual war seems to be endless, the former director of CIA, James Woolsey, asserts it is only for a few decades. He states, "This fourth world war . . . will last considerably longer than either World Wars I or II did for us. Hopefully not the full four-plus decades of the Cold war. . . . I think, over the decades to come . . . we will make a lot of people very nervous." Perhaps this understanding of war and violent act resembles, more than ever, a perpetual form of Jihad. Indeed, however, this form may turn out to be unique in its risks and catastrophic in its consequences. This is because the concept of permanent war seems to imply a profound change in cultural orientation and economic priority that has to be sustained by an overwhelming use of military power.

Most importantly, perpetual war or Jihad is expected to lead to chaos. Marshall thinks this is not an undesired outcome, rather it is part of the plan: the polarization and fragmentation of the world are not something to be avoided but something that needs to be induced. Ben-Aharon , an Israeli civil rights expert, warns about this state of affairs.

He views this development as a serious threat to world stability and security. He states that the concept of empire "..is the in thing in the current political-diplomatic discourse.

Peace, welfare, a law-abiding regime and international order will accrue to those who seek the protection of the global Western empire, while the language of force will be employed against those who reject this protection." Policymakers in Washington do not seem anxious to distance themselves from this possible scenario. Paul Wolfowitz, the U.S. Deputy Secretary of Defense, articulated this new possibility by saying that Pax Americana entailed "demonstrating that your friends will be protected and taken care of, that your enemies will be punished and that those who refuse to support you will live to regret having done so" (Quoted in Keller, 2002).

RELIGIOUS PERSPECTIVES ON JIHAD

Robbins (1990, p.222) speculates that the "first recorded act of genocide" took place in the land of Canaan when the "Hebrew escaping from Egypt invaded Canaan and killed everybody, the whole country, old men, women, children, little babies what were in arms." In more recent history, only Hitler attempted to annihilate an entire population: the Jewish people. The possibility that such human tragedy may occur is a distant memory. Nevertheless, the adage that "history often repeats itself" is noteworthy in this context. Indeed, the logical extension then and now is that, " Once religion became political, the exercise of it, too, could be said to lead sooner or later to war".

Most of the contemporary political commentators and subsequently the discourse on religion and violence seem to overlook the roots of the three religions: Judaism, Christianity, and Islam. Their roots and the environment in which they were fostered have tremendously shaped their perspectives and evolution.

The three monotheistic religions share common foundations. All trace their lineage to Abraham, an Iraqi Semitic person who claimed that Almighty God showed him a vision. All were founded in the Middle East.

Judaism was the first religion, followed by Christianity and Islam, both of whom acknowledge the influence of Judaism on the formation of their respective tenets. Unlike the first two religions, Islam is not named after a person. It strictly means total submission to the will of Almighty God. Rev. Richard Nolan argues that "Islam is the middle way between Judaism and Christianity; it restores the unity of the children of Abraham and overcomes the limitations of Judaism and Christianity." The proposition that Islam is the middle way between the two religions that preceded it may help to shed a light on the meaning of Jihad among these three religions.

JIHAD IN JUDAISM

Judaism is the oldest among the three religions. In Judaism there is an emphasis on the specific and the relevant and on the role of man on earth. Its instructions are clear and encompass moral and military conduct among other tenets. The Torah illustrates the challenges that the Jewish people faced and the action that must be taken to ensure their continuity and survival. The Jewish tribes, which were outnumbered by other tribes and communities, found that the Torah answered to most of their immediate military and political concerns. Moser argues that in the Torah, there "is the vehemence, of violence." He indicates that the second Chronicles (20:24) shows us a landscape strewn with corpses, "and, behold, they were dead bodies fallen to the earth, and none escaped." Furthermore, Rabbi Soloveichik asserts that unlike Christianity, Judaism does not accentuate the virtue of forgiveness. He states that when "hate is appropriate, then it is not only virtuous, but essential for Jewish well –being."

Rabbi Firestone asserts that anyone can find excerpts in the Torah and Talmud that "would curdle the blood of the innocent reader." He refers to Deuteronomy (7) that "calls for mass extermination, for genocide of the native Canaanite inhabitants of the land." For example, I Samuel (15:3) commands, "Now go and smite Amalek, and utterly destroy all that they have and spare them not, but slay both man and woman, infant and suckling, ox or sheep, camel and ass." Likewise, under Joshua (11: 11-12) the destruction and killings described are unimaginable by today's standard. The Bible states, "And they smote all the souls that were therein with the edge of the sword, utterly destroying them; there was not any left to breath: and he burnt Ha'zor with fire. And all the cities of those kings, and all the kings of them, did Joshua take, and smote them with the edge of the sword, and he utterly destroyed them, as Moses the servant of the Lord commanded."

W.H. Frend (1967) documents that the act of martyrdom and sacrifice is highly emphasized in the early teaching of Judaism. Both martyrdom and suicide were considered holy actions. The martyr was "regarded as representative of the people of Israel and 'an example of nobility and a memorial of virtue." Frend (p. 36) asserts that the "act of martyrdom was the means of his own entry into eternal life, and the sign that his persecutors would not escape God's judgment . . . For the victorious victim both resurrection and immorality were promised." These fatalistic attitudes and sacrifices are still practiced. Shahar Ilan quoted a religious broadcaster in Israel calling on supporters to take arms against Israeli leftists, "if we need to slaughter, we shall slaughter, and if we must be slaughtered, we shall be slaughtered."

Rabbi Firestone (2001a) insists that the notions of holy war lay virtually "dormant for most of our exilic existence." Rosenblatt argues that wars can be sometimes "necessary and even moral." Similarly, Rabbi Greenberg insists that the religious instruction regarding "a pre-emptive strike is warranted for greater security or for expanded boundaries yielding greater defensive depth against a possible future onslaught." Nevertheless, there are religious scholars who consider most of the quoted excerpts from the Torah and Talmud related to violence and war as irrelevant to today's affairs and should be viewed in their historic contexts. Most of them were instructions that were related to the process of establishing a state during primitive hostilities, dominating neighboring communities, or defending the Jewish communities from possible aggression. After the Jewish people spread into other lands, the use of holy war and the language of violence were no longer applicable. Indeed, during the Medieval era, the Jewish people posed little political and military challenge to existing powers (Royal, 1995). However, at the present time, Rabbi Irwin Kula warns against treating the Biblical teachings as especially valid. He states, "We teach a text where conquering another land and wiping out another people is something that is considered appropriate and good and even commanded by God." He suggests that this must be taught "not as precedent, but something to get better at."

Rabbi Firestone (2001a) argues that only in recent decades has the term Jewish "holy war" entered the religious and political discourse in relation to the establishment of the state of Israel in Palestine in 1948. Rabbi Firestone claims that in some quarters of the Jewish community there are those who believe in the famous statement of Nahmanides in his gloss on Maimonides' Book of Commandments who teaches "that the conquest and settlement of the land of Israel . . . is a positive commandment for all generations obligating every individual, even during the period of exile." Consequently, the conflict with the Palestinians has become the most significant issue in the Jewish discourse.

In the context of the Israel-Palestine conflict, the Jewish "holy war" may take various forms, in addition to the ongoing daily conflict in the holy land. These forms include: financial support to Israel and its settlement policies in the occupied territories; volunteering in the Israeli army, especially during the time of war; exercising political influence on governments in various countries to support Israeli polices; and media campaigns against Arabs and Muslims.

Rabbi Ariel argues that Jewish morality is based on a balance of justice and compassion. To that end, he insists, "at the fundamental moral level, Judaism does not rule out use of violence" (quoted in Sheleg, 2002). The Jewish *Forward* (see Cattan, 2002) reports that most of the organized Jewish groups espouse the war sentiment. Nevertheless, there are many religious scholars who consider war as evil and unnecessary in today's world. The Rabbinic Leader of the Temple of Universal Jûdaism, Dawn Rose, (vehemently denounces the call for war. She states that we have been told that we are "at war," and "the implication is made that innocent lives are thus expendable-especially of those people who are not American, not Jewish or Christian, and not the family down the block. We must demand that President Bush call death, death-whether it occurs at home or abroad." Similarly, Rabbi Marc Gopin argues that there must be limits on the use of violence and the Jewish "just war" tradition and the "just war" traditions of other religions, in principle, "cannot justify much in the way of war, due to collateral damage. . . . In Jewish tradition we must emphasize *pikuach nefes*, the saving and protection of innocent life, as the ultimate arbiter of difficult decisions about war and violence."

The preceding discussion demonstrates that historically the inclination for using a violent form of "jihad" in Judaism was associated with the rise of a political entity and its acquisition of a dominate power. It was during the invasion of the Canaanite land that the Jewish people fiercely espoused war and violence as instruments for territorial expansion. In the centuries following the Roman domination, the use of force by the Jewish people was not emphasized. In recent years, this has been changed. For example, the Jewish *Forward* noted in an editorial a rise in what it called "Jewish toughness." The editorial indicated that among Jewish groups "expressions of pain at the suffering of others are commonly derided as weakness of spirit" and that for these groups "peace comes only through victory."

JIHAD IN CHRISTIANITY

The environment in which Christianity first appeared had a tremendous influence on the stance of the early Christian Church relative to violence and war. The Romans were the dominant power in the area; their military and economic power was unrivaled at the time. Jesus' instructions to the faithful to avoid violence were clear: (Matt. 5:39), "But I say into you, that ye resist not evil: but whosoever shall smite thee on thy right cheek, turn to him the other also" and "Glory to God in the highest, and on earth peace, good will toward men" (Luke 2:14). Christ appeared to understand the boundaries of power. Therefore, he preached the doctrines of peace and forgiveness, and avoided confrontation with the Romans (Ali & Gibbs, 1989).

Once the Roman Empire espoused Christianity, the emphasis on non-violence disappeared or diminished. Like the Romans, the subsequent governments in the West embarked on empire building and political domination and rivalry. All used religion to justify their expansionist policies and engagement in endless war. Frend (1967) documents that Christianity adopted, in its early years, the concept of righteous suffering, martyrdom, resistance, and sacrifice from Judaism. Karen Armstrong points out that (1992, p. 22) in about 850 the concept of martyrdom became a rallying force among Christians. This took place when Spanish Christian fanatics publicly attacked the religion of their Muslim rulers and denounced the Prophet Mohamed. Armstrong indicates that the Muslims were "extremely reluctant to put these Christian fanatics to death, partly because they did not seem in control of their faculties but also because they realized that the last thing they needed was a martyr-cult."

Benjamin Kedar (1984) reports on the war against Muslims by Christian authorities during the formative years of Islam. He suggests that the Pope, about 650, attempted to convert Muslims to Christianity. A century later, Christian authorities considered the refusal of Muslims to convert "as justification for waging war on them." He (p. 8) quoted an Irish scholar active at the Court of Charles the Bald that the Muslims of the south and the pagans of the north "will bend their necks in subjection; Christ will reign everywhere; all submit to both King and God." The *Economist* (1999) eloquently shows that the Crusaders inflicted untold suffering upon Muslims. It indicates that when the crusaders besieged Caesarea, two Muslim emissaries presented a query to the Patriarch as follows: "Why do you tell your people to invade our land and kill us, when your religion says no one must kill anyone made in the image of God?" The Patriarch's answer regarding the killing was "whoever fights to destroy God's law deserves that. Give up the land, and you can go unharmed with your goods. If not, the sword of the Lord will kill you." The *Economist*, however, insists that the sword, rather than forgiveness, was the arbiter. Its quotation from European accounts of what happened when the Crusaders stormed Jerusalem is telling about the nature of violence:

Our men took many prisoners in the temple [the al-Agsa mosque], men and women, killing some and saving some alive . . .. They rushed through the city, seizing gold and silver, horses and mules, goods of all sorts. Then they went rejoicing and weeping for gladness to worship at the sepulcher of our Savior . . .. They climbed up to attack the pagans [Muslims], men and women, cutting off their heads with swords. Some Muslims jumped headlong from the roof.

Curry argues that the notion of martyrdom and death in the path of God were motivational factors for the Crusaders. He indicates that salvation through the sword was a powerful devotional element. Indeed, salvation "through violence was a revolutionary idea." He quotes (p. 39) Pope Urban II calling on all Christians to "leave off slaying each other and fight[] instead a righteous war, doing the work of God, and God will lead them. For those that died in battle there would be absolution and the remission of sins." Nevertheless, Curry suggests that this idea was without precedent in the history of Christianity.

As the search for economic interests and land became closely intertwined with the movement of the spread of religion in the Christian world, an era of colonization was initiated. As indicated in the preceding discussion, charter corporations were instrumental in spreading Christianity and enhancing Western political and military domination. Even during the Cold War, religion played a pivotal role in arousing the public sentiment against the Godless Communists. The end of the Cold War has witnessed a new era where religion and cultural sentiments have become integral ingredients in redesigning the world and restationing military forces in many of its parts. At this time, the boundaries between economic interest, greed, and religions have become blurred and the world seems to have regressed back to the era of the Crusades; though with the application of the most sophisticated technologies.

It should be mentioned that, over the years, Christian theologians have developed the concept of "just war"; a term coined by St. Augustine. For St. Augustine, the intention behind a war is an important consideration. He declares, "The passion for inflicting harm, the cruel thirst for vengeance, an unpacific and relentless spirit, the fever of revolt, the lust of power, and such things, all these are rightly condemned in war" (Quoted in Raymond, 2002).

These concepts encompass mutually agreed rules of combat between two similar enemies. The principles of just war are: having just cause (e.g., initiation of aggression), being declared by proper authority (mostly a state), possessing right intentions (done for the sake of justice and not for reason of self-interest or aggrandizement), having a reasonable chance for success (costs & benefits of a campaign must be calculated), and the end being proportional to the means used (retrieve a land that was controlled by the invading forces) (Moseley, 2001). The U.S. Catholic Bishops' 1993 statement on just war emphasized that the "Christian has no choice but to defend peace." It states that the tradition of "just war" seeks to overcome injustice, reducing violence and preventing its expansion by: clarifying when force may be used, limiting the resort to force and restraining damage done by military forces during war. For all these reasons, most of the mainstream Christian churches have stood against the call for war and expansion in recent years. These Churches believe, unlike most of the Evangelical Christian Right groups, that war does an injustice to the majority of people and results in destruction and suffering to those innocent people caught in its wake.

It is plausible, therefore, to suggest that since the era of the Crusades, the Christian world has gained considerable military power and has often used force to pursue its interests. During the inception of Christianity, however, Jesus discouraged the use of force and called for tolerance and forgiveness. In the Christian Western World, however, there seems to be a tendency to exhibit an uncompromising stance and arrogance when religion is integrated into politics. While some may consider the era of colonization as a case in point (see Amin, 2001), Nazism in Germany demonstrates that mixing religion and politics can lead to tragic consequences. Theologically, however, the mainstream religious authorities appear, in recent history, to condemn the use of violent forms of Jihad and have set certain restrictions and guidelines for sanctioning violence.

JIHAD IN ISLAM

The birth of Islam coincided with the declining influence of the Persian and Roman empires. It was revealed to Mohamed around 610. At that time, Arabia was characterized by widespread corruption, fierce tribal loyalty, abuse of power, and a complete absence of law and order. Mohamed recognized the need for establishing law and order and the necessity of emphasizing fairness and justice as preconditions for building the foundation for a new society. Armstrong (1992) believes that the immediate spread and acceptance of Islam reflected the unique message of Islam and was clearly a reflection of the genius of Mohamed. She argues, however, that the Arabs were not sufficiently developed for the sophisticated Islamic monotheism. She states (p. 53) "Christianity took root in the Roman empire where Jewish communities had paved the way and prepared the minds of the pagans. But Mohamed had to start virtually from scratch and work his way towards the radical monotheistic spirituality on his own."

Mohamed, both as a victim of violence and as a statesman, abhorred violence and instructed believers to forgive and be merciful. Both the Quran and the Prophet's sayings articulated the conditions for war and the conduct of war. Unlike Christianity and Judaism, the terms and conditions of war in Islam were specified, and gratuitous violence was condemned. Interestingly, neither during Mohamed's life nor in the first few centuries of Islam was Jihad treated as holy war. Indeed, the term was "coined in Europe during the Crusades to mean a war against the Muslims" (The Episcopal-Muslim Relations Committee, 2002). The proposition that Islam is the middle way between Christianity and Judaism is evidenced in the law that regulates war. The Torah condones territorial expansion and the slaying of those who do not submit. The New Testament, on the other hand, obligates the believer to avoid war.

The Quran instructs believers not to start fighting unless the enemy starts first, and obligates Muslims to forgive those who ask for forgiveness or cease to fight. During one of the wars, the Quran instructed Mohamed to (9:5), "Slay the unbelievers wherever you find them. . . . When the unbelievers cease to threaten you, when they cease, then remember that God is compassionate and you have to stop fighting." When the unbelievers desire to fight you then fight them (9:36), "fight ye the polytheists all together, as they fight you all together; and know that God is with the pious ones." However, when the enemy asks for a peaceful solution, the Muslims must agree (Quran: 8:61); "A·ıd if they lean to peace, then leaneth thou too it, and trust in God." Then the Quran warns that killing innocent people is a serous crime. It states (5:32); "If any one slew a person-unless it be for murder or for spreading mischief in the land-it would be as if he slew mankind as a whole. And if any one saved a life, it would be as if he saved mankind as a whole."

In defining Jihad, the Quran provides four categories: striving with one's own rebellious self-struggle within (9:41); striving with one's wealth (9:41); spreading knowledge to the benefit of those who need it; and fighting with the sword (2:216, 4:17). The first is called the greatest Jihad and the last is called the minor Jihad. The latter means that Muslims can fight only when it becomes unavoidable to defend their faith or their lives and is called Difa or self-defense (Ahmed Ali, 1988). That is, in Islam the use of force is prohibited, and permitted only in self-defense. The self-defense Jihad in Islam according to Johnson has developed along lines compatible with international law. Prophet Mohamed elaborates on the greatest striving, Jihad, by stating that one shall not cause injury to any human, either with his tongue or with his hand. In terms of spreading knowledge, the Prophet states, "The search for knowledge is Jihad" and "He who goes forth in search of knowledge is striving in the path of God."

In terms of striving with wealth, the Prophet instructs, "One who takes care of the widow and the poor person is like the one who strives [yajahid] in the way of God." The Prophet, however, insists that the best striving, Jihad, "is the uttering of truth in the presence of an unjust ruler." Those who engage in these types of Jihad, according to Islamic teaching, shall be granted a great recompense (4:74). Islamic perspectives on Jihad have not been changed from the above four Quranic classifications. For example, when the Crusaders captured Jerusalem from the Muslims, they killed most of its inhabitants and "profaned some of Islam's holiest sites." Curry (2002, p. 38) states "The al-Aqsa mosque had been used as a stable for horses." When Muslims recaptured Jerusalem in 1187, Saladin "forbade acts of vengeance.

There were no more deaths, no violence. A token ransom was arranged for the thousands of residents. Saladin and his brother paid for hundreds of the poorest themselves and arranged guards for the caravans of refugees" (Curry, 2002, p. 38). However, the Muslim countries have been subjected, since the eleventh century, to invasion and occupation by foreign forces. This reached its peak when the Western powers colonized these countries, exploited their resources and appointed dictators to rule most of them. In terms of recent history, the *New York Times* editorial (2002, July 4) states, "For too long, America has embraced corrupt and autocratic Arab leaders, asking only that they accommodate Western oil needs and not make excessive trouble for Israel.

As a result, too many young Arabs now identify the United States more readily with the repressive dictators it supports in the Middle East than with the tolerant democracy it practices at home." The Muslims have been faced with a dilemma; accepting what they perceive as cruelty and foreign subjugation, or observing their tradition that forbids abuse and sanctions self-defense.

During the decline of the Islamic empire, especially after the Moguls' invasion, some Muslims felt threatened and the Muslim community, on the verge of extinction, developed a pessimistic view. One of that period's writers, Ibn Taymiya (1268-1328) held that it was the duty of all Muslims to fight the invaders and protect their community; otherwise they were not believers. His philosophy influences contemporary extremist groups who perceive Western occupation and military subjugation and coercion as a continuation of the Crusades. Bernard Lewis (1990) indicates that the Islamic civilization, relative to other civilizations, treated religious minorities well. He explains that Muslim states, during their rise and prosperity, displayed tolerance and remarkable openness. But during their decline and defeat, they showed a rigidity and indifference to others. Consequently, zealots and extremist groups during the era of foreign occupation and humiliation found fertile ground, as simple and extreme concepts of Islam appealed to their unsophisticated minds. In our present time these groups have often adopted terms and outlooks (suicidal and violent approaches) that appear to be inconsistent with the tradition of Islam.

For example, Bin Laden and his groups find Talmudic instruction (Sanhedrin 72a), "If someone comes to kill you, kill him first" highly appealing. These Muslim radicals exhibit a disdain for the traditional Islamic view of Jihad. But ironically, violent forms of Jihad and associate messages promulgated by historian like Daniel Pipes and Barnard Lewis strongly appeal to them. The overwhelming majority of Muslims, nevertheless, appear to resign themselves to submission and ostensibly most of them are spectators. A case in point is the current Western military build up in the Middle East to attack Iraq. The Muslims find themselves in a state of fear and anxiety; confused and paralyzed. This, however, does not mean that Muslim scholars are passive. On November 21, 2002 in Cairo, hundreds of scholars from various countries issued a statement calling for lawful resistance against foreign threats. The statement stated the, "U.S. administration's insistence on using its forces to attack the countries of the Arab region reminds us of the Crusades, and the era of imperialism. At that time, the imperialist armies killed innocent people, humiliated them, created disaster in Asia and Africa and looted their resources."

Plausibly, Islam, like Christianity, did not espouse the use of force in the beginning and, like Judaism, it did not force people to convert to its faith. Indeed, Mohamed and his immediate four caliphs perceived Jihad as primarily an internal striving for the purpose of obtaining spiritual and personal improvement. Subsequent dynasties, however, have found territorial expansion a useful tool for accumulating fame and economic power. This expansion is not condoned theologically (Ahmed Ali, 1988). During their rise to power, Muslim dynasties or states exhibited a remarkable tolerance to non-Muslims and generally were not inclined to use force (Armstrong, 1992). But since the domination of Muslims by the Western World, their response to defending themselves has been erratic and unorganized. Therefore, it seems that in Islam, the violent form of Jihad is not likely to be condoned theologically during the era of the rising power and domination of an entity espousing Islam.

The emergence of zealots in Islam who champion the idea of defending the faith by force is not a new phenomenon. After the invasion of the Mogul and the collapse of Baghdad, the Capital of the Abbasid Empire in 1258, many groups emerged to defend the Muslim lands. Some of them espoused extremism and violence to defeat the invading forces but were unsuccessful. After the1860s, France and Britain started to establish a military presence in the Middle East. This development reached its peak in 1914 when most of the Arab lands were occupied by European nations.

Various nationalistic and leftists movements engaged in struggles for self determination. Freedom and liberation, rather than Islam were the rallying points. In the Arab East almost all the leaders of these movements were Christians. The occupying powers relied on tribal chiefs and corrupt individuals to sustain their occupation and managed to crush most of the independence movements. These individuals were appointed as kings (e.g., Egypt, Iraq, Libya, Morocco, and Saudi Arabia) and presidents (Syria, Lebanon). They were placed in positions of authority after the colonial European powers arbitrarily divided the Arab lands. Between the 1930s and the1950s, the Western governments utilized nationalistic movements to obstruct the growing influence of the liberal and leftist movements. After Israeli victory in the 1967 War, the nationalistic movements (e.g., The Arab National Movement, Arab Socialist Union, and almost all Palestinian political groups) espoused radical slogans and ideas. Thus, Western powers directly and indirectly encouraged Muslim- oriented political movements to counter the growing influence of political movements aligned with the Soviet Union.

Two events in the 1980s, the invasion of Afghanistan and Lebanon by the Soviet Union and Israel respectively, empowered

Islamic political movements. The Kuwaiti crisis and its aftermath, however, profoundly changed the political scene in the Middle East tilting it toward political Islam. The Arab streets are no longer dominated by the leftist and nationalist movements. Rather, Muslim political organizations have seized the political vacuum.

The huge military presence, in August 1990, of the United States in Saudi Arabia and the rest of the Arab Gulf States, initially was justified by the Wahhabi religious establishment in Saudi Arabia as necessary to defend Islam and the faithful from the Iraqi threat. After the liberation of Kuwait, political Islamic movements thought the United States would immediately withdraw its troops from the region. Since this did not happen, these organizations have channeled their wrath against the presence of foreign troops in Arab lands. Consequently, they initiated a political campaign of violence against the United States and Arab governments since 1992. This marked the beginning of the end of the formal cooperation between most of the Islamic political movements and conservative Arab governments. The region, therefore, has experienced two forms of violent Jihad with global reach. The first is waged by the Muslim political groups against the United States and Arab government camp and the second by the U.S and Arab governments against Muslim political organizations. This vicious circle of violence, in the absence of civilized dialogue, tolerance, and inclusion may ultimately engulf the whole world.

DISCUSSION AND CONCLUSION

It is without doubt that the Middle East conflict is the result of a complex interplay of politics, religion, and economic factors. Among these factors, religion seems to be the most subtle. It provides a convenient cover to otherwise unpopular hostilities. Furthermore, it furnishes an easy justification for a complex subject. Across the centuries, religion has been utilized to serve the interest of the dominate elites. Furthermore, Middle East history reveals that religion had played a pivotal role in shaping alliances and events. Today's conflict confirms too that religious sentiments in one way or another may influence the thinking of the power elites. Current trends and violence, however, give the appearance that things might get out of control. The use of force and violence arising from religious sentiments and those that are attributed to religion may, in fact, initiate the downfall of civilization if they are not rationally confronted.

Even though making precise prediction is not a primary concern of this chapter, recent events provide ample evidence that violent forms of Jihad and related Middle East conflicts are not being contained. Indeed, world public opinion and world actors, at this juncture in history, seem incapable of restraining the forces that call for perpetual Jihad.

In terms of public policy and government relations certain implications stand out. The most important implication is that governments should avoid using policy as an instrument of religion. While in most parts of the world intellectual observers and to some extent ordinary people view the infusion of religion into political discourse with suspicion, others may act upon it. This is especially true when leaders of the powerful countries give the impression that their actions are guided by a divine power. Policy makers have to maintain a separation between their public roles and personal beliefs.

Experience in most of the developing nations and in Nazi Germany provides evidence that when policy is influenced by religious beliefs, it leads to devastating consequences. In an interview with Paul Wolfowitz, the deputy secretary of defense, Keller indicated that there were three things on Wolfowitz's mind: security of Israel, invading Iraq, and reforming Islam. Whether it is right or wrong, many observers in other countries see a strong interplay between personal beliefs and policy directions. Cohen argues that when the Israeli newschapter, *Haaretz,* reported that President George W. Bush was quoted saying that he had gone to war in Afghanistan and Iraq on instructions from God, it gave the impression that this was the only explanation for "some of what Bush has done."

The second implication for governments is that short- term considerations almost always backfire. The early attempts by western and Arab governments to minimize the influence of Arab leftist and nationalistic movements by encouraging political Islam have resulted in undesired consequences. That is, policymakers, especially in international affairs, should not subordinate the vision of world peace and stability to immediate and/or domestic interests. For example, after Britain occupied Iraq in 1917 it made sure that the Iraqis would not have access to democracy. Gertrude Bell, Oriental Secretary to the High Commissioner in Baghdad of the British occupying power of Iraq, wrote in 1921 that one of the subjects that the Iraqis are "fond of expatiating upon is the crying need for democracy in Iraq-al damokratiyah, you find it on every page."

A year before, Bell had written that, "I don't for a moment doubt that the final authority must be in the hands of the Sunnis, in spite of their numerical inferiority; otherwise you will have a mujtahd [learned religious person]-run, theocratic state, which is the very devil." This short- sighted policy is probably responsible for the instability in Iraq and the willingness of the minority to use brutal force to maintain the submission of the majority.

More importantly, policy makers in Western countries must be deliberate and consistence in promoting human rights and freedom in other countries.

These policymakers have provided security for autocratic governments. Recently, Slevin indicates that historically, " U.S. Presidents have accepted the stability of autocratic rule" in the Middle East instead of promoting democracy. Furthermore, senior policymakers in Washington have repeatedly quoted the UN's *Arab Human Development Report 2002*, which states that the Arab countries experience a deficit related to freedom. Nevertheless, they overlooked a major point in the Report that foreign occupation of Arab lands is the most pervasive obstacle to security and progress in the region.

This is because (p. 2) "occupation freezes growth, prosperity and freedom in the Arab world." From a practical standpoint, foreign military occupation is a form of violent Jihad. In spirit and action, it violates basic individual and property rights. The three deficits related to freedom, empowerment of women, and knowledge that were specified by the UN in the region must be addressed by policy makers simultaneously and energetically to erode the foundations of the seemingly dysfunctional public management in the Middle East. One of the most significant implications is that the lack of democratic institutions always leads to political instability and constitutes a serious obstacle to economic growth and prosperity. Indeed, the persistence of autocratic regimes in the Arab World not only enlarges the gap of mistrust between Arab rulers and their people; but, has also been utilized to question the true purpose of the Western countries in the region and thus contributed to the growing anger at the Western governments, especially the United States.

The people in the region, regardless of their religious or ethnic backgrounds, long for freedom and peace and their experience provides them with ample reason to demand no less than full access to knowledge, economic opportunities, and political freedom. Contrasting the current developments in the region with that under Britain, Zakaria states, "America is a different country, of course—less fascinated by empire—but in one important respect it faces the same paradox as Britain. No matter how compelling America's ideals, they still come wrapped in American power. People abroad may love the former but they are inevitably suspicious of the latter. And if America falters in its application of its ideals, people around the world will believe that they are simply a smoke screen for its power."

The current discourse on Jihad is politically charged and leaves uninformed readers confused and bewildered. It is inconceivable, though urgently needed, these days to objectively discuss the term Jihad. In recent years, the term has been distorted to suit prevailing political agendas (Sullivan, 2003).

Once religion becomes politicized, reason and logic are generally overlooked. Consequently, fact, emotion, disinformation, and manipulation become difficult to differentiate with clarity. Perceptions regarding these distinct political issues have contributed to the promotion and adoption of violent form of Jihad. These issues revolve around the Israeli-Palestinian conflict, the concern for oil, and the rise of political religions. Among the three issues, the first stirs emotion among politically and religiously involved Jews and Muslims. It has also attracted Christian Zionists who believe that the gathering of Jews in Palestine will accelerate the coming of the messiah and therefore have joined the first group to discredit Muslim claims and faith (see Kristof, 2002; Milbank, 2001).

All these groups have engaged in a political and media campaign to win public opinion. In the process, political expediency and mistrust of each others intentions have become greatly engraved in their daily discourse. A case in point is an article written by David Harris , the executive director of the American Jewish Committee.

He claims that Muslim American organizations' involvement in politics and in the media constitutes a threat to Jewish American strength and ultimately to Israel. He states, there has been "a sharp increase in Arab and Muslim political activity in the United States.

These communities know they have a steep uphill struggle. They recognize the formidable strength of the pro-Israel advocacy movement in this country, but they believe it is assailable. And they have made no secret of one of their ultimate goals-to end American support for Israel... we must proceed carefully, ever alert to the physical and political threats posed by the Islamic radical network to Jews and Jewish institutions in this country."

Ironically, the state of the discourse on Jihad seems to affirm that the past is not only repeating itself. Furthermore, this discourse has the potential to dangerously affect the future if it is not wisely managed.

History reveals that powerful forces over the centuries have seldom displayed an appreciation of facts and truth, and have almost invariably been inclined to discredit their perceived enemy. Likewise, history shows that land grasping, economic greed, and religious hysteria have often opened the gate to chronic cultural and economic instability. If allowed free rein these same forces may again propel human suffering and economic chaos.

Understanding the past, however, can be a powerful arsenal in building a cooperative world community and avoiding blind rationalizations. Specifically, the most dangerous minefield is the inclination, in some quarters, to treat religion as political. Once this becomes an exercise, rationality in decision-making easily gives way to emotion and eventually leads to conflict. When war and domination become the preferred instruments of policy, stability and confidence in world institutions are threatened.

As in the past, the Middle East's religious and political disputes constitute the background that motivates and energizes powerful political leaders and commentators. Many of them see it as their religious duty to maintain Middle East conflicts (Kaiser, 2003). These forces thrive in an environment of fear and uncertainty. Politics, therefore, is seen as a useful instrument for achieving what is perceived a religiously sanctioned goal. There are two seemingly contradictory impulses in the discourse on the violent form of Jihad.

The first is advocated by Muslim extremists and treats violence as a method for asserting cultural identity and the removal of foreign dominations. The second is promoted by their counterparts in Christianity and Judaism.

These groups seem to believe that militarization of the globe and the globalization of fear is the best instrument for religious and political domination. Both impulses are a threat to civilization and established norms of the international community. Indeed, both of them constitute a major setback and threaten a return to an endless era of conflict, worse than what mankind experienced during Nazism or during the Cold War.

The globalization of fear, if materialized, may constitute the most harmful development on the global scene. This is because the world community would be subjected to three fatal consequences: restriction on the free movement of trade, capital, and labor across the globe; reductions in the flow of relevant information in and out of each society; and increases in uncertainty at national and international levels.

In short, perpetual Jihad is a dangerous trend and its consequences could impact regions well beyond the Middle East. Perhaps, its proponents believe that they are capable of containing these consequences within the geographic boundaries of the Middle East. This, however, may prove to be wishful thinking. From a distance, today's world may look large and unconnected but perceptions regarding geographic constraints have lost much of their utility. In the modern era, the world is not only finite but every part has greater proximity to every other part than ever before. Perpetual Jihad, therefore, would likely produce endless chaos/catastrophe.

The three religions Christianity, Judaism, and Islam, although they have understood the violent form of Jihad variously throughout their history in their respective ways, currently exhibit a similar trend in thinking. More importantly, Judaism perspectives on war and violence have seemed to influence the perspectives of both Christianity and Islam through out history. Generally speaking, the shift in emphasis to violence and war in the three religions seems to be associated with the rise of military and economic power and in the incorporation of religious tenets in policy. Nevertheless, the three religions offer hopeful perspectives for a peaceful world. These perspectives in an environment devoid of religious fever can facilitate coexistence and the transformation of the Middle East into a prosperous region. In their emphasis on respect for human dignity, cooperation, and the prohibition of killing of innocent people, the three religions offer reason for hope. Indeed, the relatively peaceful co-existence of the three indigenous religion communities in the region between 660-1936 evidence that tolerance and inclusion are not an alien concepts to the region. Jewish historian and philosopher, S. Goitein (1968, p. 297) argues that the Jewish and Christian communities in the Arab World maintained their freedom and were tolerated under the Muslim role.

He states, the "enormous degree of freedom of communication enjoyed by the people mirrored in the Cairo Geniza would not have been possible had it not been favored by the legal position and the general political climate in the states concerned."

Furthermore, we agree with Rabbi Kula against treating Biblical teachings as especially valid. Statements in the Bible or Quran that might seem to refer to violence should be treated in the context of their historical circumstances but not something to emulate in conduct in the contemporary world. They must be treated as a history lesson and a reflection on circumstances where primitive nomadic life and primitive conduct were the norm rather than the exception.

Nevertheless, the misreading of history and religion by politically charged power elites may, at this defining moment in world affairs, perpetuate the Middle East conflict. Historically, this misreading ended in disastrous consequences to the people of the region. Indeed, current events in Lebanon, the occupied territories, Afghanistan, and Iraq, remind us that it is often easier to embark on destruction rather than construction.

In conclusion, the Middle East conflict has been the most chronic source of uncertainty and chaos in the world. Its' persistence demonstrates that the conflict cannot be resolved through force and intimidation. The overwhelming use of force may subdue people and give a quick military victory, but it seldom eradicates the growing gulf of mistrust and mounting grievances. The severity and persistence of the conflict reflects an uncompromising view of world events and the incorporation of religious tenets into policy. Both stands facilitate the adoption and pursuit of perpetual Jihad. The cost could be immense and will not likely be confined to the Middle East.

4

Clash of Civilizations

HAS THE CLASH BETWEEN CIVILIZATIONS ARRIVED?

Almost one decade ago Samuel Huntington (*1993*) warned of an emerging "clash of civilizations" centered on religious and political economic disharmony. In the end, he envisioned a world of West versus East. Islam versus Non Islam; a Confucian-Islamic alliance on a collision course with the West.

According to Huntington the "clash of civilizations will dominate global politics". In this environment of conflict, nations are reluctant to adapt to American culture; as these nations are unable to mobilize and reap the potential economic advantages of globalization, the "clash" intensifies.

Benjamin Barber views the conflict of nations and civilizations from a different perspective. In "McWorld versus Jihad", Barber takes Huntington's prophecy to a new level. According to Barber, forces of separation and independence drive Jihad. In contrast, McWorld is empowered by globalization and the idea of a democratic free capitalism. Because these worlds are so fundamentally different, both will clash on a political level.

According to Barber, "McWorld" stands to unite the world in one common pursuit: free markets and the right to consumerism for all. It is characterized by "fast music, fast computers and fast food..pressing nations into one commercially homogenous global network" (*Barber, 2000, p 23*). McWorld ignores national boundaries, traditions, religions, and cultures while replacing them with technology, communications, commerce, and free-flowing capital. McWorld functions according to the unifying rules of democratic free capitalism, and ultimately global integration. McWorld cares little about "blue laws...pub-closing British paternalism, Sabbath-observing Jewish Orthodox fundamentalism, or no-Sunday-liquor-sales Massachusetts Puritanism" (*Barber, 2000, p 24*).

In contrast, Jihad is based on religious solidarity and local identity. For Muslim extremists this identity is secured through war against outsiders. Extremists who embrace this vision believe that the individual should acquiesce to non-secular authority. Jihad is rooted in parochialism and exclusion from the world market. Democratic principles and capitalistic economies are a threat.

Barber attempts to answer the question: can politics and democracy survive the eventually clash of Jihad and McWorld? He states,

Democracy in any of these variations will, however, continue to be obstructed by the undemocratic and anti-democratic trends toward uniformitarian globalization and intolerant tribalization that I have portrayed here. For democracy to persist in our new McWorld we will be able to commit acts of conscious political will – a possibility but hardly a probability under these conditions. Politics will require more than just a quick fix of transfer of institutions (*Barber, 2000, p. 32*).

In a study, "Economic Repression Breeds Terrorism" (*Driscroll and Holmes, 2001*), economic freedom was examined vis a vis associated levels of terrorist activity within 88 nations. The report concludes that economic repression does, in fact, breed terrorism. The authors found that economic freedom (measured by excessive government regulation, the existence of a "black market" economy) was inversely related to nation states that harbor or support terrorism (e.g. Iran, Iraq, Afghanistan, Libya and Sudan).

The September 11 attacks brought the political economic conflict addressed by Huntington, Barber, and Driscoll and Holmes to a new and real level. The world and public policy makers are reawakened. We know that the "19 hijackers" were part of a terrorist network seeking to tear down both the symbols and structure of the U.S. economy. This hideous act made Islamic Jihad known to the world. The New York Times and its series,

"A Nation Challenged", seeks to examine the events preceding and following September 11. In "Response to Attack Splits Arabs in the West", Cohen explained the nature of the September 11 attacks vis a vis the political-economic climate of the Middle East, and U.S. policy.

Cohen believed that the acts of the Saudi and Egyptian "19" were partially a response to U.S. policy with these countries. Both Carothers and Fuller echo similar points of view. Carothers states, "national origins of the September 11 attackers make clear that these nations are in fact breeders and financiers of extremism" (*Carothers, 2003, p.4)*. Fuller sees this act as the ultimate action by Islamic extremists in using general Islamic ideals as a "touchstone" for overthrowing the regimes of Egypt and Saudi Arabia. This, combined with America's support of Israel (and its inability to see lands seized in the 1967 war returned to the Palestinians) gave the Muslim extremists justification for such an irrational act as September 11, 2001. Following the attacks, Barber re-visited his "Jihad versus McWorld" theory. He concludes that the September 11 attacks brought the conflict of Jihad and McWorld to a terrifying and new explosive level. As we know, the response of the Bush Administration called for swift military action against states that harbored and supported terrorism (e.g., Afghanistan and Iraq). As the U.S. implemented this policy, its Middle East allies have removed groups that actively support terror. However, there is a continued fear that systemic crackdowns will further ignite public opinion against these governments and the U.S.

Fuller contends that unless Washington departs from policies of accommodation with oppressive and insecure regimes, popular Muslim opinion will continue to be "gratified" with acts of terrorism. Cohen offers a similar opinion. She suggests that U.S. policy must depart from past policies (socio-economic blindness) and develop alternatives, which address political and economic unrest in the Middle East.

CAN DEMOCRACY EASE THE CONFLICT BETWEEN CIVILIZATIONS?

According to Fuller , the first phase of U.S., policy in the wake of the September 11 attacks is one of engaging, military operations against state sponsors of terror (Afghanistan and Iraq) and impose a change of regimes. The policy also extends to the Arab-Jewish conflict when the U.S. successfully sought a change in the Palestinian leadership.

By effecting regime change, the goal is to "establish a successful model of Arab democracy that will have a powerful demonstration effect" (*Carothers, 2003, p.4*). However to accomplish this ultimately requires a massive, and demanding, long-term reconstruction effort. Some view these directions as "far fetched" *(Carothers, 2002, p.5)*. Others warn of the risks of supporting moves toward democracy in these countries since the outcome may be risky at best *(Kibble, 1998)*. It is clear that these propositions are being tested in Post-War Iraq.

However, effective policy alternatives require a deeper understanding of the sources of political violence and terror that mark the Muslim world today. If democracy is, in part a solution, policy analysts must ask, can democracy and Islam mutually co-exist? How does democracy fit with the vision of Islam's "new breed" of thinkers and leaders? How can we learn from the democratic lessons of Jordan and Kuwait and others? Can democracy respond to the challenges in these and other countries? Finally, should and can the U.S. "export" democracy to Iraq and other Middle East states? What are the policy issues and alternatives given these important questions?

ISLAM AND DEMOCRACY: IS THERE ANY COMMON GROUND?

According to Fuller the fact that Quran and the Hadith (traditions of the Prophet's life) direct the way in which society should be governed, makes these readings "the most powerful ideological forms in that part of the world". To the many Islamic faithful, the Quran is seen as the ultimate source of authority. Muslims do interpret the Quran and the Hadeth to derive the meaning about good governance and concepts of social and economic justice. According to Kibble (*1998*) although fundamentalism does deny democratic values, many Muslim leaders practice forms of democracy. Through Iljma, religious leaders use consensus to reach action. Iljma is acceptable as long as its decisions fit within the parameters of Quran's teachings. Unfortunately, this is where Islam's relationship with democracy begins and ends.

Other scholars (*Fuller, 2002 and Haliday, 1995*) take the position that Islam is incompatible with democracy. For example, Haliday states there are no true human rights and democratic values in a nation state that is overtly non-secular or religious (e.g. witness the Taliban's oppressive rule in Afghanistan). As an example, Iran's Ayatollah Khomeini warned not to use the word democracy, in any way, to describe his Islamic republic and revolution in Iran.

According to Fuller, the real issue is not, what Islam is, but what Muslims want. The type of Muslim leadership (radical or moderate) that addresses these needs will dictate the political/governance process (democratic or authoritarian).

In this regard, there are two possible roads for Islam and democracy. The first includes the continued practice of Islamic fundamentalist of using the general idea of Islam to attack or overthrow existing government authorities.

The second road may include the emergence of moderate Islamic intellectuals who can direct grassroots political economic change. However even under the latter scenario the result may not be ideally democratic.

Takeh believes that moderate Islam may be "democracy's last hope". According to Takeh, moderate Islam may be the only, and most effective long-term solution in the war against terrorism.

In Post-war Iraq Takeh's position is being tested. Moderate Islam in Iraq faces a watershed moment.

In a July 2003 report, Tyler explains how post war Iraq's "governing council" was formed through main Iraqi opposition groups, and the office of the American civilian administrator for the occupation.

The council is a 25-person group representing Iraq's Kurd, Shiite and Sunni populations. The council is developing a new Iraqi constitution and process that may "win the acceptance of the grand ayatollah (of Iraq)". If successful, Iraq's reform may become a model for moderate Islam to bridge and ease the clash of civilization prophesized by Huntington.

IS THE MIDDLE EAST ON A ROAD TO DEMOCRATIC REFORM?

In order to address the efficacy of democracy in the Middle East, we will look at the path of democracy in the Middle East. Attention will focus on Bahrain, Kuwait, Jordan, Turkey, Pakistan, Israel, Egypt and Saudi Arabia. This analysis may also provide valuable insight into building a post-war Iraq.

Bahrain

Bahrain had an elected National Assembly until the ruling Al Khalifa monarchy unilaterally dissolved it in 1975. Since 1975, the government has been managed by royal decree, although there is a 40-person appointed Majilis that advises the monarchy. In 1995, the Al Khalifa attempted to reach a compromise with opposition leaders. When talks failed, the monarchy began arresting scores of opposition leaders and charged them with plotting to overthrow the monarchy. Currently Bahrain is in a stall position to reinstate national elections.

Kuwait

Kuwait has a ruling monarchy that reinstated national assembly elections following The Gulf War of 1991. Initially members of three Islamist groups won 18 of the 40 parliament seats. These groups were able to retain that power with the same number of seats retained in the 1996 elections.

Jordan

Jordan has taken gradual, successful steps in introducing democratic reforms. With the 1993 elections, a number of old and new parties were legalized in the parliament. The Islamic Action Front (the political face of Egypt's Muslim Brotherhood) has emerged as the largest group in Jordan's parliament.

However, the parliament has minimal government authority. King Abdullah's vision is one of a democratically elected parliament serving in an advisory capacity to the monarchy. According to Kibble (*1998*), Abdullah "believes that Jordan might evolve as a model for democratic development in the Middle East".

Turkey

Recently, Turkey has experienced dynamic political reform and change. In 1995, the Welfare party polled over 21 percent and received 158 seats in the national assembly elections. According to Fuller , Turkey is gradually emerging as a model of democracy in the Middle East. Fuller says, "Turkey has evolved rapidly out of an initially narrow and non-democratic understanding of Islam into a relatively responsible force, whether it overlaps with American ideals or not".

Pakistan

Pakistan is moving in a unique democratic direction following General Mushariff's military coup in 1999. Mushariff has gradually reinstated elections, while ruling the country under martial law. The elections of fall 2002 saw the emergence of Islamic majorities in major regions of Pakistan. The goal of the Mushariff government is to eventually forfeit military rule and give up political power. Mushariff however has democracy on a very short leash. In the fall of 2002, he forced passage of a referendum that authorized his constitutional power through 2004.

Israel

Israel has used a parliamentary form of government since its creation in 1948. Modeled after Great Britain Israel's national elections determine the political party that leads the country. In Israel, all citizens have the right to vote. It is an open and dynamic electoral process that has led to frequent changes in the ruling political party. Currently there are two majority parties (the Likud and Labor party) competing for power in Israel politics. There are approximately 20 minority parties represented in the Israel Knesset. Religious and cultural diversity also characterizes the Israeli parliaments; there are both Israeli Jews and Arab Israelis serving in the Knesset. In fact, some of Knesset's Arab members openly oppose the government and policies of Israel.

Saudi Arabia

Saudi Arabia has experienced turbulent times in seeking a more open and democratic society. In 1992, King Fahd established a 60 person Majilis to consult with the monarchy. In 1997, Fahd enlarged the Majilis to 90 members. There is however, no elections and the Majilis serve only in an advisory capacity: The role of the Majilis is to debate policies submitted to the King, interpret laws, and examine reports delegated to it by the national authority. It is a weak parliamentary system. The current climate in Saudi Arabia is one of growing dissatisfaction with the monarchy. This has spawned the growth of fundamentalist Islamic opposition and most notably, Osama Bin Laden. Economic and social problems, corruption within the royal family, and a disparate distribution of wealth often are the focus of such criticism.

EGYPT

In contrast to Saudi Arabia, Egypt has a parliamentary electoral system The Mubarek government has suppressed all opposition to its authority. On the eve of the 1995 elections, 100 Muslim Brotherhood leaders were arrested and subject to meliorate trial. Clearly, the Mubarek government will continue its crackdown on the Muslim brotherhood as these challenges intensify.

There are grim reports of human rights violations in Saudi Arabia and Egypt. Amnesty International has condemned the use of Islamic punishments in Saudi Arabia. For example, in 1995 11 people were flogged between 200 and 1500 lashes for alleged crimes. In the same year, one Egyptian was sentenced to 4000 lashes in addition to 7 years for burglary.

In this post September 11 era the political climate in Saudi Arabia and Egypt has exposed many things. One of them is the important role that democratic and economic reform must play in their future. At the same time (as Iraq and Afghanistan reform politically and economically), real progress is needed to resolve the 50-year-old Arab-Jewish conflict over Palestine. I must note that these warnings are not old (Murphy, Gause, and Gregory, 1997). September 11, 2001 has brought a new sense of urgency to these warnings.

CAN THE ROAD TO DEMOCRATIC REFORM BE ACCELERATED?

In light of the aforementioned political climate in the Middle East, we ask; can democratic reform succeed in these countries and how? Is it in the best interest of the United States to encourage such reforms?

Currently United States foreign policy is in a "Catch 22". It must maintain diplomatic relations with long standing Middle East allies, while engaging its war on terrorism, and press for democratic reform. Fuller characterizes this environment as a "vicious cycle":

Dissatisfaction (by Muslims) leads to anti-regime action, which leads to repression, which in turn leads to terrorism, U.S. military intervention, and final further dissatisfaction *(Fuller, 2003, p.5).*

According to Fuller, this cycle fulfills Samuel Huntington's prophecy in the "clash of civilizations"; the West and Muslim fundamentalism are engaged in a collision course. In dealing with this dilemma Monshipouri et al., *(1993)* and Caruthers believe that the U.S. must balance relationships with regimes (albeit autocratic), while trying to live up to American ideals of liberty, freedom and human rights. According to Monshipouri et al., this dichotomy is likely to remain unreconciled.

Since September 11, the Bush Administration finds itself managing foreign relations within the context of this dichotomy. The pre and post Iraqi war circumstances serve as a case in point. Many feared that a unilateral invasion of Iraq (void of UN Security Council approval) would strengthen the hand of hard line fundamentalists. Although this has not occurred, with the U.S. overthrow of Sadaam Hussein, Islamic hard liners continue to call for the withdrawal of U.S. forces. These demands will only continue as the U.S. maintains its occupation force, while Iraq develops a new constitution and process. As the U.S. maintains its presence in Iraq, the existing monarchies will tighten their grip on civil liberties. Burns believes this may slow down all previous and on-going attempts of political reform.

The dichotomy proposed in this chapter is further supported by events in Malaysia. Prior to September 11, 2001 the Clinton administration criticized Malaysian Prime Minister Mahathir Mohammad's authoritarian rule. Since the September 11, attacks Mohammed began arresting Islamic militants, sharing intelligence and cooperating with the Bush Administration's antiterrorism campaign. By May 2002, the Bush Administration reversed the

1998 stance lauding Mahatir as a "force for regional stability". All of the aforementioned developments alter American policy action in two ways. The first requires encouraging existing regimes to continue to open up their political systems in an evolutionary peaceful way. The argument is made that Jordan and Turkey may emerge as models of change. This may support the goal of long-term stability, while bringing about needed democratic reform and improved human rights. The disadvantage is that America may have to live with short-term transitions that may not be in its interests until full participatory democracies are in place.

America also must encourage Pakistan's leadership and civilian population to work towards a common vision of democratic innovation. This same dialogue can occur in post war Afghanistan and Iraq. We must see if these innovations can be mirrored in Kuwait, Egypt and Saudi Arabia. In this regard, the U.S. must proactively exert pressure on these regimes to open up political dialogue and achieve real economic reform. It must support attempts to engage in dialogue with moderate Islamist groups to bolster democratic reform.

CAN REGIONAL ECONOMIC DEVELOPMENT FURTHER PURGE THE "CLASH OF CIVILIZATIONS"?

In a recent interview with television personality Charlie Rose, former Israeli Prime Minister Shimon Peres stated:

The road to peace in the Middle east partially rests on the ability of these governments to give the younger generation hope..these countries need to break out of the dark ages..innovation, product development and technology is almost non existent (*Peres, 2003*).

Peres' offers a challenge to leaders and Middle East scholars. We must determine how the principles and ideals of economic globalizations can reduce economic stagnation in the Middle East.

Ceglowski (*1998*), Ohmae (*1993*), Sachs (*1998*), and O'Meara and Krain see globalization in its most positive light. Economic globalization can raise the standard of living for developed and "developing" countries.

If done correctly, economic globalization allows a free and effective flow of goods, services and information technology across borders (*Ceglowski, 1998*). Ceglowski cites Thailand and the United Kingdom as role models for developing nations of the world.

As economic globalization unfolds, there can be noticeable gains in trade and gross domestic product growth. This may result in a "level playing field" for all nations seeking economic improvement. According to Sachs, a level playing field will result in having most nations playing an equal role in a global economy. Developed countries can reach a larger market and enjoy the fruits of innovation across borders.

As we assess the future success of globalization, we need to look at these four issues:

- Can globalization promote faster economic growth?
- Will globalization undermine or promote macroeconomic stability?
- Can globalization bring about a more equitable distribution of income?
- Can it lead to improve economic governance?

In contrast to these positive outlooks, there are also many negative considerations. First globalization may exert downward pressure on the wages of under skilled workers in industrialized countries. This can further exacerbate economic instability. According to Amsden , globalization may result in the loss of the freedom to subsidize company formation. In addition, different countries require different policies for different economic stages.

Under globalization, developing countries seeking to join the growing international economy often start with weak economic infrastructures. According to Amsden, "the poorest countries have too few skills to create professionally manageable forms to alleviate poverty".

Annan , Barber and Huntington (*1993*) all warn of the dangers that globalization may bring; it may increase the growing disparity between the rich and the poor. Kofi Annan states:

Any belief that either the end of major ideological competition or the revolutionary process for economic globalization would prevent conflict..is utterly wishful thinking (*Annan, 2000, p.125)*

Annan believes that in order for globalization to succeed it must tackle the "political roots..and economic roots of the problems now griping much of the world" (*Annan, 2000, p.125)* According to Annan, real peace is contingent on "legitimate responsive politics". Another challenge is that as countries reap the benefits of globalization they must change institutions and policies. Unless globalizers open up important "windows of opportunity", human rights and economic improvements may not follow.

As developing nations engage in macroeconomic programs like the European Union and North Atlantic Free Trade Agreement (NAFTA), its poorer neighbors will expect to see economic relief. Sachs believes that the key to unlocking the mysteries of globalization rest with the use of "trade, finance and production and growing web of treaties and instructions" with and between developing nations.

CAN GLOBALIZATION IMPROVE SOCIAL AND ECONOMIC CONDITIONS WITHIN CRITICAL MIDDLE EAST NATIONS?

Following the September 11 attacks, the New York Times' "A Nation Challenged" series examined the relationship of globalization to the war on terrorism and, issues in the Middle East. According to Brainard and Purdum and French billions of dollars in aid, and free trade agreements were instituted with Afghanistan and Pakistan to bring them into the international economic community. The goal is to bring about greater economic stability to these countries. Under these arrangements, Afghanistan and Pakistan may uncover new economic resources. The economic playing field may be leveled and provide them with greater access to the world markets. Purdum and French warn however that the brunt of this responsibility should not fall on the United States. Other European countries need to also make investments and engage in improved trade policies. The World Bank needs to open its doors to Afghanistan and Pakistan.

Another issue relating to globalization and the improvement of socio-economic conditions in the Middle East is the role oil production and profit must play in regional economic development. This is central to Iraq's development in post-war Iraq. In addition, it is important that oil-rich countries must play with its poorer neighbors. In 1993 Monshipouri et al., indicate little or no desire by Saudi and Kuwait governments to assist in development of its poorer neighbors. If these trends continue, the Middle East appears headed for new cycles of economic stagnation and militarization. In dealing with this issue, it has become imperative that American foreign policies facilitate greater cooperation between the oil-rich nations and the poorer nation states.

CONCLUSIONS

The horrific attacks on the World Trade Center by Muslim radicals placed America at the center of the religious and political conflict that has punctuated the Middle East since World War II. It also actualized scholar Samuel Huntington's theory of a "clash of civilizations" between factions of Islam and the West.

This chapter finds that American foreign policy is often the result of balancing military actions, diplomatic actions and economic development actions. Since September 11, U.S. policy has been twofold: military engagement against state sponsors of terror; and the imposition of regime change. By effecting regime change, the goal is to establish a model of democracy that may spread throughout the Middle East. Democracy and moderate Islam now face a watershed moment in post-war Iraq. A central question is can Iraq's "governing council" execute a blue print that will improve Iraq's political and economic quality of life?

At the same time let us not be naïve. We will continue to see religious resistance (both moderate and extreme in nature) to the U.S. presence in Iraq and the Middle East. Achieving a real democratic reform in Iraq requires a deeper understanding of Muslim unrest. The real issue is not what Islam is, but what Muslims want. The type of Muslim leadership that addresses these needs will dictate the political/governance process in Iraq and throughout the Middle East.

As the U.S. continues to implement these policies, it also must be prepared to deal with two likely scenarios. The first includes the continued practice of Islamic radicals using general ideas of Islam to attack the West or replace existing governments. With each passing day in post-war Iraq, this first scenario becomes likely as radical Shiite and Sunni leaders call for an Iraqi Islamic republic. The second scenario includes the emergence of moderate Islamic intellectuals who can direct grassroots political economic change. The latter may be the only way to bring long-term stability in Iraq and in the Middle East. We must find ways to open up dialogue with these moderate Islamic groups.

As the U.S. adjusts to these scenarios, it must also work closely with countries which become breeding grounds for future terrorists like the notorious Sept 11 "19". If President Bush's premise is correct (that democracy will bring regional stability), can Saudi Arabia and Egypt learn from the democratic lessons of Jordan and Turkey? Alternatively, will Iraq become democracy's template in the Middle East?

Finally purging the "clash of civilizations" also requires achieving a win-win economic solution for the Middle East people. Economic globalization can facilitate a free and effective flow of goods, services and information technology and improve the quality of life for the Middle East population. As developing nations engage in macroeconomic programs, its poorer neighbors expect to see economic relief. There has been success with the European Union and NAFTA. There are marked improvements in trade, finance and production capacities (e.g. Poland).

There is a need to apply new economic formulas in the Middle East. In fiscal year 2002 and 2003 billions of dollars in aid have been given to Afghanistan and Pakistan. For fiscal year 2004 President Bush has proposed new grants exceeding $80 billion for Iraq and Afghanistan. The key to achieving real economic stability in the Middle East rests with these countries.

However, America cannot do this alone. European countries must invest in the Middle East and engage in new and dynamic trade policies. The World Bank must open its doors to Afghanistan, Pakistan and Iraq. Improving the socioeconomic conditions in the Middle East also requires oil-rich countries like Kuwait and Saudi Arabia to help their poorer neighbors. Unless all of the above is done, we may soon see new cycles of economic stagnation and militarization. As America continues to find itself in the middle of the "clash", it cannot loose sight of its role in fostering political and economic change.

5

Case for Collaboration

The chapter elaborates on the importance of collaboration in public administration and on its meaningful theoretical and practical advantages for modern societies. Our goal is to present a program on how collaboration can be implemented in local governance and integrated with the idea of urban democracy. It is argued that collaboration can and should be fostered as the new managerial and social paradigm in the years to come which may prove useful to the problematic Middle-East region.

The chapter focuses on the local government level and provides a useful map for increasing citizenship involvement in public projects. Based on a unique experience of citizenry involvement in one ambitious Israeli project we attempts to develop a broader theoretical framework on the idea of urban democracy and collaboration with public administration. We argue that such collaboration is possible and essential, and that it may revitalize urban democracy and trust among parties of modern society. Moreover, in the context of the Middle-East and following the end of the war in Iraq we further suggest that collaboration may have an even greater potential for rebuilding citizens' trust in governance and initiating mutual cooperation that crosses feasible and cultural borders.

Finally, the chapter summarizes lessons and implications of the specific project in the context of the more general framework and tries to provide a look into the future of collaboration and at the vision of better managing local-level and national-level partnerships in modern as well as developing democracies.

INTRODUCTION

We live in an era of great challenges for modern societies. The 21st century will necessitate enormous changes in our conventional perceptions of governmental activities and responsibilities. It will similarly require reformation of the meaning of citizenship and a redefinition of the role of citizens, businesses and private sector firms, the third sector, the media, and academia. All these players, and others, will need to collaborate. Most importantly, they will need to collaborate with public administration as its impact grows, in order to provide the people with better services and high quality goods. They will have to collaborate since the economic, social, and human potential of "doing together" is much more extensive and profitable than the option of "doing alone".

What is the meaning of collaboration? Theoretically, collaboration draws substance from various disciplines and fields of knowledge, wider even than those mentioned when dealing with the eclectic nature of public administration. Actually it would be unreliable and incomplete to treat collaboration solely from an economic, political, sociological, or even psychological point of view. Rational choice theory, the conflict resolution approach, communitarianism, and real-politics analysis provide additional theoretical tools that should be applied in a useful manner if one seeks higher understanding of the collaborative process as well as its chances to endure. The literature is preoccupied with close but different terminologies for mutual effort by social players. In this sense, collaboration is only one concept that needs to be assessed, in relation to others such as partnership, cooperation, integration, or joint ventures. Thus, and according to Cigler (1999)"collaborative actions involve strong linkages among stable membership in specific and often complex purposes, and usually are long term".

However, the most prominent questions in this regard are different: Could it be that we are presenting a utopian approach, unlikely to function in a competitive environment and a free-market society? Perhaps collaboration should be left as an unrealistic prototype for the ideal society we all seek, but can never attain? Frankly, I must admit that I have no definitive answers to these questions. Indeed, it is possible that talking about a "spirit of collaboration" in public administration will in the end remain an unreachable goal, at least in the near future. However, as will be demonstrated here, encouraging experiences of collaboration exist that have demonstrated a certain level of success. Since the goal of leaders and the leadership cadre in public administration is to create vision and pave ways, the idea of collaboration seems adequate for inclusion under the concept of vision. Hence, this chapter will try to stimulate broad thinking on the meaning and potential of collaborative administration, and to illustrate its enormous potential in the local governance arena.

The idea of collaboration in public administration has close linkage with the New Public Management (NPM) doctrine or the "new managerialism". This doctrine has put serious pressure on state bureaucracies to become more responsive to citizens as clients and to direct citizens' lives with maximum sensitivity to the voices from the field. In many respects NPM has become the "religion" and responsiveness the "law". Bureaucracies have also been urged to advance beyond responsiveness and engage in collaboration with other social players such as private businesses and third-sector organizations as well as citizens. Without doubt, these are important advances in contemporary public administration, which finds itself struggling in an ultra-dynamic marketplace arena. Like any other call for reform it was caused by a necessary change in the minds and hearts of the parties involved. To bring collaboration into the corridors of public administration, many old perceptions and attitudes need to be revised and reframed.

Despite its evident advantages, the idea of collaboration also attracts heavy fire from those who believe that it is merely a utopian idea with minimal impact on the administrative process. At most, opponents suggest that collaboration is a welcome change in theory building and in practical culture reconstruction, but they add that modern societies still encounter an increase in citizens' passivism; they tend to favor the easy chair of the customer over the sweat and turmoil of participatory involvement (Vigoda, 2002).

Revitalizing Urban Democracy: Towards a Strategic Process of Collaboration in Local Government

Despite the growing number of collaborative ventures in

government and the knowledge that has subsequently accumulated, only slight regard has been given so far to the need to develop a comprehensive strategy for collaboration in and around public administration. As suggested by Cigler (1999), collaborative actions frequently emerge from disastrous events that trigger fiscal stress or perceived stress. In light of this inconsistent approach to collaboration it is easier to understand why the literature lacks a more strategic orientation to the field. The potential advantages of collaboration as a strategic apparatus for public agencies are many. It can contribute to the mutual power of public programs, increase players' commitment to a specific idea or initiative, stimulate productivity and performance by people and institutions, enhance players' image and legitimacy of in citizens' eyes, augment trust in government, and secure democratic values.

Like any other administrative or managerial strategy, our suggestion also rests on several assumptions. The first is that public administration, its agencies, and its personnel should seek higher levels of collaboration with other social players wherever possible and wherever the public interest may benefit. Another assumption, as will be explained below, is that the local government arena is a good habitat for such experiences, at least in their first steps. However, beyond the first two assumptions, which are normative, the third is much more realistic. It argues that rationalism as rooted in human nature permits collaboration only in a limited, albeit rising number of public ventures, and that collaboration is best described as a complex process with advantages but also drawbacks. There are also several preconditions for a strategic approach to collaboration. Generally we adopt Cigler's (1999) suggestion of nine such preconditions:

(1) a disastrous event,
(2) fiscal stress or perceived fiscal stress,
(3) a political constituency for cooperation,
(4) supportive capacity building,
(5) early and continued support by elected local officials,
(6) visible advantages of cooperation for participating government,

(7) existence of a policy entrepreneur,

(8) early focus on visible effective strategies, and

(9) emphasis on collaborative skill building.

These conditions set the stage for a collaborative venture and make it a relevant mechanism to deal with a public issue.

A better understanding of the collaborative process is based on systematic analysis platforms. One such platform is presented, where a general map for collaboration between public administration and others in the local government arena is suggested. This map is based on five main stages and checkpoints in the process:

(1) deciding on a fitting *issue* for collaboration,

(2) characterizing the issue by *"what and where"* inquiries,

(3) finding out *who* is involved,

(4) finding out *how* to implement,

(5) launching *implementation,*

(6) *evaluating* the process.

These stages are broadly developed below.

While collaboration can be analyzed from various perspectives, we decided to focus on the local government level. Beyond the global, regional, and even the national levels, a local governance view is the most applicable and realistic for practical and theoretical reasons. To date, most collaborative projects reported in the scientific literature have been conducted in this environment, so our present knowledge relies heavily on such experiences. Moreover, as suggested by Sobel (1993) and Etzioni (1994, 1995), the local/communal level is ideal for increasing citizens' involvement in government. It has the potential of bringing together individuals, groups of citizens, private and third-sector organizations, and public agencies, and helping them cooperate in a microcosm. The outcomes of collaborative programs in local government are manifested directly to the people. The results are more clearly observed by public stakeholders, who also develop a sense of attachment, concern, and criticism towards these programs. In the longer run these endeavors may evince relevancy and compatibility in national or federal domains.

6

Urban Democracy in Action

The idea of urging deeper and more intensive involvement by citizens has taken an interesting course in the Carmelite project as planned in the city of Haifa. Originally this project was similar to many other local government/urban development programs in the sense that all of them were private ventures asking for the approval of the city authorities. The Carmelite project was suggested by private entrepreneurs and by the owners of a piece of land on the top of Mount Carmel in the city of Haifa. This area with its breathtaking view, which for many years was held by the IDF (Israel Defense Forces) for military reasons of air control, was released and returned to its original owners in the mid-1990s when spirits of peace and silence had woven in the region. The legal owners, namely the Catholic Church and the Christian Carmelite Order, resolved to develop the area as a model for economic renewal and growth. They thus suggested a comprehensive plan targeted at building commercial centers, hotels, residential neighborhoods, as well as gardens and green areas, and they sought the formal approval of the city authorities. In an exceptional decision, supported by professionals and academics, the mayor of Haifa appointed a 12-member committee whose task was to initiate a unique public involvement process intended to probe residents' opinions of the project.

Moreover, the committee was authorized to suggest changes in the plan in keeping with the opinions of citizens and professionals. The entrepreneurs had to agree to this condition in order to move ahead with the formal request for approval by the city authorities. In any case, the entire public involvement process was designed to be activated and completed prior to the discussion in the regional Planning and Building Committee, whose task is to examine and formally approve or reject such plans. Note however that the public involvement process was not intended to replace or adversely affect the right of vested opposition by the public as sanctioned by the Israeli planning and building law (*The Carmelite plan,* 2001; p.7). The process was aimed at bringing citizens and city residents closer to decision-making centers on the local community level, providing them with the opportunity of sounding an organized voice, and stimulating a collaborative process among private, public, and third-sector organizations as well as individual citizens.

STEERING COMMITTEE AND PROCESS

As noted, the committee consisted of 12 members who directed, supervised, and accompanied the public involvement process. Of these members five were municipal representatives from various relevant departments such as the city engineering branch, the mayor's office, and the ombudsman's branch; two represented the forum of environmental organizations, which are basically third-sector bodies; three were academic professionals in the field of urban planning; one was an independent architect; and one was a lawyer representing the entrepreneurs. Members of the committee were Jews and non-Jews who also discussed relevant religious-related issues of the project. In addition, two academic experts were involved in the active process of analyzing public opinion regarding the project. The committee worked for a year and submitted its recommendations to the mayor and the entrepreneurs, and also publicized the conclusions for the citizens of Haifa. All in all, the public involvement process included six major steps:

(1) Preliminary briefing; a step in which announcements were issued to inform to the public of the preparation of the Carmelite project and of the intended public involvement process. The announcements were published in several languages (principally Hebrew, Arabic, and Russian) in local and national newschapters and on local television and radio. The announcements were also distributed to

neighborhood committees in areas located around the geographical borders of the Carmelite project. High school pupils assisted in this activity and did the rounds of placing the materials in residents' mailboxes. In addition, a detailed exhibition of the project was mounted in City Hall, with information on the public involvement process presented there and in some of the municipality's main departments. All the information was also made available on a special Internet site created for this purpose.

(2) Presenting the project to the public: two public meetings were held to present the project to the public. An open invitation was distributed to all city and non-city residents, and some 450 people attended both meetings. At these gatherings the project was presented by the entrepreneurs and by city officials, and feedback from the public was obtained and recorded. In addition, the public received information on the involvement process, its rationale, and its goals.

(3) Feedback from the public: two major methods were applied to obtain feedback from the public. First, the comments, concerns, questions, and answers voiced during the meetings were recorded and summarized in a separate document. Second, a detailed questionnaire was distributed among all those present at the meetings. This questionnaire included two major sections, one referring to the Carmelite project itself and the other to the public involvement process, its strengths and weaknesses. It is important to mention that despite previous suggestion by the professionals, who were especially engaged to conduct the public opinion survey, the committee chose to use a convenient sample of residents rather than a more extensive and representative sample. As a result, many residents who were unable to attend the meetings for various reasons obviously had no reasonable chance to make themselves heard. Finally, a total of 145 completed questionnaires were returned and analyzed. The participants were also asked to indicate if they were interested in further discussion of the project in smaller "discussion groups".

(4) Focus/discussion groups: An additional phase of hearing the public voice was accomplished through five discussion groups. These forums were composed of independent interested citizens, about 25 in each group, around a hundred in all, who had the chance to review the details of the projects, to ask questions, raise concerns, and suggest alternatives and emendations of various parts in the project. Note also that steps 3 and 4 were both managed by professionals and expenses were covered entirely by the entrepreneurs as well as being monitored by the steering committee. Participating citizens came from various religions and communities and represented the heterogeneous Haifa population that comprises of Jews, Moslems, Druze, and Christians.

(5) A summary document of public opinions: the entire public involvement process, as well as public attitudes, questions, and concerns, were summarized in a comprehensive chapter. This summary was brought to the attention of the entrepreneurs, who were asked to revise their suggestion in accordance with the recommendations. The summarizing document was also made public through the media and presented to the local Planning and Building Committee together with the revised Carmelite plan.

(6) Response by the entrepreneur – feedback to the public: The entrepreneurs examined the possibilities of making changes and revisions in the project. They were also asked by the steering committee to present a document in which they would include comments on and responses to public concerns. This document was distributed to the public in ways similar to those described above.

LESSONS

Most importantly, this final step closes a circle in the process of public involvement and collaboration among public administration agencies, private entrepreneurs, citizens, and third-sector organizations. It depends on the idea that the revised Carmelite plan will better meet the expectations of the city residents as individuals, interest groups of private or non-profiting citizens, and the entrepreneurs. The process and its results are also expected to reduce the natural resistance to change in city urban planning and development. Being a first experience in the Israeli environment, this collaborative process is also expected to suggest a practical model and guidelines for future similar ventures and decisions on both the local and national government level.

The case study of the Carmelite project is thus an example of higher levels of citizens' involvement in the community, and of a potential step towards stronger urban democratic culture in our modern society. It may thus show the road to greater collaboration in and around Middle-East countries and especially calls for citizens' involvement in various policy decisions. All in all, the collaborative process has provided the following five advantages:

(1) An increased sense of participation by city residents and by third-sector organizations (Green environment movements and other voluntary groups in the community). This is a symbolic contribution by the project but it is of prime importance due to the potential to increase citizens' trust and partnership with public authorities in similar future projects.

(2) An early understanding by city authorities and by entrepreneurs about the difficulties that the program entails and about potential ways to adjust it to become more coherent with the public interest.

(3) Better understanding by public officials that citizens are interested and willing to share knowledge, time, effort, and other resources for the purpose of building quality community life. This advantage contradicts common criticism on citizens' passivism and lack of interest in local-level and national-level affairs.

(4) As a result of this, public officials identified considerably lower levels of resistance to change in city planning. The experience has stimulated a more effective and efficient managerial process of piloting a city construction program through the halls of bureaucracy and public administration.

(5) Encouraging a more efficient strategy of policymaking and policy implementing based on relevant public inputs into the process from its very early stages. In this process,

citizens of various religions and communities worked together to accomplish a collective goal of better quality of life engaged with higher economic development.

CONCLUSIONS AND IMPLICATIONS

The end of the second Gulf War in Iraq has brought the issue of collaboration to the front stage of our nations. No doubt that one of the regions that will need to face this challenge more actively is the Middle-East.

This war was in fact one result of the simultaneous terrorist attacks on New York City, Pennsylvania and Washington DC on the morning of September 11th, 2001. It seems that a significant outgrowth of the September 11th events may turn out to be our views and perceptions of the need for better collaboration among various players in modern democratic societies. It is somehow a paradox that such a trend has been initiated when our world seemed to be progressing on the road to relative prosperity and international calm.

The end of the cold war and the firm stand against terrorist nations in the Middle-east and elsewhere such as Libya and Iraq during the 1980s and 1990s were indeed encouraging signals of the strength of democracies.

However, for many of us the challenge has come from an unexpected direction and by unconventional tools. High-level collaboration among many terrorist organizations and terrorist supporting states like Afghanistan, Iraq, Iran, and Syria, made the attack on the United States so effective and successful.

The terrorists' best weapon was international cooperation, partnership, and cohesive action of various groups. They have also enjoyed favorable attitudes and popular support of the people in extreme religious countries and regions. Thus, it's possible that only a similar counter process of collaboration among democratic nations and among their administrative agencies can resist these threatening forces and safeguard the free world.

In this conflict, as in other socially oriented conflicts and dilemmas, it is public administration that has the prime role and responsibility to provide answers to the new needs. For this purpose, public administration means a vast collection of governmental agencies that take care of our internal and external security, welfare, economy, education, and other services that citizens of modern civilizations use.

Today, more than ever before the most important goal of our governments and leaders is to enhance collaboration among various social players, and as all agree, to protect democracy by this mutual effort. We have always expected national and federal institutions to do so, and for many good reasons we expect them today to become even more energetic and involved in such trends and developments.

Today, there are several reasons for our ongoing dependence on the government and on its executive branches.

First, we simply have no other institution or body to turn to when our basic rights and needs are endangered.

Second, in the last century governments and the public sector have become larger than in any other time in the past, and they have heightened citizens' dependence on the services and goods they provide.

Third, the public sector and its administrative heads provide more services and goods than ever in the past, and they do that for larger, increasingly demanding, heterogeneous populations.

In sum, we lean on governments and on public administration bodies since we believe that they hold the answers to our questions and the remedies for our needs.

Putting it other way, citizens of modern states largely trust the systematic order and action of governments as well as their executive branches. If they can't do the right things for us, then who actually can? However, against the new and unconventional threats of terror, they need not be alone, but need to collaborate to as great a degree as possible. Collaboration is thus a political, social, and more importantly managerial craftsmanship that public administration needs to improve. It is an important tool that stands against brutality and extremism from the outside, but it can also be effectively used to fight internal fragility and intra-national social problems.

Hence, this chapter creates fresh thinking on the potential of collaboration and the way to put it in the service of our states and communities, despite anticipated obstacles. Scholars' efforts should be directed at portraying a rational and realistic map that fosters collaboration among public administration and dominant social players such as the private sector, citizens (as individuals and as groups), media, and academia. Our map, as presented here, is only one way of responding to this challenge in the local government level. In our view, such collaboration should not be considered an option for our democracies; it needs to be our bright shining choice.

This chapter contributes to the growing theme of collaboration in public administration, and possibly also a future collaboration among various Middle-East countries, by focusing on one example from the Israeli context. The Carmelite project and the method it followed are studied as one way of creating effective collaboration in the local government level. It is evident today that no renewal or real progress of a democratic nation, state, or society can be made without minimal level of collaboration among social, political and private sector parties.

This chapter has focused on the local level but in the same time it may serve as a good starting point for cultural socialization into the topic of collaboration that can latter be upgraded to the national and perhaps international level. However, one should bear in mind that the Carmelite project is only one case study that should be compared with other experiences from across the world. Like many other case studies it has its advantages (for example, pointing to a unique policy problem and the detailed way to resolve it) as well as weaknesses (for example, the problem of generalization and external validity to other cases, across time and cultures) and thus should be treated with caution.

Recent works on collaboration have encouraged public administration agencies and leaders to adopt new models of alliances among diverse groups and individuals in society. Similarly, collaboration has become a necessity in local governance owing to its growing responsibilities and the continuous devolution of central government, which transfers more tasks to local authorities. A process of reinvention in local government has thus been inspired by the increasing need to enhance collaboration. Alliances have become strategies for institutions of governance to do more with less, to create leadership systems based on steering not rowing, and to treat citizens as customers (Grubbs, 2000) or even partners equal to state and local authorities (Vigoda, 2000; 2002). It has been pointed out that the future of modern public administration depends heavily on joint forces and improved patterns of collaboration among various social players. Citizens' needs and demands, increasing complexity of public programs, and magnification of different social problems serve as main accelerators that bring citizens, public and private sector bodies, and third-sector/nonprofit organizations together. This process reflects self-derived interests but also a collective viewpoint of win-win alternatives.

For this purpose, a strategic agenda of collaboration needs to be rebuilt. Its power may draw substance from theory-anchored models and from practical and empirical experience as presented here. A core assumption of the strategic approach is that public administration can no longer settle for a limited level of cooperation among sporadic players, and thus tends to collaboration. Public agencies, both governmental-political and organizational-administrative, will need to adopt a culture of mutual effort and to put more energy into joint ventures that are inclusive and long-term. The strategic platform as presented in this chapter may contribute to the development of such an interdisciplinary orientation and increase the impact of public-private-nonprofit alliances, both instrumentally and symbolically (Grubbs, 2000).

This chapter also identifies a theoretical gap in contemporary administrative and political science literature, which frequently classifies collaboration as another technique of conflict management or conflict resolution programs (Fredericksen, 1996). The first goal of this chapter is therefore to treat collaboration as an individual phenomenon, one that deserves its own theoretical attention separate from other writings on straightforward conflict management theory. We have argued that the option of collaboration is becoming highly relevant to public administration of our times, and that it proves useful in a number of local government issues. In line with this, our second goal was more clearly to set a strategy for collaboration, one that may serve as a road map for the future, both theoretically and practically.

The importance and relevance of collaboration for public administration and for citizens in our era are not disputed. While there are equivocal attitudes on the best way to implement collaboration there is consensus on its necessity. As it progresses, public administration will have to collaborate with a variety of participants and integrate various attitudes and interests to accomplish its future challenging tasks. Traditional, albeit effective techniques of participation in decision-making or negotiation management are expected to grow and mature into a more extensive strategy of collaboration. Ambitious projects and programs for larger groups of citizens will have to rely on collaboration and support the communal "we" rather than an alienated "they" spirit in society. This is a main track that can lead public administration on its way forward.

7

Educational Governance and the New Public Management

Despite the long-held view that schools are loosely coupled organizations, recent outcomes-based accountability and school choice reforms, exemplified by the No Child Left Behind Act, represent an attempt by federal and state policymakers to employ techniques of the "New Public Management" and to impose more tightly coupled policy strictures on the educational system. The authors explore the origins of this movement and locate it within the context of an emergent neo-corporatist ideology that has fundamentally altered the traditional distinction between the public and private spheres. The authors conclude with a discussion of the impact of the NPM on educational governance and policy.

INTRODUCTION

It has long been recognized that schools—public or private—are not like other organizations. Schools are more loosely coupled than most other organizations and reflect a mass of conflicting, often indeterminate, goals and objectives *(Weick, 1976, 1982)*. Schools are organizations with ambiguous goals, unclear technologies, uncoordinated activities, and loosely connected structural elements tenuously linked to organizational outcomes *(Weick, 1976)*. Thus, loose connections exist between policy, administrative actions, and teachers. Decision-making often approximates a "garbage can" model in which problems, possible solutions, and choice opportunities interact to produce somewhat fortuitous decisions *(Cohen, March, and Olsen, 1972; March and Olsen, 1976)*.

Not only is there a complete lack of agreement on what works best, in the "one best system," but also participation in the system is highly fluid, rules are often violated, and policy implementation is, at best, uneven *(Meyer and Rowan, 1977)*. A great deal of evidence suggests that schools "lack close internal coordination, especially of the content and methods of what is presumably their main activity—instruction" *(Meyer and Rowan, 1983, p. 71)*. The work of teachers and administrators is rarely evaluated in anything more than a perfunctory manner, with few consequences for failure *(Weick, 1976)*. For example, student achievement is seldom used as a criterion with which to evaluate teachers and administrators *(Meyer and Rowan, 1983)*.

In response, federal and state policymakers have initiated a series of educational reforms designed to take "lessons learned" from successful private enterprises and apply these principles to the management and operation of schools. Adopting neo-corporatist policies and practices utilized in the "New Public Management" (NPM), policymakers are attempting to more tightly couple what has heretofore largely been a loosely coupled system *(Peters, 2001; Terry, 2003)*. Examples of these reforms include outcomes-based accountability, school choice, and merit pay schemes. Further, federal and state policymakers seem intent on blurring or eliminating many of the distinctive elements separating the public and private spheres in education.

In part, the national movement to more tightly couple the educational system, exemplified in the No Child Left Behind Act (NCLB), reflects growing dissatisfaction with the condition of education, particularly in urban areas. As Cibulka *(1997)* observed, "Public opinion in many cities favors a major overhaul if not outright dismantling of the present educational governance structure" *(p. 317)*. Similar to the private sector, educational reformers are seeking to reshape their organizations, with greater attention and orientation toward ever higher, more rigorous performance and accountability standards *(Kanter, 1989)*.

The purpose of this article is to trace the origins and evolution of neo-corporatist, New Public Management reforms in education, locating these reforms within the changing political economy of educational policymaking and governance. After examining policymakers' critiques of the "public" nature of education and delineating their efforts to incorporate neo-corporatist principles into educational governance and reform, the authors conclude with an assessment of the impact of this trend on both the nature of public education and the implications for school management and governance.

EDUCATION REFORM AND THE NEW PUBLIC MANAGEMENT

Education is big business, and educators themselves constitute approximately one-third of the nearly twenty million employees in the public sector. Given increasingly tight fiscal constraints, policymakers have sought to trim the fat from public services and have turned to the New Public Management to do so *(Peters, 2001; Terry, 2003)*. Proponents of the NPM argue that "government ought to run like an efficient and effective business enterprise" *(Terry, 2003, p. xix)*. Such thinking represents an attack on the bureaucratic public administration paradigm—an assault begun under President Reagan and continuing through the present (even "new Democrats" such as Clinton and Gore, under the aegis of the National Performance Review, advocated the NPM).

Advocates of the New Public Management assert that private sector techniques and practices are directly transferable to the public sector *(Peters, 2001)*. Educational organizations are constantly encouraged to benchmark the private sector to find ways to "be like a business" and get "hard-nosed" and "practical" *(Kaufman, 1998, p. 13)*. Merit pay and performance bonuses, practices that school districts across the nation are increasingly adopting, reflect the NPM in education. Other NPM strategies include privatization, user charges, vouchers, decentralization, and contracting out *(Terry, 2003)*.

Savoie argues that "politicians who have set out over the past twenty years or so to fix government started from the premise that bureaucracy was the problem" *(p. 8)*. The common theme of recent public sector reforms "is that the private sector is, by definition, superior to the public sector. Thus, the view has grown (widely held among the political elite) that the best way to fix government bureaucracy was to adopt private sector practices," making government more client or performance-oriented *(Savioe, 2000, p. 8)*. Critics of the public schools equate public bureaucracy with socialism *(Lubienski, 2001)*.

Terry *(1998)* agrees, observing that "liberation and market-driven management have emerged as dominant approaches in the field of public management" *(p. 194)*. Critics of pubic bureaucracies assert that the system is "overburdened by a plethora of cumbersome and unnecessary rules, regulations, and other constraints" *(Terry, 1998, p. 195)*. Freeing schools from red tape and bureaucracy, primarily through relief from collective bargaining constraints, introduces market-based practices into schools *(Fusarelli, 2003)*. The assumption of those seeking to reform public schools is that the lessons from private sector management are directly transferable to the public sector.

According to Fitz and Beers , the movement of for-profit and non-profit education management organizations into public education in the United States, England, and Wales expands the role of the private sector in the public sphere. As a result, several scholars argue that we are witnessing a redefinition of public education "from one of a public good to that of a private good" *(Lubienski, 2001, p. 636)*.

As a result, "influential policy elites are in a position to frame the problem in education as one of a government monopoly, and to locate the solution in the redefinition of public education" *(Lubienski 2001, p. 640)*. This redefinition includes charter schools, for-profit corporations running charter schools, and market-based accountability reframed as public accountability. The incorporation of outcomes-based accountability provisions into systemic reform initiatives such as NCLB is another example of the New Public Management applied to education.

THE NEO-CORPORATIST MOVEMENT IN EDUCATION REFORM

The impetus for tighter coupling of policies and processes using the techniques of the NPM in educational organizations is greatly affected by several forces, including (1) external, environmental pressures for tighter coupling, (2) the emergence of powerful new institutional actors, and (3) an emerging institutional capacity, coupled with isomorphic processes which encourage tighter institutional coupling *(Fusarelli, 2002).*

As a result, education policymaking has changed dramatically in the past two decades, with big business and large corporations becoming major players in the education reform movement, often at the expense of the traditional "Education Establishment." A confluence of forces, including increased international competition, a series of scathing reports critical of American education, and perceived dissatisfaction with public education, have encouraged big business to become major players in the education reform movement *(Mazzoni, 1995).* Throughout the 1980s and 1990s, and continuing through the present, businesses and corporations have consistently pressed for system-wide, school-based accountability reforms, linking reform to international economic competition *(Jackson and Cibulka, 1992).*

Federal and state policymakers have become increasingly involved in education through a series of mandates and the implementation of top-down command and control structures. The movement towards performance reporting is "reshaping educational politics and creating new intra-organizational dynamics between federal, state, and local policymakers—producing greater impetus for organizational change" *(Fusarelli, 2002, p. 561).* The institutional environment of education is changing, with greater emphasis on monitoring organizational performance in an effort to craft more coherent education policy. School systems throughout the United States are experiencing much stronger demands for technical performance and are under increasing pressure to improve student achievement *(Rowan and Miskel, 1999).*

Neo-corporatist educational reforms, such as higher standards, testing, and accountability, seek to improve student achievement through tightened centralized control and more effective command structures. Policymakers are "working to create coherent policy systems by aligning key policies to support demanding learning goals" *(Spillane and Jennings, 1997, p 450).*

For example, for the first time in history, the federal government now requires districts to identify low-performing schools and develop comprehensive school improvement plans

(Herrington and Orland, 1992). Under the NCLB Act, local school districts must test all children in grade 3-8 in reading and mathematics (with science added in 2005) and must provide children in consistently low performing schools with the option of transferring to another public school. In effect, the federal government will mandate that states provide parents with detailed school report cards revealing student performance by ethnic subgroup, teacher qualifications, and a host of other quality indices. The assumption is that parents whose children attend low performing, low quality schools will remove their children from those schools, forcing the failing schools to improve or "go out of business." The ideology of the market metaphor and the application of market-based principles to the operation of public education are core tenets of the New Public Management, exemplified in legislation such as NCLB.

At the state level, policymakers are incorporating principles of the NPM into state-level systemic reform initiatives. A good example of efforts to tighten up the rather loosely coupled educational system found in the United States is Kentucky's comprehensive statewide school reform, which places heavy emphasis on student and school accountability *(Pankratz and Petrosko, 2000)*. Highlighting the influence of the NPM on education reform, policymakers in Kentucky have developed a highly centralized accountability system "of interlocking policies, tying the PR [performance reporting] system into rewards for teachers and schools and sanctions for poorly performing schools" *(Cibulka and Derlin, 1995, p. 488; Minorini and Sugarman, 1999)*.

Systemic reform initiatives rooted in the NPM have been undertaken in several states, including Vermont, Kentucky, North Carolina, South Carolina, and Texas *(Fuhrman, 1993)*. Every state has developed policies to raise academic curricular standards and increase student performance *(Fuhrman, 1989)*. There has been an effort "to move away from the fragmented control system currently governing American education and to move toward closer coordination of policies about instructional goals, means, and funding" *(Rowan & Miskel, 1999, p. 371)*.

A number of studies in Colorado, Connecticut, Florida, Kentucky, Maryland, and Texas document the effectiveness of

NPM-based systemic reform initiatives in increasing student achievement *(See the National Governors Association, 2002)*. In a study of the effects of Texas' comprehensive accountability system on educational equity and student achievement, Scheurich, Skrla, and Johnson *(2000, 2001)* found that individual schools, as well as entire school districts, are demonstrating improvement under the state's systemic reform policies.

Various school choice initiatives also reflect NPM techniques to improve education. School districts throughout the country offer extensive inter and intra-district public school choice options, including magnet schools, alternative schools, and charter schools. Currently, 39 states and the District of Columbia have passed charter school legislation, educating more than 600,000 students nationwide *(Fusarelli, 2003)*. Privately-funded voucher programs operate in approximately 80 cities, with publicly funded voucher programs in Cleveland and Milwaukee *(Viteritti, 2002)*. Florida operates the only statewide publicly-funded voucher program in the United States, although Colorado recently passed voucher legislation as well.

REDEFINING THE "PUBLIC" UNDER THE NEW PUBLIC MANAGEMENT

Examining the infusion of neo-corporatist ideology, policies, and practices of the NPM in education reform, we raise a significant question as to whether the NPM will fundamentally alter or change the nature of the "public" in public schools as organizations. Further, what are the implications of this movement for educational governance? According to Roberts *(1997)*, decisionmaking and deliberation in public organizations are fundamentally different than in private organizations, since decisionmaking and deliberation in public organizations necessarily involve more and varied participants, each of whom has a say in the final outcome of decisions.

Do efforts to more tightly couple education through top-down, outcomes-based standards and accountability policies—with the federal and state governments assuming ever greater responsibilities for monitoring educational performance—weaken lay control of schools and pose a threat to democratic governance?

Furthermore, since charter schools, private, and parochial schools are not governed by locally-elected governing boards, are these schools less "public" than traditional public schools *(Lubienski, 2001)*? In sum, does the NPM essentially privatize the delivery of educational services, and what then becomes of the public character and mission of education?

Such questions raise anew whether the distinction between the public and private spheres is significant or merely rhetorical. According to Wamsley and Zald *(1981)*, public administration theory has been mired for decades in "debate over whether a meaningful distinction can be made between public and private administration" *(p. 46)*. Is administration context-specific or do such distinctions obscure important similarities between the public and private sectors? Wamsley and Zald *(1981)* assert that the distinction between public and private is significant and note that public organizations are "more dependent upon funds influenced by political processes or agents" *(p. 47)*. Furthermore, "the recipient of services is usually not the immediate funder, and the taxpayer finds it hard to discern linkage between his taxes and any benefits accruing from organizational output" *(p. 47)*, a situation that becomes particularly problematic given the increasing number of taxpayers without children enrolled in public schools.

Potential differences between the pubic and private spheres are also significant with respect to school choice. For example, whether vouchers will advance or erode the public interest depends on "our collective understanding of where our public interest lies and of the role we see for government" *(Kennedy, 2001, p. 450)*.

Another question is whether the New Public Management, with its emphasis on satisfying individual needs, adequately meets the needs of the public as a whole *(Peters, 2001)*. Does the NPM dilute the public purpose of public organizations, and does it satisfy the common good? With its emphasis on accountability and privatization, the NPM requires that public administrators, in effect, become entrepreneurs. However, Peters asks whether the demands of public entrepreneurship conflict with the requirements of democratic theory and public philosophy.

Even management theorists such as Peter Drucker *(1985)* note that managers in public institutions "tend to see their mission as a moral absolute rather than as economic and subject to a cost/benefit calculus" *(p. 179)*. Critics argue that the NPM may be inadequate in ensuring the common good or in meeting "important societal needs" *(Brown and Contreras, 1991, p. 144)*. Reforms rooted in market-based principles may be inappropriate for schools as public organizations. According to Fry *(1989)*, absent a profit criterion, "the activities of public administrators [such as school administrators] are difficult to measure" and "thus difficult to evaluate," since in the private sector, "profit serves as the ultimate test of organizational effectiveness" *(p. 1040)*.

To date, contracting out educational services to private, for-profit management companies has not proven to be an effective instrument in improving schools *(Sawicky, 1997)*. Companies such as the Edison Project, the Tesseract Group (formerly Educational Alternatives Inc.), and Alternative Education Inc. have failed to improve significantly educational outcomes of schooling or demonstrate substantial efficiency savings, contrary to expectations of the supposed efficiency and excellence of market-driven service providers in the private sector *(Fitz and Beers, 2002)*. Sawicky, himself an economist, suggests that the "legend of business expertise . . . is more appearance than reality" *(p. 21)*.

Research on vouchers suggests that market-based alternatives do not necessarily promote efficiency and tend to increase racial and social segregation in education *(Spicer and Hill, 1990)*. Various school choice plans, be they voucher plans in Milwaukee or Cleveland, public school choice plans (such as magnet schools or intra/inter-district choice), or choice provisions under NCLB, have yet to demonstrate definitively that such reforms have made the school system more efficient, more effective, or more equitable.

In fact, as in the case of the New York City high school system, the most extensive school choice plan in the United States, market-based choice options increase racial and socioeconomic segregation in public schools, with no corresponding efficiency or effectiveness benefits *(Bastian, 1990; Moore and Davenport, 1990)*.

Often, school choice creates "economically, socially, and racially stratified communities," because market-based incentives always produce winners and losers *(Brown and Contreras, 1991, p. 145)*.

Drawing from research in economics, Sawicky *(1997)* observes that markets and business organizations do not always "do a good job in satisfying public wants and promoting social welfare" *(p. 21)*. In fact, in many case, "they fail miserably" *(p. 21)*. But the ideology of privatization—that "business will always do better"—is patently false *(p. 21)*. The loosely coupled nature of educational systems, whose "educational outcomes are diverse, complex, and difficult to define, measure, interpret, and analyze," makes it difficult for private sector firms to operate effectively *(Sawicky, 1997, p. 21)*. Further, "the paths to success are shrouded in uncertainty and controversy" *(p. 21)*.

Thus, although NPM techniques are increasingly employed in education, they are not without problems. For example, numerous school districts have tried and abandoned merit pay schemes, in part due to the difficulty of measuring individual contributions to the performance of large, complex organizations such as education *(Peters, 2001)*. The scholarly research on merit pay suggests that it is an insufficient motivator to improved school system performance. As a result of such failures, management theorists recognize that many public service organizations, including schools, do not respond well to marketplace incentives *(Drucker, 1985)*. This poses a major problem in achieving the goals embodied in NCLB, since the legislation relies largely upon market-based principles as the mechanism for school improvement.

CONCLUSION

If the neo-corporatist ideology and the New Pubic Management techniques and policies fail to significantly improve schooling in the United States, as this article suggests, then many of the lessons learned about what works in private organizations are not directly transferable to the public sector. Accordingly, the public and private spheres may, in fact, be different in significant ways.

Weick was correct in his assertion that schools are not like other organizations—be they public or private. Brown and Contreras *(1991)* note that, "Education is the only public service in which individual states have a constitutional mandate to provide all children, regardless of where they live, with free quality education and to equalize educational opportunities across all communities" *(p. 145)*. This mandate and the federal government's push to "leave no child behind" distinguishes education from other public services.

Furthermore, since education is mandated and regulated by the state, grafting market-based management techniques such as those embodied in the NPM onto the educational system (as is the case with NCLB) presents a host of challenges for policymakers. Since schools, as unique public organizations, do not operate as markets do, we should not expect market-based reforms that have demonstrated success in the private sector to be equally effective when applied to schools. The challenge to educational governance and school improvement is to develop more comprehensive, systemic reforms that do not rely solely on market-based mechanisms as the vehicle for school improvement and educational reform.

8

Managing from the Inside Out

Historically, public schools have been run by an administration that made all the decisions about how education should occur. Increasingly, however, teachers are taking more active roles in decision-making at their public schools. This is often under the aegis of 'site-based management.' One important factor in site-based management is that teachers' and administrators' thoughts and beliefs related to public school management often differ significantly.

This difference can cause internal power struggles between teachers and administrators. The purpose of this study was two-fold. First, this study investigated the hypothesis that attitudes towards site-based management are consistent with teacher or administrator status in public schools. And secondly, the local data was compared to national data to determine if similar discrepancies occur throughout the country. The results confirmed the hypotheses that teachers and administrators hold different opinions towards their site-based management and that this difference in opinion is influenced by the public context in which schooling occurs.

Site-based reform has been popularized by community members, teachers, counselors, and parents since the early 1980s (Leithwood & Minzes, 1998). Creating site-based management programs within public schools can range from a total restructuring of a public school's administration to a slight shift in shared decision-making practices. A shared decision-making program can encourage greater communication among administrators, teachers, and support staff. A site-based approach is dependent upon these groups sharing common beliefs about leadership and decision-making styles.

WHAT IS SITE-BASED MANAGEMENT?

Site-based management, which is often referred to as public school-based management, is a widespread restructuring of the organizational level of the public school that involves decentralizing decision making to individual public schools and sharing decision making with a variety of groups (teachers, administrators, counselors, parents, etc.) within each public school structure (Kemper & Teddlies, 2002).

Active restructuring can include participation in reform activities, involving teachers in decision-making, obtaining parental involvement, creating a flexible public school schedule, changing the role of principals from dictators to authority figures who act as facilitators, investing in professional development for all parties, and acknowledging the efforts of all participating parties. This restructuring, as argued by those supporting the reform, cannot effectively improve the students' academic performance unless those directly involved with the students' outcomes (the teachers) have decision making authority (Leithwood, & Menzies, 1998). For the past two decades, advocates of site-based management hold firm to the ideas that the teachers can best identify and meet the students' needs, not necessarily the administration or the public school boards, yet decision making must be granted by these other entities. In summary, there must be broad-based participation by all people involved with the operation of the public school if the public school is to operate successfully under a site-based premise.

Rationale

The purpose of this study is to determine if there is a difference in opinion among teachers, administration, and counselors and their attitudes towards site-based management. West (1994) identified six characteristics that must be present for a site-based management program to occur within a public school. These characteristics are:

(1) staff development,

(2) involving staff, students, and the community in public school policies and decisions,
(3) transformational leadership approaches,
(4) coordination of strategies,
(5) inquiry and reflection, and
(6) collaborative planning.

And although the main emphasis of this research is to look at the collaboration between teachers and administrators, or perception of such, an understanding that public penetration directly and indirectly influences the management dynamics of a public school is of interest. Public schools have unique management characteristics, one being the role any community member can play which can greatly affect the decisions and teaching strategies of each educator.

THE PROBLEM

In our nation's public schools, there is an increase of stress due to the complex system of many needs, wants, and expectations. Both educators and administrators not only have to maintain their already demanding workload, but are also expected to take on extra tasks and issues that were not demanded of these types of professionals in years past. These added responsibilities create an increase of stress in an already chaotic and stressful environment (Peterson, 1996). Research has shown that administrators, teachers, and community members could share leadership responsibility within the public school so that these added stresses could be relieved (Wohlstetter and Odden, 1995). Most public schools have a unified vision of how to educate the students, yet all adults in the educational setting need to use one another's knowledge of education, of child psychology, of learning theory and of pedagogy to create a program to best teach each and every student. Legislation recently created to serve as a precursor to this premise is the "No Child Left Behind" Act (Hardy, 2002). Site-based management goes hand in hand with program built on this legislation due to the community involvement and the active role teachers play in developing a complete public school for the children.

Public penetration of values, expectations and agendas continues to complicate decisions made on a daily basis by educators. Parents today have a greater variety of public schools to choose from (Well, Slayton and Scott, 2002), and the more students in public schools, the more money the public schools receive from the government. Also, public educational institutions are based on the premise that any member of the community (parents specifically) can participate in discussions about the education of the students. Parents can provide input on policy, vote for public school board members, and even sway public school-level curriculum decisions. This community input can lead teachers to feel the parents have more input in public schools than the teachers who have been hired to educate the child. Principals know the public can impact local public schools' functioning, so they tend to cater to the public, giving more to the attention to those with greater social and political resources (Lubienski, 2001). Although teachers have contact with the students every day, they may not be the ones who are asked before important decisions are made. Site based management operates on the premise that the teachers are given a say in the decision making process, yet teachers may not feel they are a part.

Hypotheses

In order to improve site-based management within public schools, this research study identifies differences in beliefs about site-based management between teachers and administration at nine public schools. Two hypotheses were considered. The first was that the individual's position (administrator or teacher) will significantly affect their attitude towards site-based management. The second was that the data to be collected on a local level would resemble that collected on a national level.

Teachers' Opinions

Research completed through the Schools and Staffing Surveys (SASS) and Who Runs the Public schools?: The Teacher's View (Anderson, 1993) reveals that control over curriculum, hiring teachers, and discipline practices vary greatly among administrators and teachers. This research suggests that only thirty-five percent of teachers believe they have significant influence in determining discipline policy or establishing curriculum. It also shows thirty-one percent believe they have much influence in determining the content of in-service programs and only twenty-eight percent believe they are influential in setting the policy on grouping students in classes by ability (United States Department of Education, 1993). Teachers overwhelmingly note that the only real control they have, in the public school setting, is over classroom activities. These areas include selecting instructional materials, disciplining students within the classroom, selecting teaching techniques, and determining homework assignments.

Administrators' Opinions

Turning to administration and basing our findings on the same data retrieved from the United States Department of Education in 1993 in surveys administered to principals, we find that this group believes they still hold the majority of the power in the areas of establishing curriculum, hiring new full-time teachers, and setting discipline policy and procedures. Regarding curriculum, the Department of Education survey found thirty-three percent of administrators believe that the public school district (central office administration) is responsible for establishing the curriculum. This is in contrast to approximately nineteen percent of the administrators who believe that teachers and principals are equally responsible for curriculum decisions and fifteen percent who state that all parties (district administration, principals, and teachers) are responsible for the curriculum.

Principals believe in some areas the teachers have very little input. Forty-nine percent of principals feel that principals are primarily responsible for hiring yet only five percent feel teachers have any input at all for hiring new teachers. Twenty-three percent of the principals feel they, themselves, are responsible for setting policies concerning discipline and only one percent feel teachers have any say at all in this area. Kemper and Teddlies report that several of the principals in their study commented that, "Site based management allows teachers to feel as if they have a stake in decision making, but the committee itself has little impact on the decision making process."

Differences of Opinions

Site-based management success is based upon total cooperation and input from every sector that makes up the public school system. If attitudes and beliefs differ from group to group as to what individuals' real part is in the make-up of site-based management, then goals may never be met. In an analysis of data collected in 1987-88, 1990-91, and 1993-94, Mohr (1998) reports views that the administration and the faculty have on their given positions.

Principals feel that certain responsibilities have remained in the hands of principals, not simply because they choose to maintain control, but because state laws dictate it.

They state that teachers need to accept that not all decisions can be made by consensus and by letting each teacher have a say. Teachers, however, expect the shared leadership and decision-making powers that have been granted to them to provide them with greater say in public school affairs, yet these teachers feel their influence has remained the same over the past years, and is primarily confined to the classroom. Teachers see little or no change, and administrators disagree.

Teachers feel the need to share more in the decision-making process at the local level, and administrators refuse to release decision-making power, saying that laws and mandates have their hands tied. Mohr (1998) identifies factors that can create barriers to compromise.

These barriers include: 1) a gap between the senior management team and the public school; 2) a mismatch between public school goals/priorities and the role of senior management; 3) confusion about management and leadership; 4) the relationship between delegation and empowerment; 5) time-management; and 6) the gap between policy and practice. Regardless of the reasons behind the lack of cohesiveness between members of the educational community, a goal of most K-12 institutions is to provide the best education for all students. Providing this type of education means administrators and teachers working together to make decisions, solve problems, and unite the public school community, reducing the gap between what the administrator feels teachers' should be and are doing, administratively, and what administrative role the teachers feel they possess. This study looks at this administrative "gap", between teachers' role as viewed by teacher and administrator.

METHODOLOGY

Two hundred and forty administrators, teachers, and support staff from nine Midwestern suburban public schools were used in this study. Five elementary, two middle, and two high public schools comprised the total number of participating public schools. Of the participants, 41 were administrators and one 199 were teachers (Refer to Table 1).

Table 1. The number of participants in each specific category.

Public School	Administration	Teachers	Total
1	6	21	27
2	7	27	34
3	4	32	37
4	4	13	17
5	7	36	43
6	3	17	20
7	4	14	18
8	3	18	21
9	3	21	24
Public School Total	41	199	240

The design of this study was quasi-experimental with the independent variable being the position/title of each of the participants and the dependent variables being the answers on the survey. A t-test was used to show the difference of the mean scores on the survey between administrator and teacher. The survey consisted of twenty-five questions and had four major topics: knowledge of site-based management, roles, satisfaction with the program, and demographics.

The twenty-five-question survey was developed through research and review of selected abstracts from given authors on the subject of site-based management. The survey consisted of fourteen yes and no questions, seven questions that had to be answered using a Likert-type scale and four questions dealing with demographics.

After gaining approval to administer the survey by each of the principals from the nine participating public schools, it was distributed at respective public school faculty meetings by the researcher and then collected as soon as attendees completed the survey. Every participant completed the waiver form notifying subjects of his/her rights and these documents were also collected. All teachers and administrators handed their forms directly to the researchers who placed them in designated envelopes and left the faculty meetings immediately. The entire process took less than ten minutes at each public school.

Results

Table 2 shows the mean scores between the answers of the teachers and the answers of the administrators when asked two questions. The first question asked, "In your opinion, does the site-based management team really make decisions at your public school?" Teachers responded with a mean of 4.43 (SD=2.89) and administrators with a mean response score 6.95 (SD=3.08). The scale was in a Likert format, ranging from "1" (no real decision making power or no influence) to a "10" (complete decision making power). The second question asked which group made "decisions about the curriculum", and the mean scores between teacher and administrator on the survey results were also different (Teachers : M=2.53, SD=0.70; Administrators: M=1.81, SD=0.97).

DISCUSSION

The results of this study suggest that there is a significant difference between teachers' and administrators' views on who is in charge of curricular decisions. This difference was found to be significant with a sample size of 240 teachers and administrators. Similar results were found when using 588 teachers and administrators from across the United States. These results support Hypothesis 1 which stated that there is a difference between teacher and administrator belief on the function of the site based program at the local public school. In order for site-base management to function at the public school level, both teachers and administrators need to have adequate influence on certain decisions.

Perception is very important to each individual and group. If the teacher perceives they have a say in a decision, they will take greater ownership and feel more of a part of the outcome than if they perceive they have no impact. This study shows what teachers have felt for years about site-based teams. Teachers have been told by the administration that they have influence on decisions, yet they do not necessarily believe it. Teachers who are told they have an influential vote or voice expect that once a decision has been made, they would be able to feel they had an influential part in the decision. The administrators at the surveyed public schools voiced their opinions that the teachers had this voice, yet the teachers did not agree. In these public schools, it appears site-based management is not working. This supports the work done by Kemper and Teddlies and Mohr (1998) showing differences in beliefs of what is "really" happening at the public school in regards to decision making.

The finding that the national results are very similar to the local results supports Hypothesis #2 in that data collected at the local level supports that collected at the national level. Random public schools were asked similar questions (TIMSS-R), and the results showed differences in teacher beliefs as compared to those of the administrators. It appears that in the United States, a country proud of its educational system which also boasts the freedom of public schools to operate in the format each public school sees fit, deceit is present.

This deceit is evident in the TIMSS-R data where teachers feel they have little decision-making power yet the administrators report that they do. Administrators tend to say, "The teachers have decision-making power over the curriculum," and teachers say, "We have limited decision-making power over our curriculum." It appears site-based management is alive and well in the minds of the administration, but not so much in the minds of the teachers. Adding the fact that the public can make recommendations and cause changes in the public schools, the teachers have even more reason to believe their decision-making powers have been compromised. All in all, the dynamics of the public schools' decision making is unique and complicated.

IMPLICATIONS

Public institutions, such as our nation's public school system, function on the premise that all students have the opportunity to receive an education provided by professional (or at least highly trained) educators. These educators not only make their living by teaching, but have been taught, trained and mentored to make daily decisions to best educate their students. Administrators, on the other hand, have been trained in a similar educational realm yet spend most of their working hours dealing with parents, the community, and disruptive students, while planning long term goals for the public school and leading their teachers towards these goals. In most cases, public administrators have served several years in the classroom and are aware of the daily decisions teachers must make for the individualized education of each student. In this scenario, it would seem likely that principals would recognize the importance of teachers making curricular decisions, for example, allowing teachers to have a larger part in the decision-making power at the public schools.

Morale and loyalty at public schools and at public institutions have been shown to be related to job satisfaction and performance. Teachers whose views are considered in decisions should be made aware that their opinions are important. Although major decisions at public schools must ultimately be made by the principal, teachers giving input as to what is best for the students could be useful. Even more advantageous for moral would be to let the teachers know their opinions played an important role in the decision making process. The results from this study showed that at the public schools surveyed, this does not occur very well. Teachers feel they have little voice yet the principals feel they do. Possibly, better communication between the two groups is all that is needed. The results of this research should be shared with public school personnel to increase the lines of communication.

9

Decentralization and Educational Reform

This study provides empirical evidence of the implementation outcomes of decentralization and education reform policies conducted in Argentina during the 1990s. The study examines how the reform was adopted at the provincial level, to what extent policy implementation matches national official mandates, and what role organizational factors play in the processes of policy implementation and outcomes. Results shed light on the political roots of organizational adaptation that motives a decoupling between policy directives, implementation, and outcomes.

INTRODUCTION

During the past decades, policies of education decentralization have been advocated and implemented worldwide. In the 1990s, almost every country in Latin America (hereafter, LA) was engaged in some sort of education reform that included decentralization. In contrast with the effectiveness and cost efficiency arguments advocated during the decentralization policies conducted during the 1980s, democratization and participation were the generalized arguments advanced during recent educational decentralization reforms. While the rationale and rhetoric used for decentralizing education were similar across countries, actual implementation varies across and within countries. Although students of education decentralization in LA have been describing some of the differences and similarities in policy implementation across countries, still very little is known about policy adaptation and outcomes at subnational levels.

The purpose of this study is twofold. The first goal is to provide empirical evidence of the implementation and outcomes of the education reform and decentralization policies conducted in Argentina during the 1990s. The second, to examine how the reform was adopted at the provincial level, to what extent policy implementation matches national official mandates, and what role organizational factors play in policy implementation and outcomes. Argentina is an interesting case for many reasons. First, this case study shows an example of the various ways education decentralization and reform could take place and what it presupposes at subnational levels. Second, the whole decentralization and school restructuring process that took place in Argentina is a good illustration of response to global organizational changes in education than a real commitment from within. Third, this study shows how the organizational structure and politics impact on how change process unfolds and its outcomes.

The article is organized as follows. It starts by providing background information of the education restructuring process and decentralization reform conducted in Argentina in the early 1990s. A section that blends the organizational theory with my assumptions follows. In this section I argue that following global cultural changes, the Argentine government put into place at comprehensive process of school restructuring and decentralization that did not matched in practice at the provincial level. Indeed, organizational environments may provide us an explanation for that decoupling. Then, I present the methods and data collection process used in this study. Lastly, the results of the study and my concluding thoughts are presented. As result of a qualitative analysis, the case study of the province of Buenos Aires shows that political environments dictate policy adaptation and implementation. Policy adaptation and implementation responded to ways of accommodating management to individual political aspirations, which in turn make organizational changes remain unchanged to keep the status quo. The outcomes resulted in a mixed of centralized and decentralized practices that did not translate into democratization and participation at local and school levels, so prevalent in the policy discourse at the time.

DECENTRALIZATION AND SCHOOL REFORM IN ARGENTINA

The end of authoritarian regimes and the return of civilian rule in many Latin American countries during the 1980s, the developments of the Soviet Union in the early 1990s, and the decline of civic involvement in long-lasting western democracies during the last decades led to a worldwide revival of political and economic liberalization. In the political realm the emphasis was on democratization. In education, democratization became equated with decentralization on the basis of local sovereignty and increased responsiveness to the needs of diverse actors. Thus, decentralization was presented as a win-win situation helping, to maintain political stability and democratize while at the same time, improve efficiency of public services, preserve macroeconomic stability, and to respond to the interest of all groups" (Burki et al., 1999, p.17).

In the early 1990s, following worldwide and regional trends, the Argentine government continued and emphasized a process of education decentralization that started in the late 1970s. Then, the central administration, under a military regime (1976-1983), transferred the financial responsibility of primary public and private subsidized schooling to the provincial governments. This decentralizing process reached its zenith in 1992 and 1993, when the democratic government of Dr. Carlos S. Menem (1989-1999), started a second process of decentralization and restructuring of the whole schooling system.

In 1992, the transfer, as the education decentralization process is called in Argentina, delegated the financial responsibility of all public and private subsidized secondary and tertiary schools that were still under the umbrella of the central administration to the 23 provincial governments and the city of Buenos Aires. After this *provincialización*, in 1993, the *Ley Federal de Educación* (Federal Education Law No. 24195—hereafter, FEL) was passed. This law institutionalized the transfer process through a comprehensive education reform initiative. Besides the curricular reform and schooling system restructuring launched, the FEL delegated to the provinces some decision making over the management and administration of schools. The central government, however, kept control as policy maker, coordinator, and controller of the national educational design. The central administration also retained control as administrator of compensatory programs for needy schools.

In addition the FEL established a key reform initiative at the school level to foster education quality, the development of the *Projecto Educativo Institucional* (School Institutional Project, hereafter PEI). The central administration conceived the PEI as a pedagogical and school management tool that should ensure that the school organization is attuned with the organizational reform. Its purpose is to adapt national and provincial directives and curricular frameworks to the school environment and to foster democratic and participatory practices at the school level.

Theoretical Background

Much of the literature that looks at issues of decentralization, in Latin America is either interested in situating the discussion at the discourse level, establishing connections between neoliberalism and economic restructuring policies, or in showing "what works" to increase student performance. Others were simply concerned in showing the mismatch between policy intention and practice at the national levels. Less research looks at the outcomes of decentralization reforms at subnational and school levels. For the most part, analyses on education decentralization and reform efforts in Latin America have not paid so much attention to providing accounts of the nature of organizational environments and its impact on policy implementation, adaptation, and outcomes. As stated above, education policy reform in Argentina responded to a worldwide institutional change in education. In a well known work Meyer et al. (1997) argues that this global cultural change produces isomorphism of structures and policies of nation-states, which not necessary coupled in practice. On the contrary, decoupling between policy purpose and results is the most common development,

> Nation-states are remarkably uniform in defining their goals as the enhancement of collective progress... [However,] ... decoupling is endemic because nations-states are modeled on an external culture..." (Meyer et al.,1997, pp.153-154).

Consequently, world cultural dominant models may experience a wide variety of forms during the adoption process.

At central or provincial levels some external elements are easier to adopt than others, and even some of them could conflict or be inconsistent with local organizational structures (Meyer & Rowan, 1977, March & Olsen, 1989; DiMaggio & Powell, 1991; Meyer et al., 1997).

According to Ramirez and Rubinson (1979) developing nations adopt symbolic education reforms through national systems, but they experience a great difficulty in producing change. Usually, under exogenous pressures to conform to worldwide validated education paradigms, new education structures are adopted. Yet, since educational innovations usually carry high levels of uncertainty and are loosely connected to school outcomes (Meyer & Rowan, 1978; Rowan, 1982), organizations may not want to go beyond the provision of a symbolic response. Ritual compliance allows school organizations to continue its activities unchanged. Meyer and Rowan (1978) suggest that this lack of change is rooted in what they call "logic of confidence" (p.101). The confidence actors have in each other is what maintains the organization out of disruption while keeping its legitimacy.

Following the same line of argumentation, Hannaway (1993) argues that although broad institutional environments may tell us about why schools and school organizations are similar, local political environments may explain the degree of their differences. Her article examines the effects of political pressures and the system's centralization on public school districts in the United States. Evidence indicates that "the more pressured the political environment, the more likely it is that control is held by central, rather than subunit authorities." (Hannaway, 1993 p. 148) Thus, decentralization trends may experience more difficulties to succeed in politically pressured environments (McGinn & Street, 1986; Elmore, 1993; Weiler, 1993). However, how can policy success be measured in the case of interest here?

In line with ideas advanced by neoinstitutionalist students in organizational analysis, I argue that policy success in politically pressured organizational environments may not be measured in terms of the objectives of general policy mandates but in regards to the goals of its adaptation at the local level—provincial in this case. In other words, what is the purpose of policy adaptation and whose interests does this adaptation meet? I suggest that the mismatch between policy mandate and policy adoption (decoupling), or the implementation of symbolic practices that some scholars may consider "policy failure," may well serve the goals of the political elite to meet other interests and consequently to maintain the education organization unchanged. These arguments are addressed through the case study developed for this work.

10

Research Design, Methods and Data Analysis

This study uses a qualitative case study approach (Merriam, 1998). The process of building a case study involves in-depth data collection in preparation for the description of the cases of interest, confronting, validating, and generating a theoretical construct, which invites judgment and offers useful evidence for comparative analysis (Merriam, 1994). The unit of analysis in this study is the province of Buenos Aires, Argentina. Following Paton's typology of purposeful sampling (in Creswell 1994), this study uses a critical case sampling strategy. Critical cases are defined as those that can address the point of the study clearly or are particularly important to make some differentiations. Thus, this study focuses on this province for three main reasons that follow.

First, Buenos Aires is the larger province of Argentina and concentrates 38% of the country's total population. The province produces almost 50% of the country's agricultural production and 70% of Argentine cattle is raised in its lands. Buenos Aires holds 40% of the total Argentine industrial buildings and 49% of the country's total job posts, of which 70% reside in the Greater Buenos Aires (Situación Social y Evolución Social Provincial, 1998; Consejo Federal de Inversiones, 1999). However, today, the most noticeable characteristics of this province are a bankrupt economy—with an estimated fiscal deficit of 1804 million dollars for the year 2001, holding 33% of the provinces' accumulated debt and a poverty rate of 35.3% for May 2000 (Evolución Gasto Público Social, 1997; Datos Provisionales Censo, 2001).

Second, Buenos Aires has had not only importance as an economic core, but as a "political treasure" since it counts for the 37% of the total Argentine electorate. Jointly, these two characteristics, gave the provincial administration a wide margin for negotiations with the national administration, and some sort of autonomy. It should be noted here that Buenos Aires was the last province in signing the education transfer agreement with the federal government. From the total amount of school services transferred from the national government to the provinces during the early 1990s, 33% of them were located in the province of Buenos Aires. The delay could have been caused by tensions between the provincial and central administrations on the amount of extra funds that should be allocated to cover the cost of the transfer process (Dussel & Thisted, 1995; Senén González, 2000).

Third, by 1875, before the consolidation of the nation-state and the creation of a national system of education, the Province of Buenos Aires institutionalized its system of education—one of the oldest in Argentina. The provincial *Ley de Educación Común No.* 2688 (Law of Common Education) was primarily intended to organize and unify primary schooling; secondary education was initially provided in Argentina by the national government although some normal and secondary schools were created by the provincial administration. Probably the main feature of this foundational system of education was its decentralized structure of governance to the level of local school councils. However, the decision-making power assigned by law to these councils did not last for long. Even today local school councils have not regained the power they had when they were created.

Data Gathering and Analysis

During the time the researcher spent in the field, two qualitative procedures were conducted: content analysis and semi-structured interviews. The first procedure was performed during the entire period that the researcher was in the field. I used methods of content analysis to examine how national directives materialized in provincial official documents and legislation. This analysis provided me with general statements of policy rationale and objectives. This method was an important tool during the first phase of the study and provided the backbone for the design and adjustment of the semi-structured interviews questionnaire.

Following this initial stage, the researcher conducted the second qualitative procedure: the semi-structured interviews. Interviews are the primary source of data collection. The researcher used them to get information and build the case study about the implementation, adaptation, and outcomes' perceptions of the comprehensive education reform. Two waves of personal interviews—typically 45 minutes to one hour in duration—were carried out. Thirty-three key informants were interviewed. Schoolteachers, parent association representatives, ministry officials at the provincial and national level, and local and provincial school administrators were interviewed. Interviewees were selected in various ways, but primarily by means of snowball sample and geographic base.

All written and narrative protocols were coded for common thematic statements that helped analyze the content of the data by level of analyses: national, provincial, and municipal. This method was used to examine actors' accounts of the decentralization and reform processes, changes, and the consequences of them. I limited the analysis to the content of their stories and to analyze "who" tells "what" and "why." Each interview was identified and categorized by actors' location, position in the administrative structure, role, and identification number. This differentiation allowed me to identify environmental from organizational representations of the policy process and to measure the effect of environmental and organizational characteristics in determining the outcomes.

RESULTS

Buenos Aires Socio-political Characteristics and Policy Adaptation

Since 1988 the *Justicialista* party dominated Buenos Aires's political scene. It was particularly during Dr. Eduardo Duhalde's administration (1991-1999) that a process of state reform was implemented. Using the same rhetoric advocated internationally, regionally, and nationally, major changes in education took effect that included policies of education decentralization. Thus,

Duhalde's administration implemented changes in the education framework to make the federal education reform possible. These changes were blended with the provincial administration's goals of equity, administrative efficiency, and work ethics (Programa de Gobierno, 1994), which the governor foresaw as important elements that would distinguish him from the unpopular turn of Menem's presidency.

Accordingly, Duhalde implemented policies of state reform not without a quota of pure *Peronista* lineage. As expressed by a provincial official, "Duhalde could not get rid of traditional populist practices while implementing liberal type of policies, he needed them if he wanted to be reelected or for his future presidential aspirations." Students of recent neo-populism in LA agreed that although governments faced fiscal constraints in state spending they managed to create material benefits to their constituency by, among other tactics, targeting social programs for the poor (Weyland, 1996).

Various reasons allowed Duhalde to act with substantial autonomy from the national government and the national party leadership to implement a robust social program tied to educational reform and decentralization initiatives in the province of Buenos Aires. Among those are: his strong ties with the provincial *Peronist* chapter, the resources the province receives from the central administration through the *Fondo de Reparación Histórica* (Historical Compensatory Fund), and external loans. As a local party member said, "Duhalde is the boss, he has the money . . ." (EBAPVLNo.1). Indeed, Eduardo Duhalde was the boss; he was and is still today the president of the Buenos Aires *Peronist* chapter, which had controlled the provincial legislature from 1991 to 1997.

Besides controlling the provincial legislature, "the two main *Justicialista* party factions have been distributing among themselves positions within the provincial and municipal administrations and electoral lists . . ." (EBAMPNo.2). Therefore, with the control of the bureaucracy, which means control over state resources and job post used for patronage, the provincial *Peronist* chapter on his side, a discretionary use of public funds, and a provincial public debt that increased over the years—from 1112 million pesos to 3864 million pesos in 1999 (Situación Social y Evolución Social

Provincial, 1998; Dirección Provicial de Planeamiento, 2000), the governor was able to establish as *Plan Social* (social plan) side by side structural adjustment reforms.

According to official documents, the provincial *Plan Social* was based on three pillars, 1) active participation of the community, 2) creation of social welfare networks or solidarity networks at all administrative levels: provincial, regional, municipal, 3) decentralization and *regionalization* of the development and implementation of social programs. Education, of course, was at the center of the provincial social development program (*Programa de Gobierno, 1994*) and schools were an important piece in the distribution chain. In some cases, the implementation of this plan was through an *asistencialista* network (social welfare network) run by Dr. Duhalde's wife and a group of party brokers widely known as *manazaneras* (Auyero, 2000).

The *Plan Social* was clearly an exchange of favors for votes and shed light on the convergence of patron-client relations and the social welfare policies implemented by the *Justicialista* party in the province of Buenos Aries. This plan linked state funding, local political leaders, nongovernmental organizations, party brokers, and in some cases the school and local school councils. Its implementation was indeed decentralized and each unit of the implementation chain acted autonomously, but under control of the provincial executive. Duhalde and his wife soon became synonymous with the benefits distributed. The organizational structure established helped the governor to act ignoring the party's national-level leadership and to informally integrate its constituency to the provincial party structure in a disciplined manner (Levitsky, 2000). In sum, Duhalde's administration was able to adapt policy purpose to his personal political aspirations.

Policy Implementation and Educational Structure in Buenos Aires

In 1995 the provincial legislature passed the *Ley Provincial de Educación* No. 11.612 (Provincial Education Law—hereafter PEL). In terms of the proposed actions the law translated into the functional reorganization of the managerial structure with strong implications for the way schooling services were delivered. Since then, the provincial system was organized on the basis of a regional administrative decentralization. It is clear from the law that this organization was a strategic objective for the successful implementation of the provincial educational reform (Ley Provincial, Art. 46). This new regulation placed a strong separation between administrative and pedagogical functions, *deconcentrated* to the level of 134 school districts.

The new managerial structure is organized as follows. At the top of the organizational structure is the *Dirección General de Educación y Cultura* (General Directorate of Education and Culture—hereafter GDEC) with ministerial hierarchy. This unit has the overall responsibility of the education system. By its side works the *Consejo General de Escuelas* (General School Council). By law this council has the responsibility of policy planning and coordination; however, in practice it functions as a consultative body of the education executive. It is followed by sixteen *Jefaturas Regionales* (Regional Chiefs) for each branch of the education system (general basic education, hereafter EGB and *Polimodal* schools) appointed by the GDEC and reporting to the *Subsecretario de Educación* (under-secretary of education) and to the corresponding education branch directorate. These *Jefaturas Regionales* oversee the operation of *Secretarías de Inspección* (Inspection Secretariats) at the district level, and *Supervisores de Distrito* (district supervisors), selected, although not always, on a competitive basis. *Secretarías de Inspección,* through districts' supervisors, are responsible for carrying out the reform at the district level and of the bulk of administrative work in relation to the technical and pedagogical operation of the provincial education system. For example, they are responsible for filling teaching vacancies and providing statistical information to the GDEC on the standard functioning of the district such as teacher attendance, school drop outs, etc. (Ley Provincial, Art. 48).

At the district level, local elected school councils or boards initially created to be political participatory units became administrative mediators vis-à-vis the municipal administration, school-site cooperatives, and provincial authorities mostly to mobilize resources for schools within their district. Local school councils do not have budgets on their own, but they are in charge of processing funding requests for school lunches and the improvement of school buildings. Another important point to consider is that municipalities in an attempt to adapt themselves to the new provincial administrative requirements, have set up education and culture directorates or secretariats that have started to play an active role within their limited formal authority. While municipalities have only an insignificant quantitative participation in the delivery of education services, in the majority of the cases at the pre-school level, they provide additional funding sources for the schools, mostly to be used for infrastructure work and other minor expenditures. Still the bulk of public schools funding, of which almost 90% goes to pay the administrators, teachers, and school staff salaries, comes from the provincial level (Ministerio de Economía, Buenos Aires, 1995, p. 42). Additional funding sources come from the *Asociación Cooperadora Escolar* (school-site cooperatives).

Each school in the province has a *cooperadora* to which parents voluntarily contribute with time and an optional monetary amount. The amount varies across school districts and the socio-economic situation of the family (15). The role of the school-site cooperative is "to assist the school in eliminating all the causes that have a negative affect on students." (Manual de Cooperadoras Escolares, Art. 1) In addition, "the *associación cooparadora* involvement has not to address technical, administrative, or disciplinary issues unless the school requires it to do so" (Art. 4).

So even when both the FEL law and the PEL stress the role these associations have as participatory mechanisms, *asociación cooperadoras* have not been granted the authority to participate actively in the school other than with funding. Paralleling the FEL, the school unit was at the center of the reform process (Ley Provincial, Art.19); however, its centrality was to be achieved through the implementation of programs of social welfare orientation. In a context of economic hardships, the provincial social plan took different forms at the school level; school food programs for EGB schools and fellowships for students in *polimodal* education. Fellowships were administered in form of nine monthly allocations of 100 Argentine pesos to improve high school student retention.

Compensatory and social welfare programs were financed, in some cases, through alternative channels that used extraordinary funds from national transfers and external loans. These funds, instead of being distributed through the established channel—GDEC, local school councils, schools—were transferred directly from the provincial administration –sometimes through the *asistencialista* network, to either the school or individuals. As stated by an interviewee, "social plans were the direct connection between the government well, Duhalde, and the poor..." (EMPLNo.4); they have been used as a patron-client method to link the masses with the leader.

General Perceptions of Buenos Aires Administration, Policy Implementation and Outcomes

Generally speaking; education informants have a negative perception about the decentralization process and the implementation of the federal and provincial education laws. The categories identified from the grassroots as representing the provincial administration are: *extremely bureaucratic* and *inefficient, vertically* structured and *inflexible, centralized, fragmented, lack of compromise, unplanned,* devoted to political *clientelism* and *particularisms.* In the words of the education administrator, there is no clear and defined education policy in Buenos Aires . . . .the provincial administration is trapped between the inertia of the reform process and an unclear diagnosis of the system's inefficiencies . . . *virtual vs. real* policy.

Probably it is the lack of an informed policy, adjusted to Buenos Aires' educational needs and not to personal political aspirations, the causes of the inoperative and chaotic perception actors have about the provincial administration. "Improvisation rules," declared a school supervisor. Moreover, this situation could also be the reason for its inflexibility and fragmentation.

Some distinctions, however, are to be made since interviews underscore dissimilar concerns based on actors' position within the organizational structure. Criticism of general councilors, school councilors, chief inspectors and supervisors revolve around broad administrative, financial, operational and cultural issues, though not exclusively. However, both principals' and teachers' concerns are limited to the impact of the changes over the daily school life. These attitudes constitute two patterns of thinking about educational issues. First, a *macro-micro linkage*; provincial education officials and administrators think about the system's changes and outcomes as part of larger forces, including national and state general policies. Their beliefs show that the education sector alone is not responsible for the changes and outcomes, but rather broader institutional changes. Moreover, an effective change in education requires political and institutional changes as well. Second, *micro-focused affairs*; in this case, actors' attitudes are of immediate concern and although aware of macro level changes, their focus is more concerned with local and provincial level effects. While school administrators and teachers do see national and provincial levels changes as the causes of education problems they do not expect them to be solved politically but pedagogically. Actors' views about the reform implementation are as follows.

Macro-micro Linkages: Provincial Education Officials and Education Administrators' Views

At the beginning of the 21st century, education actors' views reflect the difficulties the provincial system of education is facing after the implementation of the 1990s reforms. Provincial education officials and administrators suggest the difficulties of isolating the results of the educational changes from the broader Argentine picture. Argentine institutions are in crisis, they usually lack specific planning, or when the rules are there no one respects them. Institutions work according the person that leads them. Political representation is also in crisis; unions and political parties are unreliable. Citizens are voting less and less over the years and even blank ballots are increasing in number. Besides, radical changes are implemented here that are copies, shapeless embryos, and before any result could be seen, either central authorities change and with them some minor changes occur—there is usually no continuity from administration to administration—or if the same people stay they manage to change something for electoral purposes.

According to the interviewees' accounts, this pattern is evidenced through the implementation of the educational reforms. Once schools were transferred, "the problem then became the provincial administration." Duhalde wanted to complete the process of reform no matter under what circumstances: "*without consensus* . . . it was *improvised, disorganized,* and with harmful results for the provincial education system." Interviewees' emphasized that the system is formally hierarchically centralized at the provincial level but since control mechanisms are loosely attached with one another they leave space for *personalism* and *clientelism*. Although this contradicts arguments that support decentralization, in this particular case decentralization produced a formal centralization of control at the provincial level but at the same time opened space for reinforcing traditional informal political practices. This paradox is apparent through school councilors' accounts,

> Sometimes, intentionally or by bureaucratic inefficiency, while one school receives three subsidies for repairing the same problem others receive none. Usually the rules are there, but the procedures are unclear, sometimes obscure.

Supervisors agreed that the process by which decisions are made and implemented are generally coming from the top and are not always transparent, a fact that indicates that many of these decisions represent less systematic efforts to include different sectors of the education community and consequently more short-term political investments. Supervisors and councilors pointed out that some irregularities applied to the distribution of food programs and scholarships. Indeed, a chief supervisor of *polimodal* education declared, "the problem is that those scholarships are not merit base, they have been granted without any control whatsoever."

From their arguments one can agree that administrators are not as critical of the reform in itself as they are with its implementation and practice. Provincial administrators and education leaders attributed the limited results of the reform to national-level economic conditions, market approaches implemented, and to financial constraints that the province encountered after its implementation. However, their main concern revolved around the celerity and unplanned process of reform, unsupportive environment, and the cultural shock experienced by those institutions that were previously under national tutelage, since the process was conducted by force and, without the necessary means to carry it out, it soon became a race against time, an accelerated implementation without resources and needed infrastructure, and even worse, a cultural shock that end up in a clear discrimination from both sides.

Interviews reveal a strong agreement about different cultural patterns between provincial and transferred national schools. This difference is identified as rooted in the political and administrative environment in which schools have been operating. From these arguments it is possible to speculate that, unintentionally or not, schools reproduce the pattern and act in consequence of the organizational environment they are a part. Thus, the school organization adapts certain practices that become the norm. Therefore, as soon as national schools and national inspectors found themselves in an unfamiliar environment, they not only resisted it but they also tried to reinforce previous practices to maintain their identity and status quo. In fact, the culture of national schools still persists and transcends geographical boundaries in Argentina to the extent that these schools are still informally called national schools.

The tension between organizational pressures to change and national schools' resistance was at the origin of conflicts outside and within the school organizations. The tension within the system was clearly expressed by a school supervisor, who said In the first meeting we had together, the transferred [transferred supervisors] –we called them pejoratively in that way, and us [provincial supervisors] could not understand each other, we were talking in different languages. After hours of hot discussions, a transferred supervisor suddenly stood up and said, are you [referring to the provincial supervisors] and the province going to tell us how to run our schools? But from that moment they knew there was no other option than to accept they were in the province.

Both groups—former national and provincial administrators and teachers—presented throughout our conversations a certain resentment of each other. In the words of a former national inspector, "before, administrative and pedagogical issues were handled easily than today. Here everything is based on negotiations . . . this shows the lack of administrative capacity the province has." On the other hand, chief inspectors and provincial supervisors agreed that, "in spite of the resistance, former national supervisors ended up accepting that they were doing a more desk-based type of work, but in the province you have to put your feet in the mud . . ."

As I mentioned before, the reason for this unfortunate situation was rooted in the characteristics and practices of each distinctive education system, yet schools did work under different regulatory frameworks, which generated the cultural contradictions presented.

How do the problems previously identified by supervisors, chief inspectors, general education councilors, administrative officials, and local school councilors affect the daily school operation? According to teachers and school administrators, those problems affected the schools in many ways to the extent that they produced a general deterioration of the quality of services schools provide. First, both teachers and school directors mentioned the limited autonomy they have today and the instances of control that have been added since the last reforms were in place. Before, some decisions about the management of provincial schools were made at the local level through the local school council, but not any more.

Even, "National schools used to have more autonomy, not intended though, but real." The principal mentioned that this autonomy allowed her to select her team, portrayed as "a group of committed, experienced, and motivated teachers. Today that is not the case." According to her comments, what rules is the unfortunate situation of a great number of professors' *taxi* with a negative impact on the school. "Even though teachers put so much effort from their part, it is impossible to feel attached to an institution where you only spend two hours twice a week, she said".

Furthermore, according to principals' and teachers' accounts, teachers' appointment instability affects in-school communication and collaboration, which according to the FED is a fundamental piece of the successful development of the school institutional project. Even when in many cases teachers and principals reported the successful development of the PEI, they had recognized the fundamental role principals had in its drafting. The design of a PEI requires having a permanent teaching body that could establish some compromise, something "that is not happening in a *polimodal* public school in the province of Buenos Aires today.

In addition, since "the process of teacher selection is not completely transparent—sometimes very political, and salaries grew less day by day, the teachers we receive are usually not as qualified as they used to be." This concern regarding the general deterioration of the teacher profession was also a matter of concern among other administrative officials, scholars, and stakeholders. Teachers and administrators complained about the lack of pedagogical support they received during the implementation of the reform. In spite of the courses and materials administered by the National Ministry of Education, those elements proved to be insufficient and of very low quality. The consequence then, "is more pressure on the school because at the end we are going to be blamed about the poor schools outcomes."

School administrators identified another organizational problem that leads to conflictive situations within the schools; that is, the incorporation of 8th and 9th grade to the formerly primary schools.

In many cases, as the construction of new classrooms in formerly primary schools is in process, 8th and 9th grades operate as a semi-independent unit within our *polimodal* school. So we have kids and ex-primary schoolteachers working in our school but under different rules and objectives. This [situation] is a source of conflictive relations.

It is worth mentioning that throughout the interviews issues of funding and how those scarce resources are distributed were points of concern among school administrators, particularly among those principals who cannot count on their school cooperatives and do not receive extra funds from the municipalities. Since schools were transferred and the reform implemented, more pressure was put on us to search for funds. One may say that since there is a provincial office that deals with infrastructure issues and we have a local council that acts as a liaison to place our funding requirement, things will be easier. Well, that is not the case. Depending on the type of repair needed, our request requires the signature of the supervisor and then goes to La Plata [central administration]. Moreover, the whole process is highly influenced by the connections you have; as everything in this country.

Overall, the underlying assumption from the micro level affairs is that a system that attempted to distribute bureaucratic control negatively affected schools, particularly through blending of politics, inefficiency, and a vertical accountability mechanism.

CONCLUSIONS

Recent decentralization and reform attempts in Argentina were designed at the national level under the premise that first, reforms will follow, and second that reforms will result in uniform implementation patterns and outcomes. The case of Buenos Aires provides an account of a decoupling process between national policy mandates and policy adaptation and implementation. The underlying idea presented here is that within the confines of certain geographical areas, political environments determine the actual game in town. It is evident from this study that policy adaptation and implementation of decentralization and education reforms carried out in Buenos Aires responded to various ways of accommodating managerial functions to individual political aspirations, which in turn make organizational changes remain unchanged or to keep the status quo.

From the findings presented in this study one can see that even when a formal centralized control to intermediate level units is what predominates, loose control, inefficiency, and the system's fragmentation open up space for *clientelism* and *personalistic* practices carried out through a decentralized informal organizational arrangement that, in some cases, involved the school.

However, this decentralized informal organizational arrangement did not translate into democratization and participation at the local level, so prevalent in the decentralization and school reform policy discourse. On the contrary, the organization of the provincial education system prevents that from happening, as shown through the accounts of school administrators and teachers. Indeed, former national school and local school councils lost control over the daily school operation.

Also, in-school participation and collaboration that schools were supposed to reach with the new managerial arrangement and the developing of the school PEI were rarely achieved.

Although this study was designed and meant for Argentina, its results do have significance for scholars worldwide, particularly those interested in decentralization policies and the dynamics, development, and outcomes of institutional environments. It is also relevant for policy makers in that it shows that policy design and practice do not usually match. Furthermore, the case at hand suggest that policies of decentralization aimed at promoting democratization and involvement at local levels fail to promote those expected results.

As the academic community continues studying the reforms analyzed in this study, more evidence about the pressures of the organizational environment on policy implementation and adaptation as well as reform outcomes at the local level will be provided. Further research will also shed more light on how actors' accounts about schooling vary according to their position within the educational organization, a fact evident in the case of Buenos Aires, Argentina.

11

Management of Semi-public Organizations in Complex Environments

Management activities in schools are unique compared to those of managers in other public organizations because of the character of schools as public service as well as publicly-funded organizations where high degrees of organizational autonomy and external penetration are both expected and required. There are rich discussions of various relationships between managerial activity and organizational context. And, while these discussions are not unique to the educational literature, special attention has been given to the association of managerial activities with organizational outputs of schools. There has, however, not been much attention to the effect the semi-public nature of schools has on school management In keeping with the theme of this symposium issue of Public Administration and Management: An Interactive Journal, this chapter addresses school management and the nature or influence of the public context on management activities in schools.

The bureaucratic administration of formal organizations is an important and much discussed phenomenon. Therefore, how white-collar bureaucratic organizations are managed is and has historically been of particular sociological as well as administrative interest. As a result, prescriptions for administrative as well as managerial activity are widely debated and discussed in both the organizations and management literatures. Compared to the activities of managers in other organizations, management activities in semi-public organizations, in particular, are unique because of their character as public service as well as publicly-financed organizations where high degrees of organizational autonomy and external penetration are both expected and required and because of their institutionalization across organizational environments.

First, semi-public organizations are those organizations that are governed and financed either in part or wholly by the public meaning that the general public often feels that it has a vested interest in the governance and implementation of schooling. These organizations are frequently governed by local political bodies and expected to be highly responsive to the requests and suggestions of the constituents of these political bodies. As a result of these various constituents, decision-making and other rational processes are often complicated.

Although there are many organizations that are semi-public, public schools are unique in that they are permeable to a higher degree than other semi-public organizations. This high degree of permeability results from a combination of factors. The general public is in most nations and states compelled to attend school at least through the end of primary school and through secondary school in most developed nations. Therefore, the public has had an intimate connection to schools throughout much of their lives, and often the most impressionable years of their lives. As a result, the public believes that it knows what schools do and should do. This long-term public exposure and involvement coupled with the consequent feeling of familiarity and entitlement that this exposure and involvement cultivates means that the public is comfortable discussing schools and has an opinion on most matters related to schooling, even if their opinions are not informed by the most relevant facts.

Another aspect of public schools that makes them especially permeable to public involvement and pressure is the fact that they are largely governed and financed by the public through political bodies at various levels of governance. For instance, at the national or federal level in most nations there is a Ministry or Department of Education that is responsible for national policy on education and often funds part if not all of the educational activities and schooling that occur in a nation. Depending on the particular nation, public governance at subordinate or more localized levels occurs as well.

For instance, at the state or regional level in many nations, educational policy is further refined or created, which is unique to that state or region. In addition, local regions through their own budgets often fund much of the schooling that occurs within their jurisdiction. Finally, at the local level there is often a local community governing board that makes policy implementation decisions as well as further refining educational policy from the regional and national levels. These local governing boards also make decisions regarding the use of funds and the collection of new funds for educational purposes. At each of these governance levels, the funds that are allocated to schools find their origins in publicly administered taxes or other public sources. Therefore, the public itself has a vested interest in the governance and implementation of schooling because it governs and funds schooling, be it directly or indirectly.

Secondly, semi-public organizations are often institutionalized across organizational environments meaning that the formal structure and policies related to these organizations cross traditional contextual boundaries demarcated by regions ranging from local communities to regional districts to nation-states. As a result, the contextual boundaries of semi-public organizations are frequently undefined or only vaguely defined. This means that it is difficult to talk about where contextual influences on the managers of semi-public organizations begin and end. And, in fact, previous studies have not considered the influence that the complexity of public organizational contexts has on managers' activities. The problem of broad and ambiguous definitions of organizational contexts is also significant because "environment" is a key concept of organizational and administrative theory related to managerial activity. And, although some previous empirical studies do estimate relationships between management activities and individual elements of semi-public organizations' immediate contexts, researchers have yet to determine how these managers adjust their activities in complex contexts comprising many different and even conflicting elements. In other words, the problem is that no one has yet estimated management activities based on the complexity of institutionalized organizational contexts, especially at the national and cross-national levels.

Even though levels of organizational governance, finance, and public familiarity vary by both organization and national system, public schools are ideal for the examination of the relationship between managerial activity and organizational environments. They are ideal because principals must manage their schools according to local school community contexts and immediate needs, while also considering and responding to national educational goals, trends, and expectations for schooling. Therefore, what principals do may be a response to school level needs, nation level expectations, or both. Each of these levels of needs and expectations may be called an organizational environment and at each level, varying levels of complexity characterize these organizational environments.

MANAGERIAL WORK IN SEMI-PUBLIC ORGANIZATIONS

The most obvious and important question when defining the nature of managerial work in semi-public organizations is to ask who is a manager. Stewart suggests that the two simplest definitions are that managers are anyone responsible for the work of others and managers are those above a certain level in the hierarchy of supervision. Yet even these definitions may not be appropriate given that one important managerial activity is to delegate responsibility and authority.

As a result, managerial activity according to Stewart's definition becomes ambiguous as it is diffused throughout the hierarchy of organizational supervision. This ambiguity and diffusion arises because managers pass their responsibility and authority to others who perform many seemingly managerial tasks. In other words, as managers delegate responsibility and authority, activities that may be characteristically 'managerial' may not belong to or be performed by managers exclusively. Therefore, the nature of managerial work causes a fundamental problem in identifying managerial activity in semi-public organizations.

A second important conceptual consideration is that different fields define managers and their activity differently. The context of management varies considerably, according to Stewart, over time and among people in similar positions both within as well as across nations and organizations. Noordegraaf & Stewart argue similarly that the perceptions of what managerial activity entails vary across fields within the already amorphous contextual environments of managerial activity. Of course, the obvious distinctions between the broader fields such as business, economics, sociology, political science, and education, for example, may be made, but even finer distinctions, definitions, and perceptions of managerial activity are possible. For instance, even public administration and organizational activity scholars have different conceptions of managerial activity.

Consequently, a third and more important consideration for this study is the conceptual distinction between public and private sector management and even the distinction within the public sector between the political and the social services spheres. As Hannaway (1989) and others suggest, education and schooling contexts provide situations where the activity of managers is semi-public. On the one hand is the frequent push by, for example, educational stakeholders, researchers and practitioners for the corporate model of management in schools. Yet as Noordegraaf and Stewart point out, "As traditional public sector values—such as representativeness, equality before the law, justice—are forced to compete with modern managerial values—such as economy, efficiency, effectiveness—inevitable tensions arise." These tensions are what may give rise to a loose relationship (i.e., loose coupling) or even a broken relationship (i.e., decoupling) between managerial activity and organizational environments, especially at the national level. These tensions also suggest how the environmental complexity of schools may influence principals' management activity and encourage it to couple differently with the organizational environment at different organizational levels.

Thus the conceptual considerations when defining managerial activity in semi-public organizations, and school principals' management activity in particular, are dominated by (1) the ambiguity of what constitutes managers' work or activities in these organizations, (2) the perception or relative context both of the managers and those observing or studying managerial activity, and (3) the semi-public and, consequently, tension-producing characteristics, responsibilities, and pressures of public school managers such as principals.

Management Activity

The nature of managerial work is slippery (Hannaway, 1989). And those who empirically approach management studies recognize the malleability of managerial activity even though less empirical and more policy-oriented studies do not. Noordegraaf and Stewart argue that managerial activity is oriented more toward systemic and sectorial concerns than specific problems or regions, although "extensive local knowledge" cannot and should not be discounted. They assert that "management skills are..less specific to particular problems, and more restricted to specific organizations and industrial sectors; deal with a succession of tasks in one system, rather than a series of discrete tasks occurring in separate locations; rest on a broad, diffuse knowledge base which includes extensive local knowledge." Given this study's focus on managerial activity, this is a powerful assertion. Therefore, according to Noordegraaf and Stewart, principals' managerial activity is not specific to particular problems of instruction and learning within individual schools, but is restricted to the concerns and situations of types of schools and schooling.

This concept of principals' managerial activity also suggests that while extensive local knowledge, which may include familiarity with the community and local external as well as internal school culture, is included as a part of the rationale or considerations of principals, their activity is based in a set of broad and diffuse core beliefs about the managerial activity of principals. Noordegraaf and Stewart conclude that the institutional embeddedness of managerial activity deserves attention, especially for managerial activity occurring in the public sector. This is an encouraging assertion given that this study both investigates public sector managerial activity by focusing on school principals and considers both the organizations and administrative approaches to principals' managerial activity.

Although other work focuses on the organizational embeddedness of managerial activity, each of these examples and assertions discussed above, punctuated by Noordegraaf and Stewart's conclusion suggests that the nature of managerial activity goes beyond the specific organizations in which managers are situated to encompass fields of organizations or ranges of organizations whose structures and purposes have been synthesized and scripted as part of an institutionalization process. This institutionalization of schooling structures, processes, and, in particular, principals' managerial activity suggests both the expansion of organizational boundaries and the importance of national systems in the study of institutionalized organizations such as schools.

Consequently, previous research has struggled with defining and measuring managerial activity in semi-public organizations. Although managerial activity has been defined in many ways which vary significantly depending on the managerial context or perspective of researchers and participants, the various elements of managerial activity in semi-public organizations may be divided for reasons of identification and convenience into two sets of considerations: technical management activity and legitimacy management activity.

The Institutionalization of Semi-Public Organizations

As Meyer and Rowan (1977) argue, many organizations become structured by their environments and isomorphically change with them. Of particular interest to administrators and policymakers, therefore, is the probability that structure and substance, which insinuates itself among semi-public organizations, disseminates through managers' activity. Rather than any sort of technical exchange between managers and those they manage via managers' activity and the consequences of their activity, managers' activities often reflect organizational models applied to and shaped by environmental contexts at both the local and national levels.

The significance of environmental contexts is that legitimate managerial activities depend on the institutional models developed by each type of organizational system. In particular, principals' management activities, therefore, vary depending on the national characteristics of schools' organizational environments, which are determined in part by cross-nationally institutionalized models of legitimate principals' management activity and in part by the penetration of school management hierarchies and systems by environmental conditions.

Regardless of the relationship between a manager's activity and an organization's local environment, centralization of decision-making at the national level may determine a manager's ability or opportunity to contextualize their activity. As a result, management activity is caught between local environmental pressures and national environmental pressures. So, managers of semi-public organizations respond to (1) pressures at the system level for legitimacy and (2) pressures from the local level for accommodation. How managers respond to these discrepant pressures, unfortunately, is not answered or estimated in the literature.

While some of the activity of these managers surely follows technical-rational, bureaucratic models, the more organizational and institutional elements of managerial activity are frequently described as agency-less "actions" performed in accordance with legitimate, scripted models of activity. Yet to deny that these models exist and that managers behave in a manner appropriate to maintaining not only their individual legitimacy but also the legitimacy of their organizations in both local and national contexts would be to deny the influence of organizational environment. In fact, what drives much of managers' actions is their attention to and need for legitimacy at both the local and national levels. Yet what constitutes legitimate activity at the local level may not and often does not correspond to what constitutes legitimate activity at the national level.

In fact, while certain organizational outputs may be desired at both levels, the process or method of achieving these outputs may vary significantly. This is not to say that technical output is not part of the environmental mix for schools or is not a concern of managers. Instead, a loosely coupled model suggests that many other objectives occupy managers' time and efforts, and these are often institutional requirements from the outside.

Thus, for example, the popular conception is that highly consistent or stable loci of organizational governance can simplify the external environment of schools. Using schooling as an example, in highly centralized school systems, principal management may require fewer legitimizing activities because so many of the institutional demands on schools are met at a governance level above the school. An example of this would be a nationally centralized curriculum. Political and technical conflict over the nature of such a curriculum would more likely occur at more centralized or national level arenas than at the local school level. In this case principals would not have to do the work of developing and legitimating a curriculum with both the local community and other levels of school administration. Instead, their job would be to technically assist faculty in implementing this curriculum.

Whereas, in a school system in which there was discrepancy about which bureaucratic level of governance had control over the curriculum, the environment of schooling and principals' management activity would be much more complex due to competing efforts to govern the schools from both the local and national levels of administration. This kind of reasoning about the centralization of organizational bureaucracies and management activity leads to several propositions:

Proposition 1: In organizational environments with less centralized decision-making bureaucracies, managers of semi-public organizations spend more time managing legitimacy issues and less time managing the technical processes of their organizations.

Proposition 2: In organizational environments with more centralized decision-making bureaucracies, managers of semi-public organizations spend less time managing legitimacy issues and more time managing the technical processes of their organizations.

In other words, management activity may be directed more towards legitimacy than technical process management depending on the penetration of regional or national level governance into local governing bodies. This means that organizations with fewer institutional requirements and public penetration can be more overtly accommodating to local community and cultural influences. In turn, managers of semi-public organizations in decentralized systems vary their activity more by the particular demands of their communities and clients than models of legitimate activity imposed or expected by their external governing bodies. Therefore, system or organization level inputs and resources may influence the categorical performance and production of managers, but penetration of local culture and community influences can particularize performance and activity of managers as well. As Table 1 shows, a balance between the technical organizational processes and organizational legitimacy influences may be achieved or attempted although the environments in which each is a significant predictor of managerial activity may differ: management of technical processes dominating less complex environments and legitimacy management dominating the more complex environments.

Environmental Complexity

The complexity of organizational environment has been previously defined as an increase in the number of stakeholders or other influences penetrating organizations' daily functions and administrative duties. Another previous definition of organizational complexity has been the decentralization of administrative or organizational processes and functions, meaning that centralized institutions are supposedly less complex than their decentralized partners. As a result, American schools are labeled the most complex of any system in the world because of the extreme decentralization of school governance and administration in the United States. More recent analyses, however, suggest that complexity is not as simple as that. In a recent analysis of decentralization of school policy and curricula, suggests that complexity occurs when there is a mixing of centralization levels within the same organization. In other words, semi-public organizations that attempt to centralize decision-making within nations, but simultaneously attempt to decentralize responsibility or accountability for the technical processes of schooling at the local level are the most complex. Similarly, systems that are either relatively all decentralized or all centralized are less complex because the operating system is coherent and consistent to some degree. It is when conflict arises within the administration or governance of an organization that complexity rises dramatically.

LOOSE COUPLING IN SEMI-PUBLIC ORGANIZATIONS

The relationship or association of managerial activity to the organization as well as the organization's environment is the focus of loose-coupling arguments. In characterizing loose coupling, Weick argues that "coupled events are responsive, but that each event also preserves its own identity and some evidence of its physical or logical separateness." And as Ingersoll asserts, schools embody the stereotypical characteristics of loosely coupled organizations such as: (1) unclear, diverse or ambiguous organizational means and goals; (2) low levels of coordination of employees' productive activities; (3) low levels of organizational control; (4) high levels of employee autonomy; and (5) low levels of managerial authority. Yet, coupling can occur both within and between organizational levels. Furthermore, Weick (1983) citing the influences of Glassman (1973), Heider (1959), and Salancik (1975) suggests seven characteristics of loosely coupled systems, which can be in turn translated into both local and national level phenomena. These seven characteristics are that:

(1) loose coupling allows the persistence of some parts of organizations because organizations then do not have to respond to every environmental change,
(2) loose coupling provides a sensitive sensing mechanism for adjustment to local environmental influences,
(3) loosely coupled systems are good for localized adaptation,
(4) loosely coupled systems can change more and have more unique solutions than tightly coupled systems,
(5) breakdowns in one part of a loosely coupled system are isolated and not allowed to spread to other parts of the organization,
(6) loosely coupled systems allow more self-determination by the actors, and
(7) loosely coupled systems are less expensive than tightly coupled systems because they do not coordinate people as much as tightly coupled systems.

As school managers tailor their activity to the specific needs of schools' local environments and managerial pressure from the national educational system increases (i.e., these predictors increase or combine), the complexity of the school managers' organizational environment should rise as well. In other words, the more complex schools' organizational environments are within national educational systems, the more loosely coupled the managerial activity of principals' should be to the school and national environments.

Sensitivity to organizational environments changes between types of organizations or by organizational sector. In particular, environmental influence can differ between for-profit and non-profit organizations. Hannaway (1989) as well as Lau, Pavett, and Newman (1980) argue that too much has been made of the difference between public and private organizations. In particular, Hannaway suggests that "administrative systems that are part of an organization producing goods for market exchange may behave differently at some levels, although perhaps not quite so differently at others." Hannaway continues by asserting that the evidence she finds "suggests that the similarity in administrative systems across [public and private] organizations—at least at the levels discussed here—are probably greater than the differences. These are bold assertions, which may suggest that there are institutionalized models for managerial activity regardless of organizational sector and environmental influence. These assertions, therefore, suggest a more institutional approach to school management activity than even the organizational literature typically suggests.

Across the many kinds of schools and educational environments that exist, there are often consistently similar pressures on principals to behave in certain ways and perform certain duties. In addition, principals find themselves either looking to legitimate models of school management or being taught to be effective school managers in formally accredited and scripted-for-legitimacy professional training programs. In other words, the mechanisms of institutional change, which according to DiMaggio and Powell (1983) consist of coercive, mimetic, and normative influences, may lead principals to follow transnationally institutionalized scripts for principals' activity (i.e., models of legitimate school management activity).

Following established, rationalized scripts ensures principals' legitimacy even though some activities may decouple from the legitimate model of school management activity depending on the specific school environments. This means that the activities of principals are sometimes torn between the rationalized, transnational models of legitimate school structures, processes, and outcomes and the characteristics and needs of principals' school environments. Consequently, when considering school management activities, one might expect that they would become increasingly standardized and stable over time due to institutional pressure resulting from the expanding legitimacy of mass education.

Ogawa and Bossert (1995) argue that principals' managerial activity is an organizational quality and as such enhances an organization's social legitimacy, finds strength in a network of roles throughout the educational institution, relies on individuals' resources, and leads to the adoption of structures that mirror an organization's cultural environment. By situating principals as school managers in the midst of complex, semi-public organizations such as schools, this literature questions the linkage between school management activity and either school output or organizational environment, and suggests that if school management activity and school output are related, it is because the relationship connects organizational and institutional level environmental influences (e.g., local and national environment) to individual level processes and outcomes (e.g., principal, teacher, and student performance).

School management activity may be predicted by organizational elements to which principals may contribute, but which are not dependent upon or significantly related to their activity. Instead, school level decisions and changes follow legitimate, rationalized models in part to ensure the growth and legitimacy of the organization in spite of (rather than because of) individual level outcomes such as student achievement (Ogawa & Bossert, 1995). It is more appropriate to look at organizational and institutional level characteristics that correspond with individual level outcomes independent of school management activity than to use school management activity to predict individual level outcomes. This perspective suggests that principals' individual resources and decision-making authority are not as influential on school output as the institutionalized model or environmental context in which their activities occur and to which they conform.

Consequently, the semi-public school environment or type of educational system in which students and principals work may be more predictive of the organizational output of schools such as school management activities than any proposed link between school management activities and school output. Of particular interest to educational administrators and policymakers, therefore, is the probability that structure and substance, which insinuates itself among school organizations, disseminates through school management activity. Rather than any sort of technical exchange between principals and students via school management activity and the consequences of this activity, a principals' management of instruction, for example, reflects organizational models applied to and shaped by semi-public environmental contexts at both the local and national levels.

The significance of semi-public environmental contexts is that legitimate management activities depend on the institutional models developed by each type of education system. School management activity should, therefore, vary depending on the national characteristics of schools' semi-public organizational environments. Variation in activity that is contextualized to specific school conditions and communities should also be more influential than activities that follow a strictly standardized model, which limits administrative and managerial authority. However, these school-specific conditions are nested in the larger national context determined in part by cross-nationally institutionalized models of legitimate school management activity and in part by the penetration of school management hierarchies and systems by environmental conditions.

Regardless of the relationship between school management activity and schools' local environments, centralization of decision-making at the national level may determine principals' ability or opportunity to contextualize management within their schools. The same institutional influences that contribute to the training, education, and activity of school managers like principals as rationalized and legitimate models of school administration are products of the environment and preexisting levels of school performance at least as much as they are causes of it. Therefore, principals' management of both material and personnel resources is not as influential as the environment or context, which preexists schooling processes and permeates most aspects of schooling students receive. As a result, school management activity is caught between local school environmental pressures and national environmental pressures.

Unanswered Questions

If and how school managers respond to semi-public environmental complexity within and between levels of formal school organization remains unanswered. The unique character of national organizational environments and their influences on what school managers do is less frequently studied. Also, the complexity of environments both within and between organizational levels is undefined and un-estimated. Most noticeably, however, are arguments that recognize the institutional isomorphism of school organizations while still allowing for variation within and between schools' organizational environments and the initiatives of school managers like principals. These questions lead to the need for an updated and elaborated perspective.

DiMaggio and Powell (1991) observe that while "functional explanations of the ways in which institutions represent efficient solutions to problems of governance" are frequent, "sociologists reject functional explanations and focus instead on the ways in which institutions complicate and constitute the paths by which solutions are sought." In other words, change occurs through institutions, and institutional influence is perhaps the most significant change agent among the plethora of contextual, environmental, and individual level influences contributing to each occurrence of change in society.

DiMaggio and Powell assert that "'institutionalists' vary in their relative emphasis on micro and macro features, in their weightings of cognitive and normative aspects of institutions, and in the importance they attribute to interests and relational networks in the creation and diffusion of institutions." Consequently, an exploration of new institutional theory emphasizes the distinction between technical and institutional environments. One of the clearest explanations of this distinction comes from Scott and Meyer as they define each. Scott and Meyer assert that "technical environments are those in which a product or service is produced and exchanged in a market such that organizations are rewarded for effective and efficient control of their production systems."

This technical environment is remarkably similar to the accountability environments for principals emphasized by the educational and business administration approaches to managerial activity. On the other hand, "institutional environments are, by definition, those characterized by the elaboration of rules and requirements to which individual organizations must conform if they are to receive support and legitimacy." Thus, outcomes of organizations (such as school performance or student achievement) and individual participation in organizations (such as principals' instructional management activity) are not necessarily as important in an institutional environment as they are in a technical one. This separation of process from outcome is fundamental to neo-institutional approaches to change and agency.

In fact, the aspect of most interest for this discussion is the change process and, correspondingly, which causal elements and factors lead to changes in school management activity. Jepperson (1991) argues that environmental contexts and collective agency are strong influences and can lead to action bringing change through contradictions or opposition to institutionalized social elements. He asserts that these "contradictions, or, separately, exogenous environmental shocks, can force institutional change by blocking the activation of reproductive procedures or by thwarting the successful completion of reproductive procedures, thus modifying or destroying the institution." In other words, strong exogenous influences can initiate change in institutional structures and procedures. Therefore, isomorphism through environmental context suggests that agency is at work, but more so at the collective than individual level.

Change, however, must not necessarily be initiated by severe elements outside of the institution. Although institutional forms and scripts are applied very uniformly across many semi-public environments (e.g., schools and hospitals), individuals and collectivities may 'shop' for the script or model they prefer depending on the context and situation in which they will apply it or conform to it. As a result, the interactive character of legitimacy-seeking is interesting given that outcomes of institutional structures and processes often do not change in spite of changes in form and script that may occur. Still, the main criticisms of this approach focuses on questions of rational choice and decision-making. Without actors, rational choice and decision-making cannot exist, and without the option or ability to rationally make decisions some have suggested that neo-institutional theory does not allow for the humanity and reality of change, growth, and even death that is empirically observable in every situation, environment, and cultural context and in particular in the managerial activity of school principals.

CONCLUSION

There is a relationship between the larger semi-public environments within which schools are embedded and the tasks on which organizational managers such as school principals spend their time. Hence variation in management activity from school to school, as well as from system to system, is a function of the complexity of both the institutional and technical environments of schools and schooling. In the highly charged institutional environments of schools, management activity is driven more by outside institutional pressures than internal concerns for technical output. This is not to say that technical output is not part of the environmental mix for schools or is not a concern of principals. Instead, a loosely coupled model suggests that many other objectives occupy principals' time and efforts, and these are often institutional requirements from the outside. Thus, for example, highly centralized national bureaucracies within which schools are situated can simplify the external environment of schools. Decentralized bureaucracies do the opposite. Principal management in the former may require fewer legitimizing activities because so many of the institutional demands on schools are met at a governance level above the school. An example of this would be a nationally centralized curriculum. Political and technical conflict over the nature of such a curriculum would more likely occur at more centralized or national level arenas than at the local school level. In this case principals would not have to do the work of developing and legitimating a curriculum with both the local community and other levels of the instructional leadership. Instead, their job would be to technically assist faculty in implementing this curriculum. This kind of reasoning about the centralization of school bureaucracies and school management activity leads to several assumptions: (1) the complexity of schools' organizational environments varies cross-nationally, (2) nationally decentralized educational systems create more complex technical environments than centralized systems do, and (3) in more complex organizational environments, principals spend more time managing external technical processes of schooling. Less complex environments lead to the opposite.

In other words, school management activity may be directed more towards external legitimacy than internal management depending on the penetration of regional or national level governance into local schooling and schools. This means that schools with fewer institutional requirements and penetration can be more overtly accommodating to local community and cultural influences. In turn, principals in decentralized systems vary their activity more by the particular demands of their communities and student populations than models of legitimate activity imposed or expected by their external governing bodies. Therefore, as Fuller and Clarke (1994) suggest, system or school level inputs and resources may influence the categorical performance and production of school actors such as principals, but penetration of local culture and community influences can particularize performance and activity of those actors as well. Thus, a balance between influences may be achieved or attempted although the level at which each is a significant predictor of principal managerial activity may differ: technical-rational processes dominating the school level and organizational environment dominating the national level. In general, however, the institutional environment of schools will have as much influence on public school administration and management as the technical environment.

12

The Management of Schools as Public Organizations

The public nature of schooling and its effect on the management of schools is often overlooked in discussions of public administration and management. This special symposium issue of *Public Administration and Management: An Interactive Journal* focuses on the management of schools as public organizations. As such, the articles in this symposium issue address school management and the nature or influence of the public context on management activities in schools.

Principals', teachers', and other administrators' management activities in schools are unique compared to those of managers in other organizations because of the uniquely public character of schools. As one of the few public organizations with compulsory participation all people over a significant portion of their lives, schools are also public service and publicly-funded organizations. High degrees of organization autonomy and external penetration are both expected and required of schools. The articles in this issue bring together several unique but cohesive perspectives on public administration and policy in schooling.

Lance Fusarelli and Bonnie Johnson's article, "Educational Governance and the New Public Management," looks at how neo-corporatist ideology is blending private sector administrative techniques with public sector organizations like schools. The coupling of process and product is a focus of this investigation. Ultimately, the public accountability policies for schools, such as the educational legislation known as 'No Child Left Behind,' are decoupled from the actual administration and implementation of schooling because the nature of schooling as a largely localized public service prevents strict accountability from occurring.

David Brown's article, "Managing from the Inside-Out: Debating Site-Based Management in Public Schools," steps inside schools to look at a recent trend in the administration of schools as public organizations: site-based management. Building upon the idea of private versus public spheres explained in Fusarelli and Johnson's article, Brown looks at the differences in administrative perspective that two important school managers (administrators and teachers) hold. The internal managerial conflict that can and does arise from the discrepancy in opinion between these two players in the site-based management of schools is an important consideration when discussing the public nature of school administration and management.

M. Fernanda Astiz's article, "Decentralization and Educational Reform: What Accounts for a Decoupling Between Policy Purpose and Practice? Evidence from Buenos Aires, Argentina," explores the implementation outcomes of decentralization and education reform policies in Argentina during the 1990s. In particular, Astiz asserts that policy directives, implementation, and outcomes are decoupled due to the politicization of public schooling policy and organizational adaptation. There is also a mismatch between national-level official mandates and local-level public policy implementation in schools. In particular, Astiz points out that policies of decentralization meant to promote local-level action in public organizations such as schools often do not achieve this goal. Instead, the public context of schooling frequently leads to the fragmentation of public school administration policy and activity.

Finally, Alexander W. Wiseman's article, "Management of Semi-public Organizations in Complex Environments," ties the previous three articles together by discussing the nature or influence of public schools' organizational environments on management activities in the schools. As semi-public organizations, schools are unique (1) because high degrees of organizational autonomy and external penetration are both expected and required and (2) because of their institutionalization across organizational environments (including transnational organizational environments). In particular, the idea of coupling between schooling processes and school managers' activities, which are directed toward the management of technical outcomes versus legitimacy outcomes, is discussed. This means that school management activity may be directed more towards external legitimacy than internal management depending on the penetration of regional or national level governance into local schooling and schools. As a result, schools with fewer institutional requirements and penetration can be more overtly accommodating to local community and cultural influences.

Not only do school managers have to be available to the public, but they are also expected to listen, to try to implement the suggestions (or demands) of these constituents, and to provide some evidence back to the public that their wishes have been fulfilled. These articles suggest that public policy and administration discussions should remember that the school systems in most nations, and especially in the United States, are democratic systems where there are often publicly-elected officials who have significant input into the administration of schools. School systems are also increasingly locally controlled meaning that the voice of even the least of the taxpayers is a booming voice that must be answered if not obeyed.

Schools are sometimes compared to hospitals for their degree of public penetration, but in reality these comparisons are woefully off course. While there is quite a large degree of public penetration into health care indeed, by comparison to schools the public's ability to directly influence hospital decision-making is weak. Public schools are organizations whose "clients" are generally the entire population of a nation or community. Schools are compulsory mass public institutions meaning that not only does every person have the opportunity (or right) to take advantage of this organization's services, but also everyone is also required to do so. Schooling is compulsory in most of the world's educational systems. This is dramatically different from health care or hospitals where there is no daily requirement to get a check up or complete a series of health checks. Schools are the only organizations in the world in which high degrees of organizational autonomy and high levels of external penetration are both expected and required. This public access and performance accountability make the public school administrator's job one of public service, but also one of complex contexts. This is quite the organizational double punch, and means that school administrators are double punched as well. In the final analysis, the management of schools and public organizations is not an option, but a long-standing requirement. The articles in this symposium emphasize the conflicts and contradictions in public expectations of schools in relation to the reality and feasibility of popular attempts to treat schools as if they were not public organizations at all. And, as each of these articles points out, this is a mistake that can have disastrous consequences.

The Bush Administration has shown its determination to provide direct government assistance to faith-based social service organizations, which the President believes are discriminated against in their efforts to obtain federal grants and contracts for the delivery of social services. Shortly after taking office, George W. Bush created the White House Office of Faith-based And Community Initiatives to identify and remove perceived barriers to federal funding of small religiously oriented and community based social service agencies. By Executive Order he has directed seven cabinet-level agencies to engage in proactive efforts to assist faith-based organizations obtain federal grants and contracts. Also he vigorously promoted the Charity Aid Relief and Empowerment (CARE) Act (S. 476), which the Senate passed on April 9, 2003 by a vote of 95-5. The final version of the CARE Act, which now moves to the House of Representatives, fell somewhat short of the Administration's original aspirations, but still contains some important provisions designed to enhance the ability of small faith-based organizations to compete for federal grants and contracts. The President has shown that he is willing to use Executive Orders, in addition to legislative initiatives, to accomplish his vision of greater participation by religious organizations in the delivery of social services.

The Bush Administration is particularly interested in fully implementing and even expanding the so-called Charitable Choice provisions contained in Section 104 of the Personal Responsibility and Work Opportunity Reconciliation Act of 1996, commonly known as the Welfare Reform Law enacted during the Clinton Administration. Charitable Choice allows religious organizations to use federal money to supply various social services without altering their fundamental religious character.

Advocates say that religious organizations provide important services to people in need and should have a place at the table with secular organizations. Critics argue that Charitable Choice in combination with the President's faith-based agenda has created a "slippery slope" that will lead to the use of government funds to endorse and promote religious activities and services.

THE MANAGEMENT DILEMMA

Aside from the very significant Constitutional and policy issues associated with the Bush agenda, the faith-based initiative poses a management dilemma for leaders of small religiously oriented organizations that want to enhance their social services. On the one hand, the lure of federal funding is tempting. Charities of all types, but especially small organizations, have been financially challenged by the persistent economic downturn and the uncertainty of the post-September 11 philanthropic environment.

For many of these organizations, the additional funding from the federal government would be welcome. On the other hand, many religious organizations, including some conservatives who typically support the Bush domestic agenda, are wary of taking government funds.

They fear that federal funding carries strings that will eventually diminish their pervasively sectarian values and organizational missions. Interestingly, some of the strongest support for the faith-based initiative appears to come from constituencies that are not usually aligned with the Bush Administration, including urban African American ministries.

There are at least four bodies of literature that are useful in developing hypotheses about the possible impact of federal funding on the structure and culture of faith-based organizations. Rather than an exhaustive literature review, several prominent examples from each major category are summarized below.

The Literature on Partnerships between Government and Nonprofit Organizations

There is an extensive literature cataloguing the history of government – nonprofit relations and the sometimes stormy relations between the two (e.g., Dobkin Hall, 1994). Beginning in the Carter Administration and proceeding through the early 1990s, this literature focused on the potential for constructive partnerships and strategic alliances between government and nonprofit organizations, with special emphasis on the role of nonprofits as mediating structures between citizens and large impersonal government bureaucracies (Berger and Neuhaus, 1977). During the Reagan years the literature focused on the emerging role of nonprofits as providers of public goods in an era of public sector devolution, decentralization, and retrenchment (e.g., Salamon, 1981; 1985; 1987). For the most part, this literature portrays a cautiously hopeful scenario wherein government contracting with nonprofit organizations produces a happy outcome for everyone, including citizens who will benefit from the innovativeness and responsiveness of the nonprofit sector, and government agencies that can divest themselves from the burdens of direct service delivery. In this early literature there is little if any speculation on the potential negative impacts on the nonprofit sector of growing dependence on government funding.

The Literature Outlining the Challenges for Both Sectors

Beginning in the early and mid-1990s we begin to see growing concern about the potential pathologies of mutual interdependence between government and the nonprofit sector. For government, there is the gradual evolution of a "hallow state" (Milward and Provan, 1993) in which fundamentally "public" responsibilities are delegated to the private nonprofit sector where performance is sometime suspect and accountability is difficult to trace (Gaul and Borowski, 1993). For nonprofits, research began to show a recurring pattern of negative outcomes associated with growing reliance on government contracts including increased bureaucratization, loss of autonomy, mission creep, and the inability of nonprofit boards to exercise appropriate control over the increasingly complex task of administering government contracts (Smith and Lipsky, 1993; Smith, 1994; Gronjberg, 1993; Bernstein, 1991; Salamon, 1994; Boris and Steuerle, 1999). This literature, much of which is based on high quality empirical research, posits that resource dependence often alters the fundamental character of nonprofit organizations, transforming them into quasi-governmental agencies that resemble the government contractors that support them. This body of literature is perhaps most relevant to our discussion.

The Literature on Organizational Culture, Design, and Transformation

A third body of literature, which emerged in the 1970s, focuses on the collection of values, beliefs, and assumptions that comprise an organization's unique *culture* (e.g., Geertz, 1973; Ouchi, 1981; Deal and Kennedy, 1982). Cultural theorists have explored the subtleties of organizational behavior embedded in implicit belief systems and expectations of behavior that often are shaped by external forces on the organization. A related body of literature deals with the process of organizational change, offering descriptive and normative frameworks for helping organizations "learn" and successfully adapt to changing circumstances as well as their natural evolutionary life cycle. The impact of external forces on organizational structure have been explored by Lawrence and Lorsch (1967) and many others. A useful summary of all of these theoretical approaches and their practical implications is provided by Bolman and Deal (1997). These literatures combined suggest useful templates for examining plausible impacts on faith-based organizations as a result of access to federal funding support.

Studies of Faith-based Organizations

Finally, there is an emerging literature that is focusing specifically on small faith-based organizations and their response to the new public policy environment that seems to be encouraging a partnership with them. Ram Cnaan (1999), Mark Chaves (1999), Amy Sherman , and Steven Monsma (n.d) have conducted large scale surveys to explore the types of services provided by small faith-based organizations and their aspirations for growth and partnership with government contractors. But large scale surveys are not capable of capturing rich details about gradual changes in organizational behavior that might be attributable to increased funding from the federal government. A promising approach for developing sophisticated hypotheses is to conduct in-depth case studies in one or several organizations, tracing behavior and structural changes over time (e.g., Yankoski, forthcoming)

Toward that end, as a literary devise, let's examine a fictitious case study representing a composite of congregations that are currently providing social services and might be contemplating applications for federal funding.

A FICTITIOUS CASE

Let's consider the fictitious case of Holy Cross Catholic Church, a small parish (150 families) in an industrial mid-western city. Holy Cross is 125 years old. In its early years it served the pastoral needs of immigrant families, primarily from Eastern and Central Europe, who had come to the city to take jobs in the local steel mills and other manufacturing plants. Then, Holy Cross Church was surrounded by modest but tidy row houses, nestled in the shadow of the steel mill. Over the years, and especially in the past twenty years, the socio-economic structure of the neighborhood has changed dramatically. The steel mill stopped operating 20 years ago and has been demolished. Most of the young families have moved away. The remaining population consists of retired mill workers, service workers, and unskilled laborers. The neighborhood has high rates of substance abuse, crime, and domestic violence. The population has become increasingly diverse. Now, 35 percent of the parishioners in Holy Cross are African American and a small but rapidly growing number are Asian. They are fiercely loyal to the parish and to its pastor, Rev. Andrew Healy.

Healy has been a social activist and has encouraged the Catholic Diocese to take a greater role in issues of social justice, anti-poverty, crime prevention, and economic revitalization. When the steel mills closed down, Rev. Healy led an interfaith coalition of religious leaders who pressured the large corporations to do more to relieve the pain and suffering caused by the economic dislocation. Although, Rev. Healy has "mellowed" somewhat, he continues to be blunt and sometimes confrontational on issues such as economic development, job training, environmental justice, welfare reform, healthcare financing, and human rights. His style alienates some people, especially those in positions of authority, who are the targets of his passionate sermons.

The Diocese maintains only superficial ties with Holy Cross and, in fact, has cut it off financially. The Bishop tried to close Holy Cross in a "consolidation" move several years ago, but backed down in the face of vigorous protests from parishioners and neighborhood advocates.

Under Rev. Healy's vision, but with programmatic leadership from dozens of volunteers, Holy Cross offers a modest portfolio of social services. It operates a food and clothing pantry that is open three mornings a week. It also provides a bi-weekly parent education and parental support program, an after school mentoring program for youth, and a very modest emergency loan program for families in financial distress. These services are offered free of charge to anyone in need. Less than one-fourth of the clients in these programs are Holy Cross parishioners. All of the programs are modest in scope, with a combined budget of less than $20,000. Holy Cross relies on a dedicated corps of over 50 volunteers who work 20-40 hours per month.

The management culture is fluid and informal. These programs are run by the parishioners, not under a separate 501c3 corporation. There is a paid (part-time) volunteer coordinator and a parish advisory council that plans and approves new social programs. The advisory council is chaired by Rev. Healy but decision making is remarkably democratic, and always involves direct input from the volunteers. A "faith" component per se is not readily apparent in the social service programs (i.e., there is no evangelizing), but Rev. Healy says that "all of the volunteers are motivated by a shared passion for social justice as derived from the Gospel and the life of Jesus Christ." Some of the service volunteers are more religiously oriented than others. Therefore, the way any particular client is treated with respect to the faith-component of the programs can vary significantly depending on what volunteers are working at the time. Staff meetings and advisory board meetings always begin and end with a prayer. Volunteers sometimes encourage clients to improve their spiritual condition. Training sessions for volunteers include theological teachings and reading materials, but they are not mandated to use them in their interactions with clients. There is a high level of collaboration with other churches and religious organizations in the community. Holy Cross often refers clients to other organizations and congregations when it cannot meet their needs.

Funding, of course, is a continuing problem. All of the programs are funded primarily from the donations of parishioners, collected every Sunday. Rev. Healy has a good relationship with a local grocery store chain and several restaurants, which provide food and in-kind services for the pantry. Clothing donations come from a variety of sources.

Occasionally, a "large" gift of several hundred dollars will come from the estate of a deceased parishioner or as an unsolicited and often anonymous donation; there are no formal fundraising strategies or activities other than an occasional bake sale or raffle. Expenses sometimes fluctuate, especially when needs are great or when professionals are brought in for consulting for the mentoring, parenting, and parental support programs. There have been several financial crises, but as Rev. Healy says, "The Lord seems to provide for us, just when our hope is about to run out. We operate on faith, not cash flows."

Nonetheless, Healy has been intrigued by the notion of securing government funding to support some new social programming at Holy Cross. He thinks that there might be a good chance of securing a contract from the U.S. Department of Housing and Urban Development (HUD) for transitional housing for single mothers and their children. Many of these women suffer from substance abuse, domestic violence, and severe poverty. To operate such a program, Holy Cross would need to buy and renovate a nearby abandoned apartment building, with ten units. Healy has been approached by the local Housing Authority regarding a partnership on the proposed project. The director of the Housing Authority wants Holy Cross to act as the fiscal agent and prime contractor on the project because she believes that, in the current political climate, there will be a better chance of getting the federal money if a faith-based organization submits the proposal and takes the lead.

There are some obvious benefits to the transitional housing project, but some potential hazards as well. Rev. Healy thinks carefully about the project, and especially how federal funding will affect Holy Cross Church and its social service mission. Healy is confident that government funding will not affect the "faith component" of his services. But he wonders if there are broader managerial and cultural effects that are likely to result from a government contract.

SOME PROPOSITIONS

The proposed partnership with the federal government and the local Housing Authority will result in a higher level of resource dependence, which in turn could have effects on the management infrastructure and culture of Holy Cross Church. Here are a few propositions for consideration by Rev. Healy and other leaders of faith-based organizations.

At the most fundamental level, the federal contract for transitional housing may begin to transform Holy Cross Church from an *expressive* to an *instrumental* organization. Lester Salamon reminds us that many types of organizations in the nonprofit sector, including churches, exist *not* to provide goods or services but to give their members a vehicle for collective expression of beliefs and values.

Simply stated, the *primary mission* of Holy Cross Church is to provide its members with a vehicle for the expression of their faith, not to provide social services to the community. Because the social services now offered at Holy Cross are staffed almost exclusively by volunteers, one could argue that these services provide a vehicle for the collective expression of faith and an opportunity to practice their theological belief system. In that sense, these services may be a central ingredient in the expressive culture of the parish.

On the other hand, the scope and scale of the transitional housing program will very likely require a high level of professional expertise (see discussion below) and a concentration of resources that could conceivably transform the expressive culture of Holy Cross into the *instrumental* culture of a housing and social service agency.

What types of changes in norms, language, and behavior might indicate that this organization is transitioning from an expressive to an instrumental culture? Here are a few specific propositions: From process oriented to outcome oriented: At present, the process of delivering the modest social services of Holy Cross is as important as the outcomes they achieve. In fact, the volunteers of Holy Cross have never been asked to identify and quantify the outcomes of their programs. Rev. Healy is fond of saying, "We measure our success by the smiles of our clients." Such an approach to program evaluation, while touching, is not likely to meet the specifications of the federal funders or the local Housing Authority. A kind of "bottom line" mentality is likely to creep into the deliberations driven by factors such as occupancy rates in the housing facility, job placement rates for mothers, school attendance of the children, and ultimately successful transition to permanent housing. Moreover, the federal contract is likely to come with other strings as well, including perhaps provisions for broader community participation in planning and decision making. Suddenly, a new group of constituencies and decision making processes will augment, if not replace, the current informal "all in the family" mode of deliberation. As outputs and outcomes begin dominate, there will be less tolerance for the deliberative processes and volunteer engagement that currently characterize the social service program at Holy Cross.

From core values to negotiation and compromise: At present, Rev. Healy and his volunteers are driven by a set of core values, primarily theological and spiritual in nature, which apply to all of their social programs. The Bush faith-based initiative will, no doubt, take great pains to protect the religious character of the Holy Cross program. But, the federal funding and the partnership with the local Housing Authority will inevitably introduce another set of values that will likely compete with those currently in place. Healy will need to make difficult choices among competing objectives. For example, neighboring residents may demand that certain features be built into the design and operation of the transitional housing facility in order to "protect their property values" and the safety of their children. But if one of the objectives of the program is to fully re-integrate mothers and their children into the community then Rev. Healy will need to trade off the federal guidelines (and perhaps his own values) against those of some of his neighbors. Neighborhood reactions could, in turn, have a negative impact on the existing social services of Holy Cross, again forcing Rev. Healy to make trade-offs between his current portfolio of programs and the new transitional housing project.

From a private to a public culture: Until now, the social programs of Holy Cross Church have had the luxury of operating without any public scrutiny whatsoever. Their modest scale has allowed them to operate below the radar of the media and other public stakeholders. Such circumstances have encouraged the evolution of a very informal culture among the staff and volunteers. They are accountable to no one except themselves and their clients. But that environment will soon give way to high public visibility and expectations. The transitional housing program will operate very much in the public eye and with a great deal of public oversight. The federal contract contains many stipulations in return for the funding including independent audits of financial transactions, separate accounting systems, public advisory committees, and mandated program evaluations. The local newschapter has already called Rev. Healy to inquire about rumors that he intends to apply for the federal funds. Operating in the glare of public scrutiny will likely have at least a subtle effect on everything from dress codes to governance and policy making.

As Federal Funding Increases, Faith-based Organizations Will Experience a Shift From Volunteer to Professional Cultures

The transitional housing program will likely begin to transform Holy Cross from a *volunteer* culture to a *professional* culture. Rev. Healy will need to hire professionals to write the grant application, conduct community needs assessments, and do feasibility studies and cost analysis with respect to renovating the abandoned apartment building. He will need professional assistance with financing, legal issues, architectural design, and perhaps even public relations since some neighborhood residents apparently object to the transitional housing project. If the project is ever completed, he will need to hire professionals to staff the transitional housing facility and to design and deliver so-called "wrap-around" support services to the mothers and their children. As the project progresses, he will need professional assistance in monitoring and evaluating the success of the project according to governmental goals and objectives.

Here are a few specific propositions regarding change in norms, values, and behavior that might be observed if indeed there is a shift from a volunteer culture to a professional culture:

From theocracy to technocracy: Rev. Healy's vision for conveying religious values to his parishioners through their volunteer service may give way to an increasingly technocratic culture as the sheer size of the transitional housing program, and its accompanying government standards, begins to dominate the social program agenda at Holy Cross. Healy's symbolic and spiritual leadership may also take a back seat to the technical expertise of the staff of the local housing authority who will partner with Holy Cross on the project.

From unified action to professional silos: There will almost certainly be a growing division of labor and specialization as the housing project unfolds. In its mission and scope it is both qualitatively and quantitatively distinct from the other social programs in the Holy Cross portfolio. At present, it is easy for the parish advisory council and the volunteers to exchange information and ideas on how to integrate and improve services. The current unified model of decision making may begin to give way to a divisional model of planning and implementation with specialized concepts, models of service delivery, and professional vocabulary that will make it increasingly difficult for volunteers to participate on an equal footing with the professionals.

From idiosyncratic practice to "best practice": Thomas Jeavons reminds us that faith-based organizations represent a remarkable menagerie of organizations displaying almost infinite variety in their theological foundations as well as their community outreach and their modes for delivering community services. Holy Cross Church fits this description perfectly. For example, the mentoring and parent support programs are based on principles developed by the volunteers during a weekend spiritual retreat. These programs are not based on scholarly research or national "best practice" models, but on a process of "spiritual renewal" espoused by Rev. Healy and other theologians. Most of the volunteers who designed and managed these programs grew up on the streets around Holy Cross. They based their program designs on their intimate knowledge of the neighborhood and its needs. The proposed housing program, however, will very likely introduce a dramatic change to that idiosyncratic model of design and delivery. The federal standards will require that services be made available to mothers and their children (e.g., counseling, parenting, support groups for substance abuse) that are based on nationally proven best practice models. By definition, this will introduce service modalities that are not currently used by the Holy Cross volunteers and that are not based on unique neighborhood circumstances and needs. It will also introduce a process of program design and implementation that is quite foreign to Rev. Healy and his volunteers.

From spontaneous services to planned services: At present, the volunteers of Holy Cross respond whenever and wherever the need is greatest. They don't have a strategic plan. They don't even have a "firm" annual budget. They pride themselves on responding quickly at the point of greatest need. The transitional housing project will likely change much of that. There will be huge sunk costs that will commit Holy Cross to this project for years. The federal contract will require a strategic plan, a business plan, a plan for generating local matching funds, and an implementation and evaluation plan. The spontaneous and opportunistic culture on which Holy Cross has thrived may gradually give way to one driven by prescribed goals and formalized plans to meet those goals.

As Federal Funding Increases, Faith-based Organizations Will Develop Management Cultures Driven By Cash Flows, Not "Divine Providence"

As noted above, the social programs at Holy Cross have occasionally encountered financial crises, but Healy and his volunteers have faith that "Divine Providence" will always intervene. This type of belief system, whether literal or not, creates a kind of laissez-faire management culture with steady-state features. That is, the flow (or lack of flow) of resources is presumed to be somewhat random and, accordingly, organizational activities and initiatives follow no particular pattern or cycle. With outside funding from the federal government and the Housing Authority, Holy Cross will immediately enter a new environment that will be heavily dependent on a regular cycle of cash flows with administrative and programmatic activities (planning, budgeting, staffing, implementation, billing, accounting, evaluation, etc.) that correspond to that cycle. Interruptions of that cash flow, for whatever reason, will be far more disruptive for the transitional housing program that they ever would have for the old volunteer-driven programs.

Here are some issues that Holy Cross may need to prepare for if it is to thrive in this new fiscal environment.

From steady state funding to uncertainty: At first glance, this proposition may seem counter-intuitive. After all, a large contract from the federal government would seem to give far more *certainty* to the fiscal condition of Holy Cross than its current hand-to-mouth existence. But in a curious way the current revenue streams, although modest, are perhaps more predictable than the hundreds of thousands of dollars contemplated under the proposed government contract. First, government contracts typically are not guaranteed beyond one year. Second, government priorities can change swiftly with a change in political regime. And, third, government contracts are notoriously under-funded, thereby forcing Holy Cross to seek local funds to supplement the federal grant. This high level of uncertainty can create a culture that minimizes risk and innovation, gravitating instead toward conformity as a way to reduce uncertainty. In other words, once Holy Cross obtains the federal contract, it will become *imperative* to keep it. Rev. Healy will quickly discover that the best way to keep the contract will be to scrupulously adhere to the contract specifications.

From catalyst to vendor: Holy Cross, especially under the leadership of Rev. Healy, has always been a catalyst for change in the community. The financial independence of Holy Cross has given it the autonomy it needs to challenge policies and the authorities who make and enforce them. The federal contract, however, will gradually transform Holy Cross into a vendor of a highly complex and expensive program. In turn, Holy Cross will become increasingly dependent on the cash flows from the government sponsor. In this purchaser-vendor relationship, the power balance is very heavily in favor of the purchaser. There is a chance that the advocacy role of Holy Cross will gradually give way to supplication as it tries to build a foundation for a steady, predictable relationship with the federal government and the cash flows that accompany that relationship.

From collaborative to competitive culture: No significant new federal funding has been allocated for the Bush administration's faith-based initiative. This new federal program has, in effect, established a "zero sum game" in which secular and faith-based organizations will be pitted in competition with each other for federal contracts. Formerly, Holy Cross worked collaboratively with a wide variety of both secular and faith-based organizations, knowing that its modest programs could not meet all community needs. Surely such collaboration may continue, especially in the unfunded program areas. But the fact is that Holy Cross will enter an intensely competitive arena the moment Rev. Healy decides to apply for the federal contract. Soon he and his staff will begin to think in traditional business terms like of *market niches, competitive advantages, pricing strategies, market penetration,* and *competitive threats*. If that happens, the environment of free and open exchange of information, and referral of clients, will soon give way to various command and control systems to ensure that competitive intelligence is protected.

Obviously, none of this is to suggest that there is anything inherently wrong with the transitional housing program. In fact Rev. Healy and his followers could easily make the case that this federally funded program would enrich and enlarge their spiritual mission. There is even some evidence that the religious character of services offered by faith-based organizations has not been compromised by government grants and contracts. But, from a management perspective, it is at least plausible that the transitional housing program will transform Holy Cross Church and its many volunteers into an *instrument* to achieve the social service goals and objectives of the federal government in addition to being a vehicle for the *expression* of theological beliefs and values. Also, it is reasonable to predict that the new transitional housing program and the partnership with the government agencies will introduce a higher level of *professionalism* to the existing volunteer culture of the Holy Cross social service program. Where professionals and volunteers work side-by-side, there often develops two cultures that are not always in harmony. Lastly, the financial flows associated with the transitional housing program will create a higher level of *resource dependency* that may alter the internal and external relationships of the organization.

MANAGEMENT IMPLICATIONS FOR HOLY CROSS CHURCH AND OTHER FAITH-BASED ORGANIZATIONS

Rev. Healy and his counterparts in other churches and faith-based organizations would be well-advised to carefully consider the non-financial baggage that may accompany federal grants and contracts. One is reminded of the old saw, "Be careful what you wish for, because you just might get it." Here are a few suggestions for faith-based organizations considering such a strategy.

1. Recognize that transformational change will be difficult

Even if only a few of the effects speculated above occur, Rev. Healy and his volunteers will need to embrace the notion of *transformational* change, which will affect not only programmatic agendas, but the core principles and operating philosophies of the organization. This type of change is likely to be traumatic for the organization on many levels, and may take years to accomplish.

2. Religious leaders may need to develop high-level managerial skills to deal with transformational change

Most religious leaders are not likely to possess the substantial managerial skill to lead their organizations through the types of transformational change described above. After all, they are spiritual leaders, not managers. Using a framework developed by Bolman and Deal (1997), transformation change will require a mix of skills including: (a) mastery of the design and implementation of complex organizational structures, flows, and procedures; (b) brilliant insights into worker motivation and human resource management; (c) a keen sense of political management and the role of power in organizational transformation; and (d) a theatrical understanding of the importance of symbolism and how to focus the attention of workers and volunteers on the values and philosophies that are the core of the organization.

3. Religious organizations would be wise to set up separate organizational structures for their government-financed activities

Many, though not all, government-funded programs require grantees and contractors to be formally recognized by the Internal Revenue Service as tax-exempt organizations under Section 501c3 of the Internal Revenue Code. The Bush Administration seems to be ambivalent at best about this requirement, and in fact has urged federal agencies to reexamine their statutory and regulatory practices to allow unincorporated churches and community organizations to compete for federal funds.

Despite the apparent ideological motivations of the Bush administration, there are good reasons to formally and legally separate the religious and charitable activities of faith-based organizations. Rev. Healy should seriously consider establishing a 501c3 organization to run the transitional housing project. A separate incorporation of the housing project might allow Healy to "insulate" his informal volunteer programs from the professionalized and highly public housing project. Such a move would address many aspects of accountability beyond mere compliance with the law.

CONCLUSIONS: POLICY AND RESEARCH IMPLICATIONS

From a policy perspective, the Bush faith-based initiative poses serious questions regarding the separation of church and state. Although faith-based organizations like Catholic Charities and United Jewish Federation have received various types of government funding for many years, there have been protections against the use of government funding for explicitly religious activities. The Charitable Choice provisions of the 1996 Welfare Reform Law put a crack in the wall between religiously-oriented and secular social services. Now, the Bush initiative is trying to pry that crack open to, in his words, "level the playing field" for faith-based and secular agencies competing for federal funds.

The constitutional issues are substantial, and well beyond the scope of this chapter. But the managerial issues are equally important and, in the long term, could have a huge impact on the landscape of social services and charitable activity in the United States. The stakes are high and the risks may outweigh the benefits. In the long run, the faith-based initiative of the Bush Administration may have effects that are quite the opposite of those intended by its designers and proponents, including the following:

The gradual erosion of a rich mosaic of community-based religious organizations that provide needed services to their communities, replaced by a homogenized group of government-funded agencies that may end up behaving much the same as their secular counterparts. The diversity that the Bush agenda purports to promote may actually yield to a creeping conformity of structures, missions, and values.

The gradual devaluation of grassroots volunteer activity in favor of professionalized social services. The community investments and volunteerism that the Bush Administration seems to covet may actually give way to a creeping professionalism and bureaucratization within churches and other small faith-based organizations that obtain federal contracts to deliver social services.

The proliferation of 501c3 organizations with all the administrative and regulatory complications that accompany them. There are already nearly 1 million 501c3 organizations in the nation and some estimates suggest that over 25,000 new 501c3s are formed every year. The IRS cannot possibly regulate these organizations with any real rigor and large donors in the philanthropic community are already complaining that there is redundancy and counter-productive competition within the nonprofit sector.

But these, as well as the other propositions contained in this chapter, are speculative. To date, research on these issues has taken one of two forms:

(1) large surveys of faith-based organizations, which are methodologically incapable of capturing the complex and sometimes subtle changes in organizational culture and character that may accompany federal funding, and

(2) studies conducted by researchers and institutions that are ideologically aligned with the Bush agenda and, therefore, potentially suspect in terms of objectivity.

What is needed are in-depth case studies and careful longitudinal research designs to assess over time whether the propositions expressed above have any merit. Only then will all of us be able to get beyond the ideology and the political rhetoric to explore the real impacts of federal funding on our grass roots religious organizations. I propose that the propositions stated above provide the preliminary hypotheses for such a research design.

URBAN COLLECTIVE GOVERNANCE ORGANIZATIONS

At least twelve U. S. cities have recently established community benefits district (CBD) organizations within their boundaries. The institutional arrangements of these city subdistrict organizations have been outlined but not thoroughly analyzed. In this article, we examine their institutional arrangements, defined here as rules and public policies, and show that how the organizations are institutionally structured affects the way in which they behave.

To accomplish this analysis, we examine and compare the institutional arrangements in four CBDs including Baltimore's Charles Village Community Benefits District (CVCBD), New York's 14th Street – Union Square Business Improvement District, Louisville Downtown Management District (LDMD), and Downtown Cincinnati Improvement District (DCID). Interviews with CBD organizations' executive directors and others knowledgeable about the districts provide data concerning institutional arrangements in each one. The availability of data helped to determine the four organizations examined, although the authors hope to extend the analysis to CBD organizations in additional cities in the future.

CBDs in different cities share common broad institutional arrangements, but their specific arrangements may vary from city to city. Using Baltimore's Charles Village CBD as a model, the following serve as common institutional arrangements in these subdistrict organizations (Baer and Marando 2001):

1. CBDs have the authority from a state legislature and city government to mandate an additional tax assessment levy above city-wide rates, which the city administers on all property owners, commercial and residential, within the subdistrict.
2. CBDs are created only after the service preferences of subdistrict property owners (and sometimes residential tenants who do not own property) are identified and taken into account. A referendum is required to assess property owner and residential tenant support in Baltimore. In other cities, a specified number of signatures meeting a public petition requirement or attendance and participation at city-community sponsored public hearings may be used to assess support for creating CBDs.
3. CBDs are governed by an elected or appointed board whose qualifications are specified by city charter ordinance and in some cases state statute.
4. CBDs have full- and/or part-time professional and non-professional staff to manage the day-to-day operations of the subdistrict. Commonly, CBDs are created to provide primarily "traditional" municipal services such as security and trash removal but might also provide neighborhood organizing and economic revitalization services.

Examples of city subdistrict organizations that levy an additional property tax in return for supplemental public services include Business Improvement Districts (BIDs) and the newer Community Benefits Districts (CBDs). CBDs share a common legal heritage with the BID, a structure that normally taxes and provides services exclusively to commercial property owners. CBDs are the focus of this inquiry. The success of BIDs in meeting the service needs of city merchants stimulated their widespread adoption, and there are now 15,000 BIDs estimated to be in existence in North American cities. The existing literature tends not to recognize that new BID-type arrangements such as CBDs have extended to mixed residential and commercial communities. A CBD is defined as a mixed-use city subdistrict organization whose area property owners, both residential and commercial, pay property taxes in addition to what the city levies in order to receive supplemental public services such as security, sanitation (garbage collection), and economic development.

In this discussion, we define organizational behavior as "the study and application of knowledge about how people, individuals, and groups act in organizations. It does this by taking a *system approach*. That is, it interprets people-organization relationships in terms of the whole person, whole group, whole organization, and whole social system." In other words, when we speak of organizational behavior, we are referring to the actions of the entire organization. We recognize the strong importance and influence of the actions of specific individuals within an organization, but for the purposes of this chapter, we examine organizational actions in a broader sense. However, we indirectly address the behavior of individuals, because organizational actions reflect the decisions of individuals within each organization.

THE EFFECT OF INSTITUTIONAL ARRANGEMENTS ON ORGANIZATIONAL BEHAVIOR IN FOUR COMMUNITY BENEFITS DISTRICTS (CBDS)

Substantial variation in the level of public services delivered to different neighborhoods within any particular city may occur. This fact contrasts with the way cities are often outlined in the literature as offering the same services throughout their territory. In addition, large cities increasingly rely on subdistrict organizations as structural mechanisms to provide tax and service differentiation among residents and businesses that is qualitatively different from informal approaches.

Hawkins, Percy, and Montreal offer findings that support the assumption that decentralized, specialized, and nested governance organizations are part of the "intergovernmental" system of sharing authority and delivering services. Clearly city property owners and possibly residential tenants and merchants who do not own property in a city cannot create a subunit by themselves. A "higher" level local government is necessary for creating subdistrict government. In other words, subcity interests for creating subdistricts need to be "negotiated" with officials representing city interests. And the creation of a city subdistrict such as a CBD is the result of a "compact" or officially sanctioned intergovernmental agreement involving state government as well. Thus, CBD creation reflects the results of a negotiated intergovernmental process between property owners (and residential or commercial tenants in certain cases) on the one hand and city and state officials on the other.

The Charles Village Community Benefits District:

In this section, we examine how the institutional arrangements in four CBD organizations affect organizational behavior. We begin with the Charles Village Community Benefits District (CVCBD) in Baltimore, Maryland. This CBD provides sanitation and safety services. The first institutional arrangement involved the necessity to pass state enabling legislation and a Baltimore city ordinance in order to create the CVCBD. This process of creating the CVCBD involved considerable conflict that ultimately affected the organization's behavior.

Although the proposed benefits district was located in a lower-income area, the Mayor, the city delegation to the General Assembly, and several Baltimore City Council-persons expressed concern that by creating subdistricts the city would become balkanized with white middle-income neighborhoods engaged in an elitist movement to obtain services that exclude lower-income neighborhoods. Several legislators were further concerned that such balkanized subdistricts aimed to promote lifestyle homogeneity through subtle forms of "gating" by placing an additional tax levy on property owners.4 Perhaps officials were concerned, because they believed that subdistrict creation in more affluent areas might also begin to occur. Their concerns motivated city officials to demand that an ordinance establishing subdistricts require that they be both larger in geographic scope and more diverse economically and racially than originally proposed. As a result, the CVCBD's boundaries were enlarged from a 30-block area to a 100-block area before the 1994 Maryland legislative session. Therefore, this institutional arrangement or public policy affected organizational behavior by creating a larger, more diverse district for the organization to manage.

State enabling legislation that authorized the creation of six subdistricts, including the CVCBD, within the City of Baltimore eventually passed in 1994. After passage of state enabling legislation, the Baltimore City Council adopted a local ordinance that created the Charles Village Community Benefits District (CVCBD). The CVCBD was the only subdistrict organization under analysis that experienced substantial conflict in its legislative creation process. The formation of the other districts proceeded fairly smoothly with city government support. This difference might be explained by the fact that the CVCBD's tax base includes a large share of residential property owners while the other subdistricts have a much greater percentage of commercial property owners. As a result of the high residential component in the CVCBD, city officials may have a greater fear of subdistrict balkanization by residents' ethnicity and income than in a district with a higher commercial component. In addition, the organization must manage the district so as to include the interests of a large group of residents as well as businesses.

A second institutional arrangement was a referendum in the proposed area that was a requirement for subdistrict adoption. Unlike the other three subdistrict organizations that petitioned property owners only, the CVCBD allowed both property owners and renters to vote in the referendum. One might explain the CVCBD's use of a referendum that allowed both residential tenants and property owners to vote by the fact that this subdistrict contained a much higher percentage of residents, including renters, than did the other three subdistricts. In such a broad residential community, a referendum might be the most appropriate way to assess support. Also, because residential tenants may be more mobile than owner occupants and may have the ability to easily move out of the CVCBD by "voting with their feet", those designing the subdistrict organization's institutional structure wisely gave this important group an opportunity to vote in the referendum. Thus, the subdistrict's substantial group of renters received a voice in deciding whether and under what conditions to create the subdistrict and hopefully will not choose to exit the district. The effect on organizational behavior of this policy to include renters is that this group is considered when the organization makes decisions, and renters are also allowed to be members of the organization's Board of Directors in addition to property owners.

A thirteen to twenty-five member elected and appointed Board of Directors governs the CVCBD, and the Board serves as the third institutional arrangement. The Board originates from the community-at-large with members representing neighborhoods within the CVCBD and is responsive to the community, acting as its agent in determining policy and procedures. The Board is composed of residents, businesses, appointees of the Mayor and City Council, and non-profit organizations. Up to one-third of the Board members could potentially be residential tenants. This analysis shows that residential tenants are allowed to serve only on the CVCBD and 14th Street – Union Square Business Improvement District Boards, while only property owners are allowed to serve on the LDMD and DCID Boards. This attests to the added political power that renters have in the former two subdistricts where their numbers are much higher than in the latter two. As a result, this institutional arrangement or policy affects the former two organizations' behavior by giving this potentially mobile group of residential tenants added political power and a voice in the direction of the district.

The Board also forms a selection committee to hire an executive director for the CVCBD organization. This executive director then selects additional staff members including a director of safety and an economic development coordinator who then help the executive director choose non-professional safety and clean team workers. The selection process for this professional and non-professional staff serves as the fourth institutional arrangement. The CVCBD is the only subdistrict under examination that is not connected to a broader downtown organization, and, thus, such an organization is not involved in the CVCBD's staffing. In each of the other three CBDs, its broader downtown organization is somehow connected to the CBD's staff. Perhaps these three subdistricts are affiliated with downtown organizations, because they are more BID-like or commercial compared to the more residential CVCBD. Not being connected to a downtown organization for staffing affects the CVCBD's organizational behavior, because it is more concerned with residential issues as a result and is not as concerned with the vitality of downtown businesses and growth as are the other three districts.

New York's 14th Street – Union Square Business Improvement District:

This district has 75 percent commercial properties and 25 percent residential properties. Thus, although it has a higher percentage of commercial properties than the CVCBD that is no more than 50 percent commercial, it is still a mixed-use CBD structure. In fact, it has a higher percentage of residential property owners than do the two remaining districts in this study. As a result, calling itself a Business Improvement District is a misnomer, because this name implies that only commercial property owners pay additional taxes for supplemental services. In the 14th Street district, however, both residential and commercial property owners pay for these extra services.

Like the CVCBD, this subdistrict's first institutional arrangement was the necessity to pass state enabling legislation and a local city ordinance. However, unlike the case of the Baltimore CVCBD, the legislative process to form this New York subdistrict was not filled with conflict. The state of New York passed enabling legislation that allowed the local city council to create the CBD and allow tax assessment in the area. The district was created in 1984, the first of its kind to form in New York City. The effect of this first institutional arrangement on organizational behavior was that this CBD did not have to tailor its management style to deal with the conflictual issues faced by the Baltimore CBD such as district boundary expansion and the related concern over residential balkanization by ethnicity and income.

Then, the second institutional arrangement or policy involved the requirement that property owners sign a petition favoring the creation of the improvement district. The petition was successful. If fifty percent or more of affected property owners had objected to improvement district creation, it would have been unable to form. Tenants were not involved in the petition, because state laws and local ordinances say that property owners are the only ones who may form BIDs. Thus, compared to the Baltimore CVCBD, the 14th Street district is less inclusive in its creation process since it does not involve tenants. As a result, one might expect the organization to behave in a manner that does not take account of tenants to the same degree as the CVCBD.

The third institutional arrangement, a twenty-five voting member Board of Directors, currently governs the district. All Board members except four government officials are elected at the annual meeting. The four government officials are eligible to be on the Board through statute/legislation. Fifty-one percent of Board members must be property owners. And at least one member must be a residential tenant, although up to forty-nine percent of Board members could technically be residential tenants. Thus, tenants do have representation on the Board, although this representation might be very small. As previously stated, allowing tenants on the Board affects the organization's behavior, because it means that tenants as well as property owners will have a voice and influence in managing the district. As a result, the organization needs to take the preferences of tenants into account.

The Board of Directors then selects an executive director to run the organization. The executive director in turn selects district staff. The organization provides sanitation and safety services. Under this fourth institutional arrangement of staffing, five persons including the executive director hold full-time professional administrative positions in both the improvement district and the 14th Street – Union Square Local Development Corporation (LDC). The LDC is a downtown organization that focuses on stimulating development, improving Union Square Park, and enhancing the quality of life in the neighborhood through efforts to make the neighborhood cleaner and safer. The 14th Street district's policy of being connected to a downtown organization reflects the fact that this CBD has a more commercial composition than does the CVCBD. Because the 14th Street CBD's executive director works for both the LDC and the CBD, the latter's organizational behavior should take into account the needs of businesses more than the CVCBD that is not connected to a downtown organization.

The Louisville Downtown Management District:

The Louisville Downtown Management District (LDMD) began operation in 1992 and provides supplemental maintenance, marketing, and crime prevention services in a 61-block area of the central business district. The district is composed of approximately ninety percent commercial property and ten percent residential property. Similar to the previous two CBD organizations, the

LDMD's first institutional arrangement involved passage of state enabling legislation and a City of Louisville ordinance in order to form the district. But, again, unlike the Baltimore case, the creation of the LDMD proceeded fairly smoothly. Local officials including the mayor and Board of Aldermen favored the creation of the district. In fact, creating the LDMD was part of the city's ten-year plan. This lack of conflict affected the CBD's organizational behavior, because it did not have to deal with divisive boundary issues or divided constituencies, both of which make daily management more difficult.

In early 1992, after passage of state enabling legislation and a city council ordinance, local business persons went door to door asking property owners only to sign a petition in favor of creating the district. The use of a petition serves as the second institutional arrangement. Unlike the CVCBD, tenants in the LDMD were not involved in the petition to form the district and are not on the district's Board of Directors. According to the executive director, they are not involved, because state statute does not require that they be involved. Because tenants were not involved in the petition process or other structural processes of the CBD such as re-authorization, organizational behavior is impacted in the sense that the CBD does not have to consider their preferences when making its management decisions.

A third key component of the LDMD's institutional structure is its Board of Directors. A seventeen member Board governs the district. Some Board members such as the district commander of the police department are automatically appointed, while others are elected. One residential property owner is required to be on the Board. Board members serve a three-year term. Unlike in the CVCBD and the 14th Street district, residential tenants are not allowed to be LDMD Board members. This policy affects the LDMD's organizational behavior. Because residential tenants are not on the Board, they lack power in directing the organization. Thus, the CBD does not need to take their interests into account as much as do the prior two districts.

The final policy involves the organization's hiring of professional and non-professional staff. The LDMD provides both sanitation and safety services. In selecting an executive director, a search committee first gives its recommendation to the LDMD Board. If the Board approves the candidate for the position, the person is hired. Related to this fourth institutional arrangement is the LDMD's management by the Louisville Central Area, Inc. (LCA), a major research agency for downtown organizations and city government and a downtown development organization with the task of enhancing business life. The LCA manages the LDMD separately from the LDMD Board of Directors and covers the entire downtown consisting of 102 blocks. LCA's fiscal responsibilities include developing an annual LDMD budget, monitoring property assessment collections by the City's Department of Finance and Budget, preparing and providing monthly cash flow statements to the LDMD Board of Directors, maintaining and storing LDMD financial records, and coordinating an annual audit. The involvement of a downtown business organization is most likely linked to the highly commercial nature of the LDMD. This downtown agency's involvement that includes management of the CBD affects the LDMD's organizational behavior, because such control makes the CBD more likely to favor policies that will enhance commercial rather than residential interests.

Downtown Cincinnati Improvement District:

The Downtown Cincinnati Improvement District (DCID) began operation in 1998 and consists of 330 property owners. It is a revitalization district, providing mainly business development services, although it also provides sanitation and security services. Similar to the LDMD, its properties are approximately ninety percent commercial and ten percent residential. Thus, both of these districts are more BID-like than the CVCBD or the 14th Street district, but they are still classified as CBDs since they assess an additional property tax to both commercial and residential property owners within their boundaries.

Its creation was also not conflict ridden like the CVCBD creation. In this organization, the first and second institutional arrangements are interconnected. State enabling legislation to form subdistricts had been passed in the Ohio legislature in the early 1990s, and Dayton was the first city in Ohio to form one. Thus, the path was clear to form the DCID in terms of state legislation.

The next step involved getting downtown property owners to sign a petition in favor of creating the subdistrict. In November 1996, downtown property owners were asked to sign a petition for the adoption of DCID's Downtown Services Plan listing the services to be offered and how much to spend on these services as well as a budget. At least sixty percent of front footage property owners were required to sign the petition, and the petition was a success with sixty-two percent actually signing. Tenants were excluded from signing the petition. City Council then approved the DCID and its services plan in December 1996.

The process to create the DCID differs from the other three subdistrict organizations, because property owners in the DCID first signed a petition before city council approved the district's creation. In the other subdistricts, a city council ordinance favoring subdistrict creation was required before either a petition or referendum could occur.

As a result, organizational behavior is affected, because those initiating the creation of the organization first had to lobby property owners within district boundaries before lobbying the city. In addition, because the institutional structure did not allow tenants to sign the petition, the organizational behavior of those managing the district is most likely affected as these managers do not need to be as accountable to tenants to the degree they would need to be if tenants served as a powerful political force in forming the district.

The third institutional component is the DCID's Board of Trustees that consists of nine members, four appointed and five elected. The four appointed members include the city manager, a city council appointee, a Hamilton County representative, and a representative from the Building Owner and Management Association (BOMA).

Thus, local government officials have a substantial role on the Board and influence in managing the district. As a result, the CBD must consider the desires of these officials when making its daily operational decisions. At least one of the five elected Board members must be a residential property owner, so residential property owners receive at least a small share of power on the Board. However, the district excludes tenants from serving on the

Board of Directors. Therefore, tenants lack a voice in governing the organization, and the CBD Board and staff do not need to devote much consideration to the preferences of tenants as a result.

The final institutional arrangement to be considered is staffing. Since DCID itself hires no staff and instead has only volunteers, the Board's relationship to DCID's employees flows through Downtown Cincinnati, Inc. (DCI), a downtown advocacy organization established in 1994 as a result of the city's loss of retail tenants. Donations from major corporations in the city and tri-state area fund DCI's operation.

To acquire employees, the CBD Board hires or contracts with DCI. The president of DCI then runs the CBD organization and hires its employees. The staff includes ten professional, full-time employees and nine non-professional clean team and safety team employees. Because the president of DCI, a downtown business organization, directly hires CBD employees, it is likely that these employees will focus more on commercial or business interests than on residential ones.

DISCUSSION AND IMPLICATIONS:

Overall, the current inquiry shows that CBDs share four similar broad institutional arrangements outlined earlier in the chapter, and that these arrangements or policies affect organizational behavior. However, several key differences exist in the institutional arrangements of the four CBDs under analysis, and these differences affect policy implementation.

First, the CVCBD is the only organization to require a referendum for subdistrict creation. The other three CBD organizations instead use a petition. Second, residential tenants as well as property owners are able to vote in the CVCBD's referendum, while the former group is not allowed to sign petitions in the other three subdistricts. Third, up to one third of the CVCBD's Board of Directors may be renters, and up to forty-nine percent of the 14th Street – Union Square Business Improvement District's Board members may be renters. In contrast, both the LDMD and DCID allow only property owners to be Board members. The first difference in institutional arrangements may be the result of the

CVCBD's position as a subdistrict with a greater balance between residential and commercial property owners. In fact, in order to create the CVCBD, organizers demanded that the subdistrict boundaries include a balanced mixed-use area. By way of contrast, the LDMD and the DCID developed in heavily commercial downtown areas with only a very small portion of residential property. The 14th Street – Union Square Business Improvement District lies between the two extremes in terms of its mix of residential and commercial properties. Thus, a referendum may prove more conducive in the CVCBD as a method to gauge a broader array of residents' support for the organization, and petitions may be more amenable for use in the heavily commercial districts.

In terms of the second and third difference, one finds that only the CVCBD and the 14th Street – Union Square Business Improvement District are institutionally required to be accountable to renters. Unlike the other three subdistrict organizations, the CVCBD allows renters to vote in the referendum along with property owners. And both the CVCBD and the 14th Street – Union Square Business Improvement District allow a substantial proportion of their Board of Directors to be residential tenants. As a result, residential tenants have a potentially strong voice in both the creation and operation of the CVCBD and in the operation of the 14th Street – Union Square Business Improvement District, but they lack such a voice in the other CBD organizations. Again, this is most likely due to the fact that renters compose a larger group in both the CVCBD and the 14th Street – Union Square Business Improvement District. And because renters may generally be mobile, these two subdistrict organizations designed institutional arrangements to give members of this group a voice so they would not move out of their subdistricts.

As a result of this analysis, we find that the CVCBD and 14th Street-Union Square Business Improvement District are more inclusive, because they are accountable to renters. This inclusiveness affects the two organizations' policy implementation in a favorable way, because the two CBDs take account of renters, an important part of their constituent base, in addition to property owners. Because the other two CBDs' institutional rules do not mandate that they be accountable to renters, they are less inclusive which may negatively impact their policy implementation. However, because the number of renters within their boundaries is so small, this lack of inclusion does not create as great a problem as it would in districts with a larger base of renters.

CBDs have the potential to stabilize areas containing both residents and businesses. If all areas of the city are able to form subdistricts, a CBD's obvious benefits may outweigh potential abuses involving exclusion or balkanization. If city property owners and possibly residential tenants do not form CBDs and, therefore, do not receive needed and desired supplemental services, they may find themselves living and working in areas that are becoming more and more unstable. Or they may simply decide to "exit" the city for the suburbs consistent with the polycentric model. Alternatively, through "voice" CBDs with the potential to help stabilize and prevent population decline and business closures in the inner city may be created, and these CBDs may even attract new residents and businesses from outside the city. Because many inner cities continue to experience instability, population loss, and business closures, CBDs may serve as a structural policy option to aid in stemming these trends.

13

The Development of Nongovernmental Organizations

CENTRAL AND EASTERN EUROPE UNDER SOVIET DOMINATION

The implementation of soviet communism in Central and Eastern Europe resulted in the transformation of the existing political, economic and social structures of the region, including the virtual elimination of all nongovernmental organizations (NGOs). Under the new soviet regimes, all political, economic and social activities were controlled by a totalitarian state dominated by a single party. The communists sought to establish a new social order in which private property and competition were abolished, money and credit were centralized in the hands of the state, and all children were educated by the state.

In establishing this new social order, the soviets radically changed the existing social capital of the Central and Eastern European countries. The soviet system changed the informal norms within Central and Eastern European societies by replacing them with formal norms – new rules and laws decreed by the state without popular participation and consent. Sovietization was forced on largely unwilling populations through the restriction of political debate and the expansion of the soviet security apparatus. The soviet system, which bound the soviet-dominated nations of Central and Eastern Europe and guided their political, economic and social development during the course of more than seventy years, was instituted by the soviets using an extraordinarily brutal paradigm of an onslaught of mass terror, succeeded by generalized terror and subsequently held in place through selective repression.

Excessive force and mass terror were used to eliminate anyone who "displayed an independent mind about public affairs" and it was used to establish soviet control in all of the countries that came under soviet domination. Generalized terror was used to further eliminate anyone capable of challenging the soviet regime, to dissolve existing social relationships and to completely subordinate the individual to the state.

The soviet state aim was to break society down into a collection of individuals, which acted "collectively only when mobilized by party and government." It sought to control every unit of social life, consciously seeking even the disintegration of family loyalty; the soviet state was to supersede all else, and the individual was to become an accessory of the state.

The soviet state targeted all of those viewed as potential opponents of the soviet system – former government officials, former army officers, soldiers, former members of the judiciary, former police officers, former political party members, active members of student organizations, landlords, merchants, bankers, businessmen, wealthier farmers, anyone who had fought against the soviets, and anyone resisting collectivization, industrial-ization, and secularization of society – as well as their families, colleagues, friends and neighbors.

Constant fear of repression, the soviet demand for "not only submission, but also complicity" and progressive soviet subversion of previously existing social ties, spurred an increasing sense of isolation among the soviet dominated peoples and succeeded in obliterating a general sense of trust within the soviet-conquered societies.

Once the general population of a country had been terrified into submission and was too fearful to oppose the soviet regime, selective repression was used to maintain that fear. Anyone willing to overtly challenge the soviet regime was condemned. Dissent was punished. Privacy disappeared as the state encouraged people to monitor and report on their neighbors, friends, and even family members. Consequently, trust eroded; conversations became guarded; and, associations faded. As the soviet state strove to increasingly control both the public and private spheres of life, the soviet dominated peoples learned to avoid even the appearance of having independent opinions, to fear showing initiative, and to live with a "deeply ingrained sense of impotence, because of the official power of retaliation, and the assertive intrusion of officialdom with personal lives."

The sovietization process was, in many ways, analogous to battering. Batterers seek control of their victims through the exertion of excessive force, or an unusual amount of control over their victim's activities, finances, contacts with others. Usually, there is a determining event that convinces the victim that the batterer can cause them tremendous harm, and the fear that it generates forms the foundation of the batterer's control over his victim. Once a victim believes that they are in imminent danger from the batterer, the victim lives in constant fear of incurring the batterer's wrath, of enduring another violent episode, and strives to protect themselves and their family by learning to censure their speech and actions in accordance to the batterer's demands. The batterer's control over the victim is maintained through explicit or implicit threats of harm. This battering paradigm is shown by the Power and Control Wheel presented below.

The effect of sovietization is also analogous to battering; in both cases, targets are subjected to prolonged victimage, and exhibit signs of post traumatic stress – fear, helplessness, horror. Both paradigms create an imbalance of power in which the target is made dependent on the dominant entity for survival. In both cases, the target is made to feel powerless. Fear, despair, distrust, a sense of isolation and depression characterized early soviet society to the point that even the closest of personal relationships were subordinated to obedience to the state; battered victims live in fear, isolation and depression. Soviet terror pushed Central and Eastern European populations into a state of depression and apathy; battered victims live with a sense of helplessness and defeat. Just as the batterer seeks to control his victim through complete dominance, so did sovietization implement totalitarianism in which "the state breaks down the barrier between public and private spheres to control not only the outward flow of social life, but the inner lives of individuals."

The imbalance of power established through the soviet policy of terror was institutionalized politically, economically and socially, giving way to the development of a "suspicion-ridden, corrupt, and exploited new society . . . living in a state of fear and frustration." It had an important impact on how societies under soviet rule were structured politically, economically and socially; on how their social capital developed, and on the type of human capital (skills, etc.) that was fostered.

The soviet state created and controlled all social organizations, using them to indoctrinate, monitor and control the soviet-dominated populations. Unlike any natural community, soviet society was an "artificial social unit" – planned, deliberately structured and constantly monitored. Due to its artificial nature, the structure of soviet society was quite complex. Each of its subsystems was developed as a virtual replica of the central system and each of its members subject to a distinct hierarchy of authority. The soviet social structure was constructed so that each social unit, down to the individual, was effectively an auxiliary of the state, controlled by the center through edicts enforced by the secret police. Thus, soviet society was structured as a formal organization and its culture was formed, transmitted and enforced through formal mechanisms.

The soviet system was a self-reinforcing and self-perpetuating system in which political, economic and social policies were closely intertwined and used to promote subservience, compliance, conformity, uniformity, and passiveness in soviet-dominated populations. The soviet political system shaped and controlled the economy and society. All soviet-based societies were state-funded and state-organized. The government assigned jobs, paid salaries, determined production quotas, issued payments for production resources, allotted apartments, cars, systemized education, social clubs and health care. The individual was made completely dependent on the soviet state for survival.

Over time, people born into the soviet system had little or no knowledge of alternative political, economic or social structures. Their perception of how government, the economy and society function was formed by the soviet system itself. Daily existence taught them how to function within a system that fostered uniformity, conformity, subservience, passiveness, and discouraged individual initiative. Isolated from the rest of the world, people living under soviet domination were

"expected to join what Havel's friend Ivan Klima called the 'community of the defeated,' and to abide by its basic rules: that there would only ever be one governing party, to which everything, including truth itself, belonged; that the world was divided into enemies and friends of the Party, and accordingly, that compliance with the Party policies was rewarded, dissent penalized; and, finally, that the Party no longer required the complete devotion of its subjects, only the quiet acceptance of its dictates."

For nearly five decades, the people of Central and Eastern Europe lived in command societies in which most social, political and economic decisions were made for them, and individual initiative was discouraged. Their societies were dominated by a single party which controlled all resources and employment opportunities, controlled social interaction, controlled the availability of information, controlled freedom of movement, and used its economic power to promote "correct attitudes among the masses, by inducing conformity of thought and action." They managed their affairs within a narrow scope of approved activity, with no freedom of association, and no real possibility of forming nongovernmental organizations.

DEMOCRATIZATION AND THE DEVELOPMENT OF NONGOVERNMETAL ORGANIZATIONS (NGOS) IN POST-COMMUNIST CENTRAL AND EASTERN EUROPE

The collapse of communism in Central and Eastern Europe released the fifty-year soviet grip on the region and the process of transforming the countries into democracies with market-dominated economic systems began. New constitutions replaced those implemented during soviet rule in the region, creating legal frameworks for the development of democratic societies. Laws and institutional structures were changed, and soon the basic hallmarks of democratic societies – the right of association, freedom of assembly, numerous political parties, free elections, the rule of law, and peaceful transfers of power – were acknowledged and evident in the post-communist Central and Eastern European countries. Changes in laws and institutions eliminated some of the former structures and relationships that existed in the soviet system - multi-party systems replaced the single-party soviet political system and people regained the right of association, freedom of assembly, and freedom of movement - but in and of themselves, these changes did not transform the post-soviet Central and Eastern European countries into democracies. Many of the countries experienced partial democratization; formal democratic procedures and institutions have been introduced, but everyday practice lacks the democratic spirit.

By 1997, it was clear that "economic and democratic reform were complementary and heavily correlated," when the Freedom House Nations in Transit 1997 rankings showed that the Central and Eastern European countries that were guided by the rule of law and were successfully consolidating their market economies, were also making progress in their transitions to democracy. Less clear was that the transition from an authoritarian system of rule to a democratic system also depends on the emergence of a strong nongovernmental organization (NGO) sector. NGOs serve three vital roles in democracies: they convey public opinion to lawmakers formulating public policy; they advise the public of public policies and serve as an instrument of policy implementation; and finally, they independently fund and deliver services. In post-communist Central and Eastern Europe, the emergence of NGOs marked a shift from the previously existing balance of power in which the State was the dominating entity upon which citizens depended for survival, to one more conducive to a partnership between citizens and State; a shift away from totalitarianism toward a democratic form of governance.

Interestingly, despite the abundance of NGOs in the post-communist Central and Eastern European countries, the effectiveness of the NGO sectors in post-communist Central and Eastern Europe remained underdeveloped. This was due in part to the legislation passed with regard to the third sector, and in part due to the expectations of the NGOs themselves; in pushing for government funding, the NGOs remained closely tied to the government, rather than forming a truly independent sector. Many Central and East European governments tried to develop an adequate legal and institutional framework for the NGO sector (Romania, Poland, Hungary, Lithuania), but initially there seemed to be an undue emphasis in forming NGO/Government partnerships, in which NGOs were funded from the state budget (International Center for Not-For Profit Law, undated) and operated with a high degree of government oversight.

In light of the previous soviet-imposed system, this is not surprising. In the soviet system, state funds had been used to underwrite every official aspect of society, and to eradicate all that which was not state-sanctioned.

The soviet system had discouraged innovation, experimentation, as well as independence of action and thought, and had fostered subservience, compliance, passiveness, uniformity and conformity. While the fall of communism in Central and Eastern Europe disturbed the existing status quo, the soviet culture of dominance and dependence did not disappear with the soviet system. As would be expected, those in power continued to hold on to it, protecting the rights and privileges that the soviet system had provided them.

Those used to being dependent on the government continued to cling to it for support. And finally, by attaching NGOs to the government, each side took out a form of insurance – the government effectively maintained control, while the new NGOs gained a sense of security, because they were clearly government-sanctioned. This interdependence slowed the development of civil society and democracy in post-soviet societies.

As the NGO sectors continued to evolve in the post-communist countries, their very existence contributed to the process of democratization. Those post-communist countries that have encouraged the growth of the NGO sector (Lithuania, Latvia, Estonia, Hungary) over the past decade have made tremendous progress toward becoming democratic societies in a relatively short span of time. Those countries in the post-communist region that have actively quashed their NGO sector through legislation (e.g., Belarus), have progressed little along the path to becoming democratic societies.

The World Democracy Audit shows that Lithuania, Latvia, Estonia, Czech Republic, Hungary, Poland and Slovakia rank among the 34 countries that are listed as "unquestionably free," while Bulgaria and Romania are classed as "free but with a distance to go" (based on Lindley 2002 and World Audit 2002). Democratization has not progressed as far in the countries of the Confederation of Independent States (CIS). Russia ranks far below the post-communist Central and Eastern European countries, at 101 on the list of countries audited, but ranks ahead of seven other former soviet republics (Azerbaijan, Belarus, Kazakhstan, Kyrgyzstan, Tajikistan, Turkmenistan, Ukraine, and Uzbekistan). Moldova is the only one of the CIS countries that ranks among the "free, but with a distance to go" countries.

STRENGTHENING THE NGO SECTOR IN CENTRAL AND EASTERN EUROPE

Developing adequate legal and institutional frameworks for their NGO sectors is an important step in developing a climate conducive to private initiative and the growth and development of the third sector in post-communist Central and Eastern European countries. Equally important is the development of public policies specifically geared toward undoing the soviet legacy of subservience, compliance, passiveness, uniformity and conformity, and the development of policies that return power to the people, creating a solid partnership between citizens and State. Koestenbaum (1991) provides a simple formula for empowerment:

Empowerment (E) is the product of autonomy (A), direction (D), and support (S), or

E = A x D x S

To promote *autonomy,* the Central and Eastern European governments should focus on projects that come from the initiatives of their citizens, rather than trying to create NGOs that fulfill government initiatives. In terms of *direction,* more than anything else, governments should pave the way for philanthropy by creating tax incentives (i.e. income tax deductions) for individuals and enterprises to support NGOs financially. Income tax deductions for charitable giving would make plain that the government respects individual choice, and encourages philanthropy. They would also serve to decentralize the current system in place in several countries (e.g., Hungary) where the government allows individuals to designate one percent of their personal income tax to the civil sector (only to NGOs that meet the government's beneficiary criteria) and an additional one percent to churches, which the government then distributes. Note the difference between this practice, and those of old democracies, such as the United States, where funds are given directly by the donor to his or her NGO of choice and a tax deduction subsequently taken. Finally, government should *support* the third sector by providing tax relief to NGOs, particularly public benefit organizations.

CONCLUSION

Public policy continues to impact organizational behavior in Central and Eastern Europe, because as the state sector shrinks in Central and Eastern Europe, room for NGOs expands. By taking themselves out of the third sector, Central and Eastern European governments will create a political climate more conducive to private initiative and to the growth and development of NGOs. NGOs will form a true third sector – a sector active between the state sphere and the market sphere – and increasingly involve citizens in democracy through active participation. NGOs will also be free to convey public opinion to lawmakers formulating public policy; advise the public of public policies and serve as instruments of policy implementation; and, independently fund and deliver services. This, in turn, will increase democracy in post-communist Central and Eastern Europe.

14

Rogue Corporations, Corporate Rogues and Ethics Compliance

SOCIOPATHOLOGY

The Sarbanes-Oxley Act was one year old on July 30, 2002. Promulgated by Congress as statute and signed into law by President Bush after the corporate scandals of 2002, *"this law says to every American: there will not be a different ethical standard for corporate America than the standard that applies to everyone else. The honesty you expect in your small businesses, or in your workplaces, in your community or in your home, will be expected and enforced in every corporate suite in this country."* Its aim is deterrence—"[to] *adopt tough new provisions to deter and punish corporate and accounting fraud and corruption*". Sarbanes Oxley is the most sweeping attempt to regulate and make ethical public markets since the Securities and Exchange Act of 1934. The Sarbanes-Oxley Act has two broad categories: accounting oversight, and corporate governance.

Within these domains is regulatory guidance on CEO/CFO accountability, audit committees, external auditor independence, corporate governance and increased financial disclosure transparency. In setting these standards, this Act adopts a new standard for corporate financial reporting accuracy.

Titles VIII, IX, and XI, which cover white-collar crimes are the criminal enforcement tools that attach liability to senior leadership for violating reporting requirements. While this is a necessary condition for corporate responsibility, it is insufficient. Public policy, merely addresses the manifestations of corporate social pathology. The cause itself lies in the stickier region of institutional visions, values and beliefs, as modeled by the top executives in corporations. Addressing these issues will be a longer-term effort to change cultures, shared meanings about profit and loss, and social responsibility that must be spearheaded by the highest levels of corporate governance.

How well has Sarbanes Oxley performed to date to mitigate or outright prevent corporate fraud and create a climate for corporate ethics? A look at the issue a year later in this chapter reveals complexities and unintended consequences of trying to regulate morality in business.

At the same time, it must be stated that it would be naïve to think that that the issue of corporate roguery can be looked at through the simple frame of pure *theoretical* ethics—where it is easy to distinguish between right and wrong. Rather, to talk about corporate ethics is to encompass it in its *applied* state—namely, a multi-dimensional field replete with many voices, value quandaries, moral mazes, complexities and rapid change. The companies such as Enron and WorldCom, whose actions catapulted the Sarbanes Oxley Act, 2002 into life, had fundamental cultural problems viz., corporate cultures that operated on the basis of one set of values to which they gave lip service, while in actual organizational practice, the structures and processes reflected a different set of values.

CORPORATE SOCIAL RESPONSIBILITY

The Problem of Leadership

Leaders set the tone for the organization and the culture of the organization develops primarily via the executive's vision, values, and morality. Sociologist Robert Jackall (1988) argues that characteristics of CEO personality and behavior filter down all the way to the shop floor,. Legal writing in this area is in agreement, "Top Management, and in particular the chief executive officer ... set the corporate ethical tone". Also, in this context, Peter Drucker (1973) has suggested that managers being professionals, must be guided by the *"do no harm"* principle as their first responsibility. Drucker sees the executive as wearing a "*badg*e" of distinction and privilege. As such, he or she can be held to a higher standard, and should expect a heftier punishment for wrongdoing.

Ralph Nader has labeled the latest corporate criminal behavior as "*greed on steroids*". How can such colossal greed be punished? Stiff financial penalties and long jail terms have been recommended. In addition, there are arguments in the legal literature for "*reintegrative shaming*"–a process by which the criminal himself/herself acknowledges wrongdoing and pledges corrective action. Theatrical-style shaming, in the presence of the national media, with enough drama and pageantry could be very useful as effective deterrence for white-collar rogues. The very anticipation of shaming, and of one's family being embarrassed in the community might by itself, be a restraining instrument for greed. Barnard argues that public shaming, in courts, directed at individual corporate CEOs who commit wrongs is particularly effective. Edward Rock has noted that public disgrace shows such individuals up to their small, close-knit, rarefied community-of-interest, where "*the role of reputation is significant.*"

There is also argument in the legal literature in favor of shaming members of a corporation's Board of Directors, and sentencing them along with the executive management. This is because these board members implicitly accept the obligation to ensure that their companies conduct their businesses ethically and comply with legal standards. Thus, their culpability should be acknowledged as well.

Others present the counter claim that unless something really egregious is occurring that is clearly visible, these board members may not be able to *detect* wrongdoing. To this one might point out that via the evaluations they make of executive personnel, the standards they set for the institution, and the policies they instigate, they can do much to improve the corporate culture and to reduce organizational wrongdoing.

Another suggestion for board-level governance is to have it set up an ethics and policy subcommittee to alert itself to, as well as to inoculate against, wrongdoing. This committee can be similar to others that already exist on many Boards of Directors—subcommittees on the environment, on personnel, health and safety issues, for example come to mind.

The Problem of Structure

Corporations set up systems in which certain practices are encouraged, and people are pressured to do things they might not ordinarily do. For Manuel Velasquez, the issue of corporate ethics is a *systemic* matter and not a matter of *individual* character flaws. *"Unethical practices arise when corporations fail to pay explicit attention to the ethical risks that are created by their own systems and practices."* In such systems the culture is so structured that management finds it easy to provide rationalizations for deviant demands. Lower functionaries feel pressured into doing things (in the name of the business) that they would not otherwise do. The problem is not a new one, nor is it limited to Enron, WorldCom, Quest, Adelphia, etc. Because of the breadth and scope of these recent scandals, one might easily forget that the last century was beset with indictments of big business for ethical violations. Most of these arose, like Enron, from a *"culture of corruption."* The culture of corruption begins as a small act of stretching a fact or two about products or revenues. *"Little lies grow into bigger ones* and such stretches of truth eventually get out of hand and turn into big problems. *"Corporate cultures condition people to think that it's alright to lie. One little lie, deemed to be innocent, grows—and then one day an Enron happens."*

The Game of Managed Mendacities

Business has long been likened to a game. This game played out in the competitive arena uses sports analogies and other gaming activities, with rules of its own, say analysts. In his 1968 *Harvard Business Review* classic, Albert Carr suggests some businessmen believe that since all players know the game, and if bluffing is part of the game, then bluffing is ethical in this context. Like bluffing in a game of poker, such deception does not *"[seem to] reflect on the morality of the bluffer."* British statesman, Henry Taylor suggested "falsehood ceases to be falsehood when it is understood on all sides that the truth is not expected to be spoken" (*ibid*). However, "all players" in this context really means all the *major* players, and not necessarily the rank-and-file employees who are the ones truly hurt by the deceptions. Robert Jackall suggests that rules-in-use are contextual and situational guidelines and are "the ropes to skip and ropes to know" in a modern corporation.

These become the social morality, or the business ethic that guides the organization through its quandaries and vicissitudes. In a multinational global environment, most of these quandaries involve competition, success, and marketshare. Bluffing, and other deception in this environment become everyday rules-to-know. Nevertheless, misleading statements about financial losses twist reality and damage the public trust.

The sour mood of the investment market can only be reversed when the public get concrete examples from CEOs that they are moving from hoaxing to honesty, *"along with real changes in corporations that address compensation and accounting."* Looking at this dynamic through a Johari Window the cell showing Public Information (openly disclosed information) would be miniscule in Enron's case. In contrast the same Johari Window would show the Private Information Window (Known to Self and Unknown to Others) as a vast domain, wherein managed mendacity typical nestles down. Carr's argument concludes by arguing that bluffing is another way of saying that someone is lying, and such deception is to be avoided in business at any cost,.

Another issue concerns prevarications, ambiguities, exaggeration and concealment that are common forms of business behavior when it comes to product/service promotion and advertising. Here reality, not to mention, morality and ethics, seem again to be discarded with impunity. Much advertisement today is based on illusion, or tongue-in-cheek, inevitably employed to mislead. We, the public, accept these "falsehoods" and have become almost immune to their (so called) *ironies* and we are consequently misled with impunity. In the case of Enron's purposeful mendacity, to create the illusion of financial stability, the deception was planned via stages. Double-speak was employed—but not in one fell swoop. Rather, *"they concocted their stories carefully, neither stretching too much at a time."* Thus, *"their reports seemed reasonable, directionally right. Falsehoods concealed among accurate facts."* Enron did not see this as conspiring. It was merely "managing its earnings". This was done of course by communication that *"fostered the illusion of exploding cash flow," and, as noted by Mitchell, it "...is the new American corporate creed: maximize stock price. This is a norm of behavior that is not legally mandated, [and] is only the product of the last several decades, and, as we have seen and may continue to see, is very bad for business."*

Has the policy intervention helped make corporations accountable by promoting new ethical standards, and correlated corporate structures to meet compliance? We turn now to results of 3 surveys that give a barometer for how the Sarbox is influencing corporate social responsibility in terms of: (1) New ethical standards; (2) Corporate structures to meet the new standards; and, (3) Costs of compliance.

THE IMPACTS OF SARBANES OXLEY

Survey Data on Current Corporate Ethical Climate

This legislation is only a year old, hence, definitive studies do not exist that directly show the impact of Sarbanes-Oxley on ethics in corporate life. However, good indirect measures can be utilized from the general business climate vis-à-vis ethical standards. For the purposes of this chapter, the periodic National Business Ethics Survey (NBES) data is being used. NBES does periodic surveys on the larger business environment, and its 2000 survey, which was pre-Sarbanes-Oxley, can be compared to its survey in 2003 after the law was promulgated.

The NBES survey asked employees in the 48 contiguous states to share their views on ethics within their corporations, using specific questions. These have been combined to show how organizations distinguish between ethical and non-ethical behavior, management actions and influence, decisionmaking, and values like honesty and respect. The survey of 1,500 participants specifically focused upon the following categories:

Interpretation of Findings

Management appears to have become more ethical in 2003 as compared to 2000. The difference could be imputed to the Sarbox policy intervention. Employees also noted that "actions count", i.e., when management actually models ethical behavior, versus just simply talking about ethics. Here observed misconduct was shown at 15% when management is proactive, versus 56% when management merely paid lip service to ethical standards.

The availability of formal ethical programs in an organization has the effect of higher reporting of misconduct. Conversely when there are written standards + one other category in place reporting goes down to 67%. When there are written standards only it was 52%, and when there were no programs reporting was low at 39%.

Table: Impact of Organizational Size on Ethics Programs, 2003

Categories	Large Orgs. (500+)	Small Orgs.(-500)
Training	67%	41%
Anonymous Reporting Mechanisms	77%	47%

Interpretation of Findings:

Size apparently matters in terms of the breadth and scope of organizational ethics programs that can be provided and larger companies show higher reporting rates than smaller companies with fewer ethics programs.

Table: Types of Organizational Intimidating Tactics, 2003

Abusive/Intimidating Behavior	21%
Misreporting of Hours Worked	20%
Lying	19%
Withholding Needed Information	18%

Interpretation of Findings:

Overall 3 additional useful findings arise from this survey.

(1) Nearly 1/3 of respondents say that tacit agreements with questionable practices still exist. They impute this by organizational respect bestowed upon those who achieve success by using such tactics. However, this is likely to be reduced as more companies fall under the penalties of Sarbox.

(2) Another useful finding was that younger managers (under age 30) with less than 3 years tenure in the organization are twice as likely to feel pressure to compromise ethics standards.

(3) Finally less than 3 in 5 employees (58%) who report misconduct are satisfied with the response of their organizations.

Survey Data On Compliance Strategies: A was survey undertaken in June 2003 by PeopleSoft and Business Finance Magazine which involved more than 880 Chief Financial Officers and senior Information Technology executives about their corporate strategies designed to comply with Sarbox. Responses were elicited in the following categories:

Organizational implementation or evaluation of a compliance project: Results reveal that 86% of respondents were engaged in either evaluating or implementing a compliance project. Out of these 56 % were planning to implement a project in the next 6 months.

Importance Placed Upon x404: Section 404 requires business process audits and documentation to support internal controls certification. In response, 71% of respondents believed that this is the most important part of the Sarbanes-Oxley Act.

Need for Process Improvements: Respondents believed by an overwhelming margin of 65% that process improvements in how financial data is managed as mandated by Sarbanes Oxley will increase business efficiencies and competitive advantage.

Organizational Perceived Need for Upgrade of Compliance Systems: In order to achieve compliance 40% of survey respondents believed that they need to upgrade current systems for: (1) business performance management solutions; (2) internal compliance portals; (3) enabling workflow systems; and (4) replacement or upgrading of financial systems.

Interpretation of Findings:

Corporations appear to be seriously concerned about their organizations' internal controls matching the requirements of reporting placed on them by Sarbanes Oxley. Most companies (86%) are already engaged in evaluating or implementing an internal controls project, while the data shows that 40% intend to upgrade current processes and systems in their compliance efforts.

Survey Data On Costs Of Compliance: Compliance with any policy instrument comes with costs, and Sarbox is no exception.

A survey executed by Price Waterhouse Coopers in July 2003, shows corporate impressions of cost of compliance with Sarbanes-Oxley:

Table: MNC Senior Executive Survey

Not Costly	12%
Not Particularly Costly	44%
Somewhat Costly	39%
Very Costly	5%

Table: Report on Cost by Company Size

Company Size	More Costly	Less Costly
Smaller Companies (RevenuesUnder $1 billion)	58%	—
Larger Companies (Revenues over $1 billion)	—	38%

Table: Cost Breakdown By Functional Area

Type of Corporate Activity Somewhat Costly/ byExecutive Report

Internal Resources	76%
External Assistance	24%
Documentation	74%
Legal Compliance	72%
Policy Development	65%
Self-Assessment	62%
Certifications	52%
New Tools and Technology	41%

Interpretation of Findings:

Sarbanes Oxley has been costly for companies, but executives surveyed expect future annual costs for the Act to stay about the same or decline. Overall, executives reported that total costs for control and compliance were expected to average 10.4% of their management controls budget over the next two years.

COMPLEXITIES OF CORPORATE CULTURES

The Complex Universe of Corporate Ethics

Talking about a "corporate ethics" today might well be met with skepticism given the scandals of 2001-2002. Nevertheless, corporate ethics—or lack of such—is of vital interest to the public these days. Lack of basic ethics and fair play has been major factors in leading vital organizations to rapid entropy within the span of just a year. The issue of corporate ethics is not as simple to achieve as one might be led to believe given the twin realities of modernity inherent in mega corporations of the 21st century. These issues of modernity are organizational complexity and rapid change.

It must be acknowledged at the outset that complex organizations face issues that are ill-structured in nature with choices that are intransitive. Here we find simultaneously in existence multiple competing issues whose outcomes are uncertain. Any given choice could lead to immediate disaster. Taken in combination, this puts any organization, in tenuous equilibrium, teetering like a see-saw. Into this volatile mix also, throw in unethical, self-serving leadership, and dangerous invalid, not to mention immoral, organizational practices. One is then confronted with an Enron, a Worldcom, an Arthur Andersen, and the like.

In this chapter for the purposes of simplification, the issue of corporate ethics is being broken down into two very distinct realms. On the one side, we have management ethics—or *individual values*, standards, and beliefs of corporate executives. This raises issues of rights and responsibilities of executive personnel as well as their propensities for malfeasance and mischief. On the other side, we have the notion of corporate values and standards. These are the *collective values* of the juristic, yet living, entity—the mega corporation. These are the standards that have accrued to it via time, tradition, and day-to-day decisionmaking. The nature of economic means-ends chains relating to competitiveness and productivity are also important as a springboard for discussion, as are organizational structural imperatives.

Together these individual and collective behaviors and policies form what we recognize as the *"culture"* of the organization. All of the issues stemming from individual and the collective wrongdoing—involve ontological, epistemological and methodological choices that were made. In the case of the rogue corporations, the methodology of producing the information was deliberately flawed. Complexity and rapid change then led to entropy.

Furthermore, it must be stated that "law is but a 'moral *minimum*'" (Madsen and Shafritz, 1990). Law cannot legislate corporate morality completely. It can and does, however, as the title of this chapter suggests, restrain or inhibit the propensity to immorality. Sooner or later under the hands of clever accountants and lawyers the intent of the law will be thwarted by the greedy and self-serving that have economic access to millions of dollars. Even the most carefully prepared legislation is less than comprehensive and optimum and simply satisfices—or is merely *sufferable.*

Impacts on Human Resource (Intervening Variables)

Wholesale destruction of a corporation's major capital resource—its personnel—has been a disturbing trend of mega corporations in the last decade. Hersey and Blanchard, 2002, describe this as the destruction of organizational "intervening" variables. *Intervening* variables are the human resources of the organization—its very nuts-and-bolts, so to speak.

In the drive to show short-term profits that form the end-result, or *output* variables of a company, leaders manipulate the *input* variables (the causal or stimuli variables—in this case false reporting of profit and loss.

In the process, the intervening variables, the people and the plant, which take a long time to develop and to build up are unprotected, and often are destroyed. In the cases under discussion, short-term self-interest over long-term corporate interest was the *modus operandi.* At Enron, this form of selfish manipulation was done by "moneymakers" on a "*'five year' mission. Their goal was to manage an initial public offering, take over a solid publicly-traded company, push the stock to the sky, and cash out.*" Thousands of intervening variables—i.e., employees, communities and lives were thus destroyed.

The Reagan Legacy of Corporate Covetousness:

Corporate selfishness, evident in the mantra perpetuated in the Reagan years of the 1980s, is captured in the refrain in the film Wall Street –"*greed is good*". Even the lip service given by the former generation of the 1950s, 60s and 70s, to ethical values and standards became muted during the 1980s. It is not surprising, therefore, to see big lapses in business ethics, such as the insider trading scandals in the Reagan years. Professor Lawrence E. Mitchell has likened the Reagan credo to be the "*rough equivalent of telling an alcoholic that The New England Journal of Medicine had reported the health benefits of excessive consumption of liquor.*" We go back to the days of "honest graft" practiced by politicians of the Boss Tweed era.

Reform the Via New Policy Instrument:

The Sarbanes-Oxley Act calls for improved financial reporting, independent audits and accounting services for public companies. In addition it also attempts to short-circuit individual and collective wrongdoing in the following ways:

- Creates a Public Company Accounting Oversight Board to enforce professional codes, standards, and ethics for the accounting profession and its professionals.
- Strengthens the independence of firms that audit public companies.
- Increases corporate responsibility and the usefulness of corporate financial disclosure.
- Increases penalties for corporate wrongdoing.
- Protects the objectivity and independence of securities analysts.
- Increases Securities and Exchange Commission resources.

Already critics claim that like the Patriot Act of 2001, this bill too was passed in haste. This, they say, creates many uncertainties that will have to be sorted out over the years. All this comes about because the Sarbanes-Oxley Act is only partially *self*-executing and it contemplates *other* executions via SEC or stock exchanges. Thus the full impetus of this legislation cannot be considered either by itself, or immediately, as it is part of a broader effort that includes SEC rulemaking. The latter part is not effective immediately but will be soon, as SEC adopts the relevant rules within a given time frame of 30 days to 12 months. Also required are DOJ input, stock exchange listing standards proposals and private group actions.

The addition of Section 906 of the Act, regarding certification of books by CEOs of large corporations was introduced as an amendment by Senator Joseph Biden of Delaware. This is now catching some companies by surprise, because it sweeps into the mix those corporations that were not included in the SEC's previous targeted list of 947 corporations that were required to certify their books.

CEOs scrambled around to certify their books in compliance with the Act, because the effectiveness of the Section 906 of H.R. 3763 was immediate. Some CEOs had just hours to certify their books. To make things worse even companies among the 947 targeted by the SEC perceive the section as requiring them to re-certify books to satisfy the Sarbanes-Oxley Act, 2002. Additionally, critics question whether validity and reliability of the documents will be compromised by the broad statement that precedes the CEO's signature: *"to the best of my knowledge."*

To complicate the issue further, Section 906 is to be enforced by the Department of Justice, not the Securities and Exchange Commission. The net immediate result of the passage of this statutory law is to have regulators stepping over one another.

Influence of the Intellectuals

One issue that needs to be addressed more directly concerns the blind faith of neoclassical economists, clustered around our universities and think-tanks, in the efficacy of markets—despite lack of evidence. Here our neoclassical legal brethren have also joined in, maintaining that the workings of capitalist markets have built-in safety systems that would effectively punish corporate pathogenetic-types who put their own self-interest over that of their shareholders. This view naturally suggests that government intervention is not needed. Such thinking, again arising from the Reagan era, influences much of the relevant scholarly literature of the last decade. It has proven itself wrong.

RECOMMENDATIONS

The hard-bitten French skeptic, Montaigne, once argued: "Man is an amoral creature inevitably committed to the moral enterprise." Montaigne was actually declaring that predatory and degenerate as man might be he cannot live without certain ideals. These ideals could not have been developed had there not been a germ of this idealism in the very make-up humanity itself. The capacity to feel shame and guilt when men fail to live up to their moral codes demonstrates that men are creatures of conscience. It is this sense of shame and guilt that one can appeal to, not only via public laws, such as the Sarbanes-Oxley Act, 2002, but also through the urgings of our fellow citizens.

Earlier it was noted that the law can only provide for *moral minimums* as far as rightdoing is concerned. Laws are but a caricature, or small approximation of what is needed to correct social wrongs. Thus, in addition to statutory disincentives to wrongdoing such as H.R. 3073, 2002, and other regulations, some additional preventative inoculations that individuals and groups can take are given below. They require that the sovereign people take a proactive stand: (1) via their elected representatives, (2) via their corporate votes as investors, (3) via their professional and employee associations, and (4) their voiced dissent via the various forms of the media. Some of the recent recommendations that have arisen from town meetings throughout the country in late summer of 2002 are provided below:

1. The public must resist further de-regulations, which keeps the governmental watchdogs out of corporate crime investigation because of the self-interestedness of corporate leaders.
2. In a regulated industry "watch the watchdogs" so their independence is not compromised and captured by corporate leaders.
3. Shareholders must exercise their power more forcefully by demanding more disclosure and information-sharing, so as to prevent mega corporations from running amok.
4. Employees must take proactive stands through their professional and employee-based associations to demand corporate responsibility.

5. Hold elected representatives to standards of independence and accountability.
6. Employees and investors alike must be vigilant in managing their financial affairs—one aspect of which is to keep their financial eggs in different baskets. Never again overload retirement investments into a company's stock or any other single stock source.
7. Protection must be ensured for those employees who have been laid off without pension and are ill, and thus have no means of support.
8. The practice of using board members who serve on other corporate boards must be so as to prevent *"dispersion of interests"* as well as conflicts-of–interest.
9. CEOs need to be reminded that when they decide to go public and sell the company's stock that the company now belongs to the public and no longer to them alone.
10. Periodic business ethics courses must be given to all managerial staff of corporations.
11. Business ethics courses must be included in the curricula for students in colleges and universities, especially for those business-related disciplines.
12. Academics and other intellectuals need to mobilize themselves and demand more government funding to offset corporate-funded research with its potential for conflicts-of-interest.

While lawyers and accountants try to deal with unknowns in the aftermath of Sarbox, corporate executives try to change to best practices to implement it, the audit committees must in the end rely on the information provided by these groups—they cannot manufacture these data.

Ultimately it will depend on how willing key individuals are to set aside self-interest for collective good. Congress can create laws for us, but "until individuals are willing to increase their ethical behavior, the public may not obtain the level of protection that they desire...what is needed is a change of heart" to change individual behavior and ultimately to change organizational culture. Changing this, however, is a slow process.

15

University, Industry and Government Alliances

INTRODUCTION

Economic globalization is not new; nor are corporate partnerships with governments or universities. However, the geometrically increasing speed of technology transfer has added new dimensions to corporate relations light years from the time when the English and Dutch governments granted charters to their merchant companies in the fifteenth and sixteenth centuries. High technology has dramatically shortened the time from discovery to practical use in fields as diverse as microelectronics, telecommunications, biotechnology, and information technology. The concept of "intellectual property," in turn, has altered the relationship between academic researchers and both government and industry.

This interdependency is not merely symbiotic but a matter of survival for all parties involved. Since World War II, the costs of doing basic research have become so great that the federal government has played a key role in both industry and university research. While at one time it was even considered "improper if not unconstitutional" for private universities to receive government grants, key arenas of scientific research can now only proceed largely with such funding. The instability of government funding, in turn, has made corporate funding indispensable to university research. Corporations, for their part, stand to benefit from both the prestige and cost-savings gained from having their research objectives met in university settings — and could not conduct their research otherwise.

In many rapidly developing areas of technology, research breakthroughs are so broadly distributed across both disciplines and institutions that no single firm has all the necessary capabilities to keep pace..Consequently, in such fields as advanced television systems, biotechnology, computers, optics, and semiconductors, firms are turning to cooperation with former competitors, and to partnerships with universities and government institutes.

How well does this interdependency and division of labor serve the public interest? On the one hand, this interdependency has further blurred the distinction between basic and applied research that once distinguished academic from business research. By the early 1980s, the distinction was variously described as elitist, "outdated and pernicious", or else "fanciful" and irrelevant to protecting science from external control. While there are good reasons for abandoning the distinction, there is evidence that where industry has sought short-cuts to market, this has entailed circumventing basic research.

Part of this chapter, for example, discusses how pharmaceutical industries have sought to identify new uses for existing drugs. The objections to such research practice lie in the fact that basic research questions are bypassed by efforts to apply a "drug solution" to a particular problem for which that drug was not originally developed.

The lure of commercialized research is more apparent than the risks to the public interest. In 2001, 149 universities reported collecting $827 million from payments derived from licenses on inventions, the top three earners being Columbia University, MIT, and the University of California system. Private corporations have become a major voice in those collaborations where government-university-industry relations (GUIRs) are the primary conduit for private contracts: "although the government usually supplies the greatest share of the money, corporations usually have the most powerful voice in defining the project and universities often contribute most of the knowledge or expertise, sometimes contributing money as well". If this is true, then such alliances pose a significant risk to the public interest.

Entrepreneurial ventures may be an important means for generating university revenue, but still wanting are systematic checks to ensure that business pressures do not interfere with the normal scientific research process, whether it is the cumulative development of theoretical knowledge or the ethical responsibilities of disclosure. The Nancy Oliveri case is discussed to illustrate the clash between a university researcher's fundamental loyalty to her patients and the confidentiality clauses routinely written into university-industry contracts. While the case is unique in the publicity it received, it represents the tip of the iceberg, where researchers have otherwise been cowered or muzzled by the threat of lawsuits into suppressing findings unfavorable to a company's product.

At least regarding the most public face of their relationship, GUIRs relations have been framed by their mutuality (as "partners") rather than by implicit conflicts of interest. However, where conflicts of interest surface, they clearly show how the public interest is at stake, and where oversight is needed.

Concerns surrounding corporate lobbying have prompted explicit moves (e.g., campaign finance reform) to address the fact that much public policy gets determined by corporate interests in the context of closed-door discussions rather than by public debate. The latter part of this chapter focuses on the National Science Foundation (NSF), for many years the premier guardian and sponsor of scientific research, especially in the science and engineering fields.

By the 1990s, however, it would meet scandal when its own internal research, unduly influenced by the industry perspective, led to ill-advised government immigration policies involving increases in temporary visas for scientists and other knowledge workers. Because this policy created a glut that led to massive unemployment, the case would prompt Congressional oversight into possible conflicts of interest.

There is a growing body of evidence that the relationship of government and universities to the public has been negatively altered by their relationship to industry and by corporate values. What are some of the risks to the public as revealed by this larger social perspective?

CORPORATE JUGGERNAUTS

While chartered merchant ships of the 15th and 16th century exercised sovereign powers in the name of the crown, their modern-day counterparts would successfully maneuver for greater freedom and protection from government. By 1973 the most successful corporations were growing at an average rate that was "two to three times that of most advanced industrial countries, including the United States." Of the world's 100 largest economies, 52 are corporations. Overshadowing governments as shapers of public policy, transnational corporations view political structures such as the nation state as unnecessary obstacles to their efforts to centralize operations in a "rationally integrated" world economy.

Academic opinion on whether economic globalization is in the public interest ranges from qualified optimism to ambivalence to undiluted criticism. What is clear is that public trust has eroded as corporations increasingly became big business, accountable more to shareholders than to the public.

An 1886 Supreme Court case (*Santa Clara County v. Southern Pacific Railroad)* marked a major reconfiguration of power by paving the way for corporations to gain unprecedented status as "persons." Previously treated as a legal fiction or as artificial entities, they had been strictly regulated by state legislatures as bodies accountable to citizens. Once corporate personhood was assumed, however, the door was open to their claiming protection under the Bill of Rights. By successfully claiming First Amendment rights to free speech, corporations were empowered to lobby politicians. Fourth Amendment rights to privacy enabled them to close their records or facilities to government inspection.

Fourteenth Amendment protection against discrimination enabled a chain store to challenge paying a higher business license fee than that paid by local stores. The implications continue to be far-reaching. In the California Supreme Court case of *Nike v. Kasky*, the sports apparel giant recently responded to charges of false advertising and unfair competition by claiming free speech protections. Having misinformed the public and select customers that workers in its overseas factories were paid the minimum wage and received free health care, Nike then sought exemption from accountability on the grounds that these statements did not appear in paid ads and that the labor practices themselves were publicly controversial.

If granted the First Amendment license to misrepresent, corporations could effectively lie to the public on the grounds that their practices had become publicly "controversial." Government's power as federal regulator in the public interest has been whittled down as corporations buy control or assert certain constitutional rights. The institution that has historically spoken against corporate power and acted as the conscience of society — the media – has had its own credibility and independence vitiated as their financial ties to corporations have increased. For universities, too, these ties have erected barriers to free speech.

The intrusion of industry interests into the core mission of the university is not new. However, the possibilities for open and uncensored discourse were significantly altered as university-industry partnerships were taken to a new level by legal developments in the 1980s. These included the Bayh-Dole Act, which facilitated the commercialization of university research, the Stevenson-Wydler Act, which opened up research at government-operated labs to industry, and the Cooperative Research Act, which enable university-industry collaborations to sidestep the risk of antitrust litigation.

In general, these changes are the ripple effects of more global changes. The small businesses that represented Adam Smith's competitive ideal still exist but they are eclipsed by the corporate juggernauts of today, whose huge capital investments and global presence have fundamentally altered the nature of competition. While some might argue that competition envelops even the largest companies in certain industries (e.g., telecommunications, computer software, airlines, steel, and automobiles), it is anything but a level playing field. For one, the advantage of sheer size and concentration of power mitigate against competition, allowing a few companies (and countries) to dominate an industry (e.g., AT&T, Microsoft, United Airlines, U.S. Steel, General Motors). Speaking to this very issue of economic concentration, Richard Barnet and Ronald Muller (1974: 229) stated: "the power accumulated by giant oligopolies by the late 1950's to control supplies, set prices, and create demand had made an anachronism of the classic concept of the market even before Big Business became global. But globalization completed the process."

The ability of large firms to buy out other firms removes these competitors, and the pace of acquisition and mergers has accelerated with globalization. Second, large companies have frequently sought government bailouts (e.g., Chrysler, United Airlines) and other protections generally less available to small businesses. The U.S. steel industry, for example, has sought to extend existing tariffs, even though critics have argued this rewards inefficiency and noncompetitiveness, and is in violation of international trade rules.

Multinational corporations have a poor record with respect to public interest issues such as sustainable environments, public health and safety, democracy, civil rights and human rights, and social equality, there being nothing in international trade law to protect the public interest. Furthermore, measures of material progress, such as Gross Domestic Product (GDP), perversely convert social costs into income.

Thus, because car crashes, family breakdown, divorces, and prison construction involve lawyer bills and spur the growth of certain industries, they are treated as "economic gains" not as unfortunate human and social costs. More subjective measures indicate that quality of life and psychological well-being as well are adversely affected by commercialization. Disparities in wealth, moreover, are increasing. In 1998, the top one percent of U.S. households owned 38 percent of all wealth; with the level of inequality in 2003 double that of the mid-1970s. The two hundred richest corporations in the world, moreover, have double the assets of the poorest 80 percent of the world's population. Jeff Gates, founder and president of the nonprofit Shared Capitalism Institute, questions the very goal of growth and material prosperity without regard to how that wealth is distributed. The value of Bill Gates, Jr's projected individual wealth is staggering in and of itself but also because our cultural values have sanctioned such accumulation without regard to public interest values.

What's the point of prosperity in a democracy? Is it a success no matter who reaps its benefits? Apparently so. If the value of the Microsoft stock owned by Bill Gates continues to grow at the same torrid pace as it has since Microsoft's 1986 initial public offering (58.2% a year), he will become a trillionaire ($1000 billion) in March 2005, at the age of forty-nine, and his Microsoft holdings will be valued at $1 quadrillion (that's a million billion) in March 2020, when he turns sixty-four. Or is prosperity an opportunity for widespread economic advance and social accomplishment? Apparently not. Today's rules are clear: Making the already-rich endlessly richer is now the best use to which our expanding prosperity can be put. That's what today's policymakers have concluded. How much is a million billion? The 1998 gross world product was just $39,000 billion (less than 4 percent of a million billion). In May 1997, the journal *Nature* concluded that the planet's ecosystems provide a range of environmental and resource services worth $33,000 billion each year. If that amount were capitalized using the interest rate paid on U.S. treasuries, that puts the value of all creation at about $500,000 billion, one-half Bill Gate's projected net worth in 2020.

Private corporations justify their profit by their philanthropic gestures and by their alleged efficiency, rationality, and economy. Bill Gates, Jr.'s six billion dollar donation towards drugs for AIDs patients presumed to accomplish all these ends. There is pathos, irony, and public appearance windfall from this gesture. Gates' donation will save only a fraction of the over 25 million South Africans infected with the virus, but he stands to benefit enormously from a World Trade Organization (WTO) rule that erects trade barriers that will prohibit AIDs patients getting the cheaper drugs they need. The reason is TRIPS (Trade-Related Intellectual Property Rights), which bars countries from buying cheaper medicine from other sources because this would mean buying or selling outside zones carved out by brand names.

COMMERCIALIZATION OF ACADEMIC RESEARCH

In the U.S., the Reagan policies of the 1980s began a process of radically realigning government in the service of big business. Despite free market rhetoric, large corporations effectively became the beneficiary of subsidies, entitlements, protective legislation, and other business friendly tariff or immigration policies. These policies have facilitated sales operations overseas and provided cheap domestic labor for high technology needs in the U.S.

Government and higher education officials, persuaded of the greater "efficiencies" to be gained through privatization, have outsourced many services they formerly provided for themselves. Oddly, for the past five years, there has been a precipitous decline in information and accountability, as far as how much the federal government spends on private service contractors.

Meanwhile, an emerging literature has developed, documenting the rise of the corporate university. The effect of downsizing on the University of Pennsylvania from 1994 to 1998 was to create enormous pressures for this nonprofit academic institution to operate as a business, an effect so devastating that it was dubbed by one critical analyst as "the neutron bomb theory of excellence". In much the same vein, Massachusetts governor Mitt Romney has proposed a major reorganization of the state's public higher education, including the University of Massachusetts' five campuses. While some, like UMass Boston's Chancellor Jo Ann Gora, have argued that the dismantling would not alter the basic mission of the research institution, others have resisted the overhaul, precisely because they represent moves to run the university like a corporation. Such developments have radically altered the political economy of universities not only in the United States but elsewhere.

The North American Free Trade Agreement (NAFTA) has enabled American transnational companies to penetrate and commercialize education in Canada. For example, NAFTA conferred upon these companies *national treatment rights*, which means that the Canadian government cannot give preference to domestic companies even if a Canadian perspective was considered vital. Bids for educational services must be open to competing firms from the entire continent. Thus, when the government of British Columbia needed to prepare its twelfth-grade provincial examinations, it decided to contract this out to a foreign provider. The Department of Education cannot return this function to the public sphere on the grounds that cultural issues would be better served by local firms. To do so before the expiration of the contract would require financial compensation to the company involved. Moreover, once the contract expires, it would once again have to be opened to firms competing from non-Canadian companies.

Other kinds of school support services that are presently affected include food services, school-bus transportation, computer services, building maintenance, cleaning, and consulting.

Historically in the United States, the federal government has played a major role in the growth of universities, first through the conferral of land grants and then through the funding of research. The American university that was taking its earliest shape at the end of the eighteenth century was a private institution with a primarily religious mission (training students for public service) and a faculty composed almost entirely of the clergy. As the federal government began donating public lands to states to develop secular and public degree-granting institutions, universities would continue to pursue their primary mission of educating students but would also begin to serve the public interest through conducting vanguard research, which in the nineteenth century meant agricultural and mining interests. In both religious and secular instances, a strong humanistic tradition developed, promoting the free exchange of ideas, critical thinking, and service or research on behalf of the society at large. This was true, even though this tradition was often contested, sometimes undernourished and besieged, and in the last half of the twentieth century witnessed notable erosion. Though a chartered corporation, with a history of its own internal sources of ideological repression, the university would continue to fulfill a crucial and unique function as a center of independent inquiry and public service, with free speech as the lifeblood of intellectual exchange.

A dramatic turning point in the history of American universities occurred in 1980 with the passage of the Bayh-Dole Act. The brainchild of corporate CEOs, backed by a select group of university administrators without faculty consultation, it would give private companies easy access to publicly funded research. Specifically, Bayh-Dole granted universities title to inventions developed from federally funded grants, whereas previously these inventions belonged to the public. Up until then, universities had been agents of the government, representing the interests of the public whose tax dollars paid for their research. Once designated owners of this research, the universities became less beholden to the public as their faculty became oriented towards selling their discoveries to corporations. One effect has been to increasingly divert scientific attention away from basic research towards short-term marketable products, without considering the long-term public interest. Second, as academic discoveries thus became transformed into "intellectual property," corporations, in turn, leapt at the chance to obtain the exclusive license to manufacture. A sharp growth in university patenting can be traced directly to Bayh-Dole. Previously such licenses were sold only on a non-exclusive basis, enabling greater market competition, thereby protecting the public from monopolistic pricing.

A third effect of Bayh-Dole was to introduce a culture of secrecy and confidentiality aimed at protecting proprietary craft knowledge, and to raise the specter of possible conflict of interest as faculty became increasingly involved in commercial ventures, including the launching their own companies. Problems presently facing higher education are to varying degrees discernible as connected to this singular change in the incentive structure of universities. The problems of higher education – the fraud, the tuition increases, the falsified research, the transformation of teachers into workers, the scramble to steal intellectual property by administrators from faculty and students, and by colleagues from one another – are all new problems. Bayh-Dole leads to the displacement and subordination of the humanistic tradition and collegial society integral to the university, and will never be identified as the source of the problem. The public knows very little about it and the university community most affected was – carefully – not consulted. To this day, the public knows little about the act or its effects, and most faculty have never heard of it.

In exchange for the passage of the Bayh-Dole Act, industry assured government that it would protect American jobs from foreign competition, once it gained the "competitive edge" in the global market. It was this promise, along with lobbying by university presidents, which won over then President Jimmy Carter. The U.S. economy at the time had been declining, and American corporations were faring poorly against their German and Japanese counterparts. According to one interpretation, American business had refused to plough their profits back into basic research, as was the norm. According to others, it was global rivals that allegedly did little of the internal research but were "quick to exploit the developments of others." In either case, the legislative maneuver now enabled industry to benefit from an academic research infrastructure already in place, paying only a fraction of what it actually cost to conduct the research. Big business failed, however, to live up to its promise to protect American jobs. As we shall see in the latter half of this chapter, the National Science Foundation (NSF) would help support an industry agenda that brought access to cheap, highly skilled immigrant labor at the expense of American jobs. That it did so by suppressing respectable research serves as yet another example of how commercialization undercuts academic integrity.

INDUSTRY RESEARCH: "NEW USES" FOR EXISTING DRUGS

The distinction between basic and applied research fades as commercialization blurs the traditional division of labor between academia and industry. The loss of this distinction in drug research sharply illustrates how, in their rush to market, drug companies have increasingly bypassed basic research focused on finding cures and shifted their attention towards marketing existing drugs for new uses. These new uses are presented as "therapeutic breakthroughs," which presumably warrant the exorbitant costs patients must pay.

Federal Drug Administration (FDA) approval for a new use or "indication" takes less than 18 months, as opposed to eight years to bring a drug from lab to pharmacy. The selective serotonin reuptake inhibitors (SSRIs) are a case in point. This family of pharmaceuticals, which includes Paxil, Prozac, Zoloft, Celexa, and Luvox, were originally approved simply and solely for use as antidepressants. Brendan Koerner explains how SmithKline Beecham was able to increase Paxil's market share, when in 1993 Paxil lagged behind its competitors — Prozac (an Eli Lilly product) and Zoloft. SmithKline subsequently found two disorders in the *Diagnostic Statistical Manual of Mental Disorders* (DSM) for which Paxil might be prescribed, namely, "social anxiety disorder" and "generalized anxiety disorder." It would not be long before Pfizer, in turn, would seek a new use for Zoloft, specifically as a medication for "posttraumatic stress disorder."

Although DSM entries are shaped by social and cultural norms, and the politics surrounding them (e.g., homosexuality was diagnosed as a mental disorder up until 1973), the DSM notation is considered sufficient proof by the FDA that a disease actually exists, and in-house corporate studies are basically unquestioned, even when companies fail to make their data or methodologies available to other members of the scientific community, as would be essential for professional academic acceptance. In August 2002, escitalopram became the sixth member of the SSRI family. Its birth came about as a result of another kind of pharmaceutical marketing and development strategy. The strategy is not to find new uses for an old drug but to push an old drug as if it were new. Drug companies do this by manipulating a chemical molecule known as an isomer and then selling what amounts to a chemical mirror image of the original drug. An isomer..is, chemically speaking, a molecule containing identical atoms to another molecule, but differently arranged: a mirror image, to be precise. Consider two isomers of a certain molecule to be like a pair of gloves – same number of fingers, just arranged differently. Separating these mirror images and selling only a single mirror image as a "new " drug is a successful business scheme, *not* a strategy to improve public health. This may be likened to selling one glove and claiming that it is as good as or better than two.

The Public Citizen Health Research Group (2003: 4) advised against the use of this drug until 2005: "for practical purposes it is the same drug as citalopram and it has no therapeutic or safety advantage over citalopram or other SSRI antidepressants."

Because corporations have become primary funders of biomedical research, their impact on public health is enormous. Yet their obligations to the public have not matched their rhetoric of public service. Not surprisingly, corporations have sought to disguise their influence when their public image is tarnished. Performing its own form of "smoke and mirrors," tobacco manufacturer Philip Morris renamed itself Altria in order to portray itself as an objective source of information about the dangers of smoking. The company has unashamedly continued to promote the industry's interests in minority communities and developing countries. Moreover, in March of 2003, it was ordered by an

Illinois judge to pay $10.1 billion in the first consumer fraud class-action lawsuit involving "light" cigarettes to go to trial: the company was found guilty of intentionally deceiving smokers into believing that "light" cigarettes were less dangerous than regular cigarettes. Philip Morris is currently asking the Illinois Supreme Court to prevent the plaintiffs from enforcing the $10.1 billion judgment. The funding of proprietary research has led the push to subordinate academic science to corporate values and agendas. With Bayh-Dole, knowledge within the university was no longer common property but intellectual property. Scholars were discouraged from sharing their findings with their colleagues, and could no longer be completely trusted as the purveyor of disinterested knowledge, especially when their research findings threatened corporate profits. To dispel the appearances of ethical impropriety, university administrators have called for disclosure, but this is limited to private disclosure within the university (e.g., reporting to some supervisory authority or administrative head), not public disclosure. The issue of what is a conflict can get murky...so many university scientists have started their own companies that deans of medical schools no longer talk about eliminating conflict of interest; the current buzzword for dealing with conflicts is "management." The primary management tool, university officials say, is disclosure. But that means disclosure to supervisors – not to the public.

OLIVERI: ACADEMIC FREEDOM BLOODIED

As the incentive structure within the university shifted towards the market, it altered the academic culture, creating conflicts of interest particularly for medical schools and research centers with ties to pharmaceutical companies. In general, scientists are strongly motivated to publish their results and to do so quickly in order to be credited with their contributions to scientific knowledge. At issue in the case of Nancy Oliveri, A University of Toronto clinical researcher, was whether she could promptly release her results *not* to this group of scientific peers but rather to (a) investigators administering the same experimental drug at collaborating research centers as well as to appropriate regulators and (b) patients being exposed to newly discovered risks in these clinical trials. Certain contractual constraints with her corporate sponsor, however, impeded her ability to exercise this academic freedom. Beginning in the early 1990's, the University of Toronto had discussed the possibility of a multimillion dollar donation from Apotex pharmaceuticals to build a biomedical research center. The Oliveri controversy eventually led to suspension of such discussions. Dr. Oliveri attracted public attention in mid-August 1998 when it was learned Apotex had tried to suppress adverse findings uncovered in the course of the clinical trial conducted under a grant secured by her co-investigator, Dr.Gideon Koren. Two unexpected medical risks would be discovered in connection with the randomized trial of an experimental iron-chelation drug that seemed to be a promising alternative to a more onerous but standard drug administered to transfusion dependent patients.

Oliveri's patients suffered from a genetic disorder, thalassemia, which required regular blood transfusions. The transfusions themselves brought an increased risk of long-term damage to bodily organs from too much iron in the blood, something iron-chelation drugs seek to offset. The experimental drug aimed at countering this problem, however, were discovered to have two main side effects: the loss of sustained efficacy and an increased risk of liver fibrosis.

Oliveri's 1993 contract with Apotex had a one-year, post termination confidentiality clause. Her 1995 contract with Apotex had no confidentiality clause though the pharmaceutical manufacturer reserved the right to terminate the trial at any time. It did so abruptly and stopped supplying the drug — but without notice to patients, who were left in an uncertain situation – issuing legal warnings to Oliveri for which there was no contractual basis.

Obligated by the requirements of informed consent, Oliveri sought to exercise her academic freedom to counsel her patients and publish the adverse findings. By contrast, Dr. Koren sided with their corporate sponsor by publishing an article that testified to the drug's efficacy. No mention was made of Apotex funding nor Oliveri's opposing findings. Details regarding the dispute are documented extensively by a committee which investigated the case over two years (Thompson, Baird, and Downie, 2002). Neither the University of Toronto nor the Hospital for Sick Children, the affiliated teaching hospital where Oliveri conducted her clinical trial, supported her on the issue of academic freedom and protection of the public interest. The Hospital, to the contrary, took active steps to remove her from the program directorship and to disrupt and discredit her work. The only legal support forthcoming came from the Canadian Medical Protective Association, which was primarily mandated to reduce her legal risks as an individual client rather than to protect the larger public or societal interests. The case, in short, pointed to a systemwide problem where those directly or indirectly involved were unable to resolve the conflicts of interest raised by corporate sponsorship. A major lesson from this case is that confidentiality clauses for clinical trials are inappropriate. Oliveri had signed different contracts with Apotex: she should have refused to sign, without modification, those contracts which contained post-termination confidentiality clauses, one of which was a three-year, post-termination confidentiality clause inconsistent with University of Toronto policy.

The Hospital's Research Ethics Board, for its part, approved these contracts without ensuring that there were provisions to protect trial participants in the event of premature termination of the research. In short, policies and procedures needed to be in place at every level (investigator, research ethics boards, universities, hospitals, regulators, federal and provincial governments, industry) to ensure that contractual agreements related to communication and disclosure did not have clauses or protocols to restrict communication. The committee report concluded with a series of recommendations outlining a structure of accountability whereby various stakeholders party to a company-sponsored relationship would each have some individual or institutional role in the oversight process, specifically to ensure that contracts did not require secrecy.

In a parallel move to ensure data access and publication among researchers involved in multicenter studies, a group of Duke University researchers reviewed U.S. medical schools for their compliance with guidelines laid out for academic-industry partnerships and developed by the 2001 International Committee of Medical Journal Editors (ICMJE). The results of this evaluation study were "dismal": there was little if any compliance; researchers had severely restricted access to data, and the requirement to publish their data were often nonexistent. To put it mildly, the results were dismal...The universities reported that a median of 1 percent of their studies had provisions for such access. In one study that was not a focus of the report, even the principal investigator did not have unfettered access to the data, forcing him to publish a chapter with only 90 percent of the data. The agreements were often lacking other crucial elements. Only a median of 5 percent of studies addressed plans for data analysis and interpretation, opening the doors to industry mischief in the forms of data massaging or the reaching of conclusions with an eye on marketing rather than science. Extraordinarily, a median of 0 percent of study contracts required the data to be published.A median of 0 is technically not the typical statistical median, which designates the midpoint. As The Public Citizen Health Research Group (PCHRG) noted, this was "extraordinary," yet another measure of the dismally low rate at which study data were made available. Like the Oliveri Committee, the PCHRG offered several recommendations to ensure publication and disclosure of data. These included (1) the development of a standard contract by the Association of American Medical Colleges, (2) accreditation denial to those universities failing to develop such a contract, (3) denial of National Institute of Health (NIH) funding to those failing to implement a contract, (4) publication refusal by medical journals unless authors have met all ICMJE guidelines, and (5) further studies by ICMJE to determine the extent of compliance. A recent report offering an overview of the state of medical research ethics confirmed these observations – that academic researchers cannot meet their scientific or ethic responsibilities largely because the guidelines in place to prevent conflicts of interest with corporate sponsors are "written vaguely and enforced half-heartedly."

INFILTRATION OF THE NATIONAL SCIENCE FOUNDATION

The National Science Foundation has been a putatively objective, neutral evaluator of research, historically providing federal support to academic institutions for basic research. Since the 1980's, it has been a chief architect of the research arrangements involving government, university, and industry relations (GUIRs). According to Stephen Stigler, the NSF presumably found it "easier to explain large-scale projects and research centers to Congress than to argue convincingly for the diffuse benefits of a broad-based funding of individual projects..." NSF-sponsored centers would eventually require an industry component and a review process involving corporate participation in the evaluation of a proposal's merits. In 1992, NSF was found to be engaged in partisan research that promoted industry interests. Not only was this research tainted with bias and flawed methodology, but the effect of policies issuing forth from it was to create a market glut of workers, which benefited employers.

Although industry was a major beneficiary, it was not alone. The resulting scandal involved a wider network of stakeholders that included government and universities. Relevant to the discussion here is how these interests were accommodated and furthered by NSF under former director Erich Bloch.

Eric Weinstein (n.d.) reports that beginning as early as 1975-76 and continuing from 1986-1990, employers in government, industry, and universities engaged in discussions that would lead to policy depressing the wages of scientists, engineers, programmers, and information workers.

Industry claimed that higher education was not producing a sufficient number of graduates in these fields, projecting the specter of a labor shortage that would slow economic growth. Genuinely alarmed members of Congress responded to this desperate call for assistance by passing the Immigration Act of 1990. The Act, among other things, greatly simplified the process by which employers could hire foreign workers. The effect was to flood the labor market. In the ideal free market situation, employers typically respond to labor shortages by increasing salaries and other terms of employment so as to attract the necessary talent, thereby honoring a basic relationship between the law of supply and demand. Neither government, industry, nor higher education, however, saw it in their interest to compete with one another in a tight labor market.

Their shared interests were explored through a Government University Industry Roundtable convened and headed by NSF Director Bloch. Working scientists were never consulted, although the final policy outcome would adversely affect the careers of students and workers, domestic and foreign. Under the directorship of Peter House, the Policy Research and Analysis (PRA) division within NSF would generate an in-house study supporting industry's claim of imminent labor shortages. Based on "supply-side" economics, the PRA study predicted that between 1986 and 2011, there would be a shortage of almost 700,000 bachelor degrees in science and engineering (S&E). The scarcity study, however, was contradicted by an internal NSF statistical analysis that did not foresee such a shortage. As Joel L. Barries, who supervised this report, testifies, the PRA and its director, Peter House, moved to actively suppress this competing evidence.

After PRA began doing its modeling work, our work [that of the SRS statistical subdivision] was scaled back, and PRA began to interfere in the text of the section on the science and engineering workforce in Science & Engineering Indicators and other SRS work through the review process. It was at this same time that former NSF director Erich Bloch was trying to get Congress to appropriate money to revitalize science education programs.

It worked as follows: SRS publication underwent "anonymous" review by the Scientific, Technological and International Affairs Directorate (STIA) of which both it and PRA were a part. However, this "anonymous" review was usually done by PRA. After beginning the scarcity studies, PRA and Dr. House began to force changes in Science & Engineering Indicators that weakened our conclusions, based on past history and likely projected supply/demand scenarios that the labor market would adjust to any spot shortages in personnel.

For example, in 1989 I supervised the preparation of a report entitled "National Overview of Scientific and Technical Personnel," which had a new section on the projections based on the SRS model. The report did not project any significant personnel shortages. Mysteriously, it was held up for a year in STIA's "anonymous" review process. Finally, William Stewart, then SRS director, arranged a meeting with Peter House to see what the problem was. At that meeting, Dr. House said the problem was that the report did not support the director's position that there would be serious personnel shortages in the 1990s." Even if the more pessimistic claims of a shortage were substantiated, it did not follow that extraordinary corrective measures were needed. As Weinstein points out, other PRA analysts had in fact carefully analyzed the demand side of the equation as well and explicitly stated that shortage could be offset if employers increased wages or salaries at almost double the 1982 salary level. PRA director House, however, prevented the publication of this report and circulated it only to select representatives. University of California President Richard Atkinson was one of the few PRA outsiders to receive a copy, and he too would reject the market solution as a corrective measure: "Market mechanisms will no doubt reduce projected shortfalls between supply and demand, but they will be slow in coming and expensive. [P]rudence suggests, therefore, that we pursue intervention strategies to increase the future supply of Ph.D.s". It is ironic that while anti-trust laws have prohibited business from forming monopolies that interfere with the natural workings of wage and price dynamics, NSF succeeded in obstructing this very dynamic. During the 1992 Congressional oversight hearings investigating how NSF predictions could have gone so awry, Representative Wolpe poignantly expressed his disappointment in this highly respected and trusted scientific establishment in his comments to Peter House, NSF's chief policy analyst. "Hundreds if not thousands, of people believed that your study had something definitive to say about the scientific and engineering needs of this country. Science education, immigration policy in this country have been affected by the study and by the number that was its product.

One has the sense that the goal was to create the impression of a crisis to lend urgency to the effort to double the NSF budget; nothing inherently wrong with such an activity. It happens, as some people have noted, on Capitol Hill every day. Democrats and Republicans will selectively present any set of numbers in a different way to make their case.

But the difference here is that everyone up here is well aware of how that game is played. We look at each other's numbers with a great deal of skepticism, and the media shares that skepticism sometimes to a fault. But no one expects the NSF to play that game or to take a study that has been so severely criticized from so many quarters and to pretend as if there is nothing wrong and to go forth with that in advancing its own agenda. The NSF is the nation's premiere scientific agency. Everyone, including I think most of the media, accept as a given that NSF's pronouncements are the result of good science, really analytic kind of work.

This was not good science, this study that you produced. It has been relentlessly criticized by labor market experts both inside and outside the NSF. If you had performed this analysis for a member of Congress privately as a private kind of action, initiative, you wouldn't be here today. But you work for the National Science Foundation, and a different standard, I think, must apply as we deal with this question."

In sum, Eric Weinstein's research reveals how the mission of one of the country's premier publicly funded institutions was deflected by NSF staff research which was both methodologically flawed and propelled by political biases sympathetic to industry. The high-level secrecy not only betrayed the scientists it was entrusted to support but other staff researchers who had little to do with the misdirected study. The effect was twofold: (1) to give the nation's major employers the wherewithal to exploit lower salaries available through a global labor market, and (2) to produce massive layoffs and double digit unemployment derailing careers and other "forgotten stakeholders," i.e., the families of scientists and engineers. In January 2003, the *Chronicle of Higher Education* reported that fewer and fewer U.S. students are seeking degrees in science and engineering (Potter, 2003). While industry rhetoric has supported educational initiatives that encourage students to enter math and science careers, employers have been unwilling to retrain or raise wages and salaries to draw more students into these fields. The shortage claim that originated around natural scientists and engineers has also affected knowledge workers in the information technology field, especially programmers. As evident in subsequent layoffs, this claim too was a self-interested product of industry myth-making. Computer science professor Norm Matloff thus testified:

When the industry claims a shortage of programmers, what they mean is a shortage of cheap programmers...The fact that the industry cries of "shortage'" were nothing more than a political ploy was illustrated by the fact that heavy layoffs in the industry began around January 2001, just two months after the industry lobbyists were insisting to Congress that there was a '"desperate" shortage.

The present recession has prompted Congressional moves to recognize employer abuses of these foreign visas and to consider eliminating them. Where NSF is concerned, The National Academy of Public Administration is seeking to address key issues revolving around the impact of NSF's organizational structure and management processes on research opportunities, including whether the recruitment of short-term managers from academia poses a real or perceived conflict of interest.

Yet as long as corporations exert their influence through interlocking directorates, their formal and informal influence will be felt in a number of high-level structures, university bodies as well as government. Among the nation's top universities, twenty-four out of fifty of its presidents served on corporate boards; and CEOs are the largest single group of university trustees. Not surprisingly, universities have been strongly motivated to tow the industry line as a leverage for more resources, from both government and industry.

Bibliography

Adam, R.: *Elements of Government*, New York, Random House, 1960.

Amartya Sen: *Action and India: Economic Development and Social Opportunity*, Delhi, Oxford University Press, 1999.

Benefits Agency: *One stop. Benefits Agency delivery*, Leeds, Benefits Agency, 1992.

Chandra, R.: *Judicial System in India*, Lucknow, Print House (India), 1992.

Davies .A.: *Telecommunications and Politics. The Secentralised Alternative*, London, Pinter, 1994.

Foreman-Peck J. and Millward, R: *Public and Private Ownership of British Industry 1820-1990*, Oxford, Clarendon Press, 1994.

Goldman, H.: *Co-ordination of Computerization of the Criminal Justice System*, London, Home Office, 1986.

Hazard, J.N.: *The Soviet System of Government*, Chicago, University of Chicago Press, 1960.

Keane J.: *Democracy and Civil Liberty*, London, Verso, 1988.

Lipietz A.: *Mirages and Miracles*, London, Verso, 1987.

Mary, W.: *Asian Power and Politics: the Cultural Dimensions of Authority*, Cambridge, Belknap Press, 1985.

Politt. C: *Managerialism and the Public Services*, Oxford, Blackwell, 1993.

Rosen, P.: *Societies and Military Power: India and its Armies*, Ithaca, Cornell University Press, 1996.

Simon, D. : *Public Administration*, New York, Knopf, 1950.

Thomas, R. : *Elements of Government*, New York, Random House, 1960.

Wade, R.: *Public Bureaucracy and the Incentive Problem*, Washington, D.C., World Bank, 1994.

Index

C

Civil Liberties, 41, 55, 56, 57, 58, 59, 60, 111.

Civilizations, 77, 92, 103, 105, 111, 112, 115, 116, 128.

Company, 113, 243, 245, 246, 249, 257, 261, 262, 264.

Complex Environments, 174, 193.

Contribution, 6, 10, 13, 14, 15, 16, 20, 65, 126.

D

Democracy, 12, 21, 25, 40, 49, 50, 60, 78, 92, 97, 104, 105, 106, 107, 108, 109, 115, 116, 117, 119, 122, 128, 231, 232, 234, 255.

E

Environmental Pressures, 2, 135, 181, 188, 194.

F

Foundation, 42, 90, 208, 228, 252, 260, 265, 269.

Freedom, 44, 61, 74, 94, 97, 98, 101, 104, 111, 113, 151, 230, 231, 253, 262, 263, 264.

I

Industry, 248, 250, 251, 252, 254, 255, 259, 260, 264, 265, 266, 269, 270.

J

Jihad, 52, 71, 74, 75, 76, 78, 82, 83, 86, 90, 91, 92, 93, 94, 95, 96, 97, 98, 99, 100, 101, 102, 103, 104, 105.

N

Nongovernmental Organizations, 226.

P

Performance, 2, 3, 5, 7, 18, 19, 22, 23, 26, 27, 28, 29, 30, 31, 32, 33, 34, 35, 36, 37, 38, 40, 74, 120, 133, 134, 135, 136, 137, 138, 141, 144, 152, 156, 183, 186, 188, 189, 191, 195, 197, 242.

Politics, 1, 11, 12, 13, 16, 21, 27, 40, 42, 60, 63, 71, 73, 75, 76, 89, 90, 95, 99, 100, 103, 104, 109, 114, 118, 136, 154, 172, 261.

Public Management, 2, 13, 18, 19, 20, 21, 23, 24, 97, 135.

S

Small Businesses, 235, 254, 255.